Christianity: A Comparative Study

*Forthcoming titles*

**Masao Abe** Buddhism and Christianity
**P. S. Alexander** Judaism and Christianity
**John E. Smith** Humanism, Marxism and Nationalism:
Quasi-Religions
**A. V. Williams** Zoroastrianism and Christianity

# Sikhism and Christianity

## A Comparative Study

W. OWEN COLE

P. S. SAMBHI

First published 1993 by
THE MACMILLAN PRESS LTD
Houndmills, Basingstoke, Hampshire RG21 2XS
and London
Companies and representatives
throughout the world

ISBN 0–333–54106–5 hardcover
ISBN 0–333–54107–3 paperback

A catalogue record for this book is available
from the British Library

Printed in Hong Kong

Piara Singh Sambhi died on 30 November 1992. When we last met he said that this book symbolised many aspects of our work together and might be described as our crowning achievement. Be that as it may the task of taking it forward to publication has been an act of love and respect and if it furthers the causes of Sikh studies and inter-religious understanding in any way it will be a comfort to me and to Piara Singh's family. A friend, Professor Bakshish Singh, has suggested the appropriateness of the following words as an epitaph:

Blessed, blessed, is the gursikh who falls at the Guru's feet.
Blessed, blessed, is the gursikh whose mouth speaks the
     Name of God.
Blessed, blessed, is the gursikh whose soul achieves bliss
     through hearing God's Name.
Blessed, blessed, is the gursikh who serves the Sat Guru.

(AG 593)

The gursikh is one who learns the gurbani, teaches it, and
     records it for others.

(Bhai Gurdas, Var 20, pauri 6: 4)

OWEN COLE

# Contents

# General Editor's Preface

A series of monographs on themes in comparative religion might possibly give rise to misgivings in the minds of some readers because of misconceptions concerning the nature of comparative religion. It is often maintained, for example, that comparisons are odious; that religious comparisons are more odious than most; and that those who are concerned with comparative religion are only comparatively religious. The aim and purpose of this series of monographs, however, is not to present a comparatively religious outlook, nor to engage in odious comparisons which could result in one religious tradition being elevated to a position of superiority over others. The intention rather is to look at what might be called 'family resemblances' that pertain in the major religious traditions of the world.

Contributors to the series were asked to examine certain basic themes in the different world religions from an empathetic standpoint – that is, so far as possible, from within the religious traditions concerned and in a way that would meet with the approval of adherents of those religions. Since Christianity is the basic religious tradition of the West it was considered appropriate that the comparative thematic approach adopted by the series should involve Christianity on each occasion, and that religious themes in the different religious traditions of the world should be related to similar themes in the Christian tradition.

An indication of this approach would be the way in which the mystery of divinity takes different forms and finds expression in a variety of ways in different religious traditions. The Tetragrammation or Logos of the Judeo-Christian tradition, for instance, might take the form of the Tao of the Chinese religious tradition, or the Brahman/Atman synthesis of the Hindu way of life, or the Kami of Shinto. A similar comparative approach involving 'family resemblances' would apply to other themes, such as creation and emanation; death and immortality; liberation and salvation; revelation and enlightenment; ethics and morality; the Kingdom of God, moksha and nirvana; and the ritual practices involved in the realisation of ultimate goals.

Naturally the choice of themes for the different monographs in the series, which include a comparison of the relation of Hinduism, Buddhism, Islam, Judaism, Japanese religions, Chinese religions, Sikhism, Zoroastrianism, primitive religions and Humanism with Christianity, would depend to a great extent on the way in which the different contributors to the series approached their subject matter. But the concept of empathy prevails throughout and the odious kinds of comparison sometime associated with comparative religion, albeit mistakenly, are excluded.

It is hoped that this open-ended thematic approach to comparative religion will prove helpful to the enquiring mind. In the pluralistic religious situation of today, with its great variety of religious experiences, we ought to be able to escape from the small island of our own culture, and from the ghetto mentality that would confine us to the insights of a single religious tradition. Such a mentality simply isolates us from the richness and diversity of other cultures and from the deep, spiritual insights of other religious traditions.

GLYN RICHARDS

# Preface

The authors have been constrained by a number of considerations in writing this book. The first is the recognition that readers may not have as easy access to primary or secondary sources for the study of Sikhism as they may have for Christianity. Most books on the subject are published in India. Even if booksellers have good contacts in the subcontinent and can locate them, availability is often affected by small print runs of only a couple of thousand copies. We have therefore tried to write a book which is self-explanatory, though occasionally references are given to other sources where we think that readers might find them helpful. For this reason we have also confined ourselves more to the fundamental teachings of the religions, especially Christianity, rather than to exploring developments. Our discussion of grace, for example, would have constituted a book in itself, if we had given attention to the views of Christian theologians during the last two millenia.

Sikhism is a very scriptural tradition. Comparison with it from a Christian position must, therefore, concentrate on this area. We have therefore given much attention to the teachings of the Bible and of the Guru Granth Sahib. Sikhism confines itself to the re-examination and re-expression of scripture. Consequently, the kinds of development in the area of textual criticism which have taken place in Christianity since the Enlightenment have no parallel in Sikh studies.

Translations of the *Guru Granth Sahib* into English tend to use archaic language or to seek to retain the poetry of the original. Like the King James version of the Bible they may possess majesty but the impact of the message upon the reader is less great than it might be. We would hope that before long an international team of experts might produce an English edition which would do full justice to the revelation contained in the Sikh scripture. Meanwhile we have consulted the translations listed in the Bibliography and the original text, and offered our own reading. Our purpose is to present the message plainly to the reader. In doing so, therefore, we have aimed at communicating the message rather than at literal precision. The Revised English Bible has been used for the Christian scriptural quotations.

We realise that the convention of italicising words is related to whether or not they are found in the Oxford Dictionary, but we would argue that this can be misconstrued as Christo- or ethnocentricism. In a book of this kind especially, any differentiation would seem inappropriate but it has been necessary to conform to convention because some Punjabi words are identical with common English ones, notably *man*, meaning mind, heart, soul, or psyche.

The use of BCE for Before the Common Era, and CE for Common Era, has been followed, replacing BC and AD in keeping with the usual convention in religious studies nowadays.

We have also tried to use the terms which belong to the respective religions. Baptism and *amrit pahul* are not the same thing. To speak of Sikh baptism would only be to arouse visual images and theological ideas in the minds of Christian readers or students who had studied Christianity which we would then have to dispel before the Sikh initiation ceremony could be understood. Readers are warned that the media, at least in the west and in India, is fond of using the phrase 'Sikh priest' (there is no such person), and that Sikhs may use Christian terms in an attempt to be helpful. We must plead guilty to committing some errors of this kind during our twenty-year writing partnership!

As this is a comparative study and not an introduction to each of the religions, readers must not expect to be provided with such an account of them within the pages of this one book. For that they must turn to the reading list which is supplied at the end of the book. However, a brief introduction to the two religions is provided in Chapter 1.

Finally, we would like to thank Peggy Holroyde who brought us together through the Yorkshire Committee for Community Relations. We are also grateful to the many people who have enhanced our understanding of Christianity and Sikhism and so enabled us accomplish this task, and especially the Reverend John Parry for his comments on the initial outline. The anonymous reader who commented upon the first draft of the book for the publishers, and Tony Grahame, the editorial consultant, must also be thanked for helping us to produce a much improved text. We must, of course, absolve anyone but ourselves from the faults which remain.

As Piara Singh Sambhi's death approached we became more grateful than ever for the opportunity which Glyn Richards and Macmillan had given us to share the result of our experiences and knowledge with others. We have written for A-level students, undergraduates and the general reader as requested. Hopefully, we have provided them with some indication of areas deserving of further exploration and the stimulus to take the work forward into the next century. We express our gratitude and good wishes to those who come after us.

To our wives, Avtar Kaur and Gwynneth, as always, we express our gratitude for their love and patience. We hope that the book, which has been the result of our experiences as well as study, will be of value to students, and to Sikhs and Christians, as they learn to live together and with people of other faiths and none in our one world.

W. OWEN COLE AND PIARA SINGH SAMBHI

# 1

# Introduction

The authors of this book are friends who have worked together since the quincentenary celebrations of Guru Nanak's birth in 1969. Consequently, the form chosen is one of interaction and dialogue. There will be times when a section refers solely or mainly to the beliefs and practices of one of the two traditions being discussed but there will be many other occasions when they are considered interactively. In preparing and writing this book we became more conscious than we had been before of the remarkable similarities which exist between Christianity and Sikhism, or at least between some forms of the two traditions. However, besides noting these and analysing them we shall also take cognisance of the differences, though our purpose is to understand and explain, not to criticise or score points at the expense of one another.

We have decided to begin by providing a brief introduction to each of the religions under discussion as we cannot assume prior knowledge of either on the part of users of this book. In doing so we acknowledge the besetting problem which faces anyone who writes a book about any faith, political party, or nation, namely that of stereotyping. It may be true that there is no such thing as Christianity and no such entity as Sikhism, there are only Christians and Sikhs. However, adherents do have some kind of model in their minds, for some it is a vision to which they aspire, for others it is an image they react against, believing that the spirit is threatened by formularies and practices which they condemn as 'religiosity'. In these outlines we simply hope to convey a general picture of the Christian or Sikh.

Each human being has a particular way of looking at the world. This world view is influenced by many factors, history, geography and personal experience being only some of them. The one that concerns us most is, of course, the impact of religious belief.

In this book we are looking at Christian and Sikh responses to the one world in which both religions exist and examining their

1

similarities and differences as they interact with the world as
well as between themselves, though the history of Christian–Sikh
dialogue is recent and their encounter dates only from the early
nineteenth century. Both religions have provided definitions of
orthodoxy which influence the individual adherent's outlook. This
may conform with it wholly, partially, or almost not at all! Faced
with such variety, and the need not to confuse the reader unduly,
we have kept certain norms in mind. From the Christian position
this is the person who respects the authority of the Bible and the
teachings contained in the historical creeds. Our Sikh is one who
believes in the ten Gurus, the Guru Granth Sahib, and respects the
Khalsa ideal. In Chapter 10 the consequences of choosing this stance
will be considered in detail.

When readers meet Christians or Sikhs they can discover the
extent to which the orthodoxies presumed in this book apply to
them. By the end of it they may understand how and why their
conformity is limited, if at all. If they get to know the person well
they may then be able to discover what they mean by saying 'I am
a Christian/Sikh'. Meanwhile we can only offer these substitutes.

## CHRISTIANITY

The focus of Christianity is Jesus of Nazareth, a Jew who was born in
Israel about 4 BCE. He was a religious teacher in the Jewish tradition.
He proclaimed the imminent coming of the Kingdom of God and
gathered a following of disciples which included women and 'tax
collectors and sinners', a phrase denoting compromisers in their
relations with the Roman occupying power and laxity in observing
the Torah.

After a preaching career of no more than three years Jesus was
executed by the Roman authorities (probably 29 CE) on charges
brought by some Jews who feared that claims that he was God's
promised deliverer, the Messiah, might lead to an insurrection
which would be suppressed by Rome and could result in them
losing their remaining power and influence.

Jesus' disciples, who had all deserted him at his arrest, rallied,
asserted that he had been raised to life from death and that this
demonstrated that he was not only the Messiah but also the one
sent by God to bring spiritual salvation to the whole of humankind.
Within twenty years this message was being preached to non-Jews

and the new religion based on it was spreading westwards throughout the Roman Empire. Gradually the Jewish heritage was replaced by beliefs, practices, and a church order which owed much to the Graeco-Roman culture to which most Christians now belonged. An interesting vestigial link with Judaism remained in the name 'Christian', which is derived from the Greek word for 'Messiah', 'Christos' and which had been used initially to describe those who claimed that Jesus was the 'Christos'! Terms like 'Son of God' or 'Lord', more meaningful in the new ethos, became popular descriptions of Jesus. As Christianity moved further away from its Jewish parent it began to imbibe the anti-Semitism of the Roman world. Jews came to be called 'Christ killers' and for about sixteen hundred years were submitted to forms of discrimination culminating in the Holocaust of the twentieth century.

In 313 CE the Emperor Constantine legalised the Christian religion, which became the recognised state religion of the Empire by the end of the century. Attempts were made to define and codify Christian belief at Church Councils and through such formularies as the Nicene Creed. The concept of Christendom developed, a relationship of church and state combining to create nations ruled on Christian principles. Although they achieved some degree of harmony under the authority of the Bishop of Rome, the Pope, no form of political unity or cohesion was reached.

The eastern churches finally rejected the supremacy of the Pope in 1054 but the most serious challenge to the remaining unity of Christendom came in the sixteenth century when a number of people known as reformers or protesters, pioneered by a German monk, Martin Luther, questioned the Pope's authority. Their studies of the Bible convinced them that the medieval church had developed a momentum of its own, often contrary to scripture, and was in need of reform. The result was that while the church which acknowledged the Pope as its head, now called the Roman Catholic Church, remained by far the largest, many other denominations emerged. For centuries these reformed or protestant churches existed as rivals but during the twentieth century a spirit of ecumenism has developed resulting in harmony and cooperation and sometimes in structural unity.

Within the Christian spectrum exist a number of groups which are particularly active in missionary work and which place the power of the Holy Spirit and their understanding of Christian truth above ecumenical concerns but many regard the Pope as 'anti-Christ'.

4 *Sikhism and Christianity*

Among these are some Evangelicals and Pentecostalists. Other movements such as Jehovah's Witnesses and Latter Day Saints (also known as Mormons) are often considered to be outside the limits of Christianity by many of the major denominations.

Christian worship varies from one denomination to another. It is always congregational but the focus may be on the Last Supper which Jesus shared with his disciples on the night before his death, or on an exposition of the Bible.

Not surprisingly, ethics featured prominently in the teachings of Jesus, for they were an important aspect of his heritage. He often clashed with his co-religionists over interpretations of the ethical teachings of the Torah. He did not give his followers particular precepts but invited them to base their attitudes on the principles of love for God and for one's fellow human beings. Christians define 'love' in terms of Jesus' own example. He is their role model. For much of the period since Constantine became emperor, Christians enjoyed favoured political status aand power, and were able to influence government policies. In matters of personal morality Christians would agree that things like theft, murder and adultery are wrong. With regard to the punishment of criminals, pacifism, abortion, euthanasia, and many other issues, including cohabiting in a stable relationship outside marriage, however, many views have emerged in recent centuries. There is also considerable debate as to whether Christians should use any power they may possess to impose their beliefs in these matters on others through influencing politicians. In some parts of the world there are Christian religious parties. On the other side of the debate are those who find it impossible to endorse any political world order as being Christian. They are critical of all regimes and parties.

Glancing towards the future one might say that the concerns of Christians will be relations with other Christians, the environment, racism, the ministry of women, attitudes towards and relationships with people of other faiths, as well as ongoing attention to poverty and social issues, particularly those raised by medical advances in the west. This is a western agenda; perhaps Christians in Africa or Asia would have different perspectives and will increasingly express their views in the next decade. The consequences of the fact that most Christians are not white or European has not yet begun to be felt. It might be, if eventually the Roman Catholic Church elects a black Pope.

## SIKHISM

Sikhism is the expression of the vision of Guru Nanak who was born into what is sometimes described as a middle-class rural family in the Punjab region of north west India in 1469. He was followed by nine other spiritual guides, or Gurus, who preached and developed his message according to the needs of the time. These were, in particular, the lack of spiritual hope of men, and even more so women, who were at the base of the caste system, or outside it. The line of human Gurus came to an end in 1708 with the death of the Tenth Guru, Guru Gobind Singh. Some time before his death he ordained that the teachings compiled by him and earlier Gurus should be adhered to and that it should be recognised as the Guru. This scripture is now known as the Guru Granth Sahib. He further taught that in matters where direct guidance could not be had from the scripture, decisions should be made by the Sikh community as a whole, the Panth, in the light of the general spiritual and moral principles laid down in the Guru Granth Sahib. Those who commit themselves to follow this teaching are called 'Sikhs' a word which is derived from the Punjabi verb *'sikhna'*, to learn.

Guru Nanak was appalled by the prevalence of a multiplicity of ideas about God and the resultant conduct which divided people into hostile groups, placing the emphasis upon sectarianism rather than the unity of humanity and the unity of God. The Guru stressed the worship of the one almighty God, *Akal Purukh*, the One Beyond Time. He also called people to forge themselves into one spiritual family, discarding all those kinds of social distinctions and racial prejudice which perpetuated inequality and injustice. To this end, stress was placed on collective worship where men and women of all castes and sectarian groups, be they Hindu or Muslim, praised the one God. He also introduced the practice of commensality in a further effort to break down social barriers. A logical consequence of Guru Nanak's stress on one God and one humanity was his teaching that men and women are equal.

Ritualism was discouraged. One of the Guru's main arguments with the Hinduism and Islam of his day was that they placed excessive emphasis upon formalism, correctness of observance, whereas he taught that sincerity of heart and mind were the principal requirements for approaching God. His method of preaching was popular and direct, using the language of the people (though he knew *sanskrit*), and easily memorised poems set to music by a Muslim companion, Mardana.

Sikhism strongly advocates the institution of the family and sees no conflict between the pursuit of the spiritual life and that of a householder's obligations to family and society. At a time when asceticism was popular, Guru Nanak denied its efficacy. Instead he taught that it was God's grace which enabled men and women to live godly lives and to achieve liberation, not austere self-effort.

Brahminical Hinduism and Islamic orthodoxy felt threatened by the teachings of the Gurus whose growing influence may have been regarded as a challenge to the stability of the Mughal Empire.

In 1606 Guru Arjan, and in 1675 Guru Tegh Bahadur suffered martyrdom. As a consequence of developments in the seventeenth century, the Sikh movement took to arms and Guru Gobind Singh created the Khalsa in 1699. Sikhs often describe it as a 'brotherhhood' but the term is inappropriate because its membership is open to women as well as men. Khalsa describes those Sikhs who have been initiated and taken vows in a ceremony known as *amrit pahul*. The distinctive turban and beard, together with a sword worn on the left hip, have become the hallmarks of a male Sikh since 1699, but this aspect of Sikhism should not make the observer, or Sikhs themselves, forget that spiritual liberation is the primary message of the Panth. Its struggle is against injustice in all its forms, not only the military might of the tyrant. The Khalsa ideal should not blind the observer to the fact that although all Sikhs should aspire to it, the number who have received initiation may be a fairly small percentage of the total membership of the Panth (though no records are kept). There are also many Sikhs who do not keep the uncut hair.

## BASIC SIMILARITIES AND DIFFERENCES

From the foregoing outlines it will be apparent that the religions share several similarities. These will simply be noted here, as will the differences, to be dealt with in more detail later.

- Perhaps most striking is the way in which both Christianity and Sikhism developed historically from other traditions, namely Judaism and Hinduism. This meant that each had to search for and assert a distinct identity as well as going through a process of alienation from the parent faith, and rejection by it.

In the case of Christianity the rejection was mutual, but Hindus have seldom regarded Sikhs as other than Hindus in matters of religion or socially. The affirmation that 'Hindus and Sikhs are brothers' has survived the communal violence of the last decade.

- There has also been a need for each to assert and establish a claim to a distinct revelation, whereas the parent sees both as heterodox movements. Each offspring has had to formulate some kind of theological response to the tradition from which it came. From their own standpoints Christianity and Sikhism also claim to be protest movements reacting against formalism and ritualism. Each has devised its own structures and is open to the criticism of having accepted the very things which it rejected; there are both Christians and Sikhs who strongly condemn these developments while their supporters, in each case, justify them on the very highest authority.

- Jesus and the ten Gurus are historical figures and history is a matter of considerable importance to their followers. Sikhism may not seem to have an eschatology in which the temporal process reaches a goal, the establishment of the Kingdom of God, but whenever the congregational prayer, *Ardas*, is offered at each act of worship, the hope is expressed, 'may the kingdom of justice come'. 'Khalsa', meaning 'the pure ones', is explained by some Sikhs in exclusive terms whereas others would include within it all people who are inspired by sincere devotion to God and are committed to the service of humanity.

- The ancient Christian statement that 'outside the church there is no salvation'[1] is also variously interpreted. A popular usage refers to the rejection of the view that there is any such thing as a private Christian isolated from the rest of the community. The Salvation Army and the Society of Friends, denominations which do not accept even the two sacraments, are nevertheless firm in declaring the value of fellowship. The Greek word *ecclesia* carries with it the notion of election, calling, and corporateness. Similarly, a Sikh is a member of the Panth. The word has the literal meaning of 'path' or 'road'. Gradually it came to denote the community which followed the way of spiritual liberation taught by the Gurus. It is the community called into existence by God. Sikhs should demonstrate their vocation by sharing in the life of the *sangat*, the local Sikh community which meets to worship and to provide sustenance both spiritual and human, for its members. There are clear parallels between the *ecclesia* and the Panth. Both are communities which have been established by grace, they are custodians of a teaching, and they have a salvic role to play in communicating the message which they have been given to the world at large.

• Congregational worship and consciousness of belonging to a community are strong characteristics which both Sikhs and Christians share. In both the scriptures are very important. The presence of the Guru Granth Sahib is an absolute requirement, as it is at every other Sikh ceremony other than a funeral. If a householder does not possess a copy for use in private devotions, a compilation of some of the major compositions, recommended for this purpose, will be used or they will be known from memory. An outsider viewing Christian worship might not always immediately notice the use of the Bible, which may not always be physically present, but it would take only a short time to discover that it features prominently in the liturgy, either directly, through being read, or in the singing of psalms or the use of hymns inspired by scriptural passages or in the sermon which may be the exegesis of biblical verses.

• A key Sikh doctrine is the oneness of God. Sikhs are categorical in affirming this teaching. They would also argue that their monotheism differs from that of Christianity, however, being inclined to class the latter with Hinduism, which they might describe as polytheistic.

• Strong humanitarian concerns lie at the heart of the teachings of Jesus and Guru Nanak and his successors, so much so that it is easy to emphasise their teachings on the kinship of man and woman, and overlook their claims to be providing spiritual sustenance and a way of salvation. Care for the needy features strongly in these teachings and those Christians who value the work ethic find much that is congenial to them in what the Gurus taught.

• A major difference between the religions is the obvious diversity of Christianity and the apparent cohesion of Sikhism. It has to be recognised here that one is four times the age of the other, but, perhaps more important, it should be remembered that for many centuries from the time of the Emperor Constantine to the sixteenth-century Reformation the unity of Christendom was asserted and fiercely defended often by outward force. In more recent times there has been no lack of groups which have proclaimed themselves to be the one which conforms to the New Testament Church in faith and structure. There is a similar eagerness within the Panth to affirm unity of belief and practice. It has remained within the Punjab until very recently and is still composed almost exclusively of people whose homeland lies in that part of India, even if they left it three generations ago. Punjabi remains the language of worship. These are two reasons why there is much more cohesion than diversity, making it easier to make fairly categorical statements about Sikh beliefs and practices than those of Christians, where almost every one must be prefaced by warnings that 'some' or 'many' do not hold this view! This, of course, raises problems in writing this book and presents difficulties for people actually engaged in dialogue. While many Christians see diversity as being of the essence of their religion, pointing perhaps to the existence of four canonical gospels, not one, some others are embarrassed by it. To make a fairly sweeping generalisation, representatives of religions sometimes play upon diversity in another religion as a weakness and consequently attempt to conceal the usually lesser variety which exists in their own traditions.

There have been challenges to the unity of the Sikh Panth from earliest times. Guru Nanak's son, Siri Chand, rejected his father's teachings and founded a movement of *udasis*, ascetics, which has survived to this day, being now part of Hinduism. Such movements are often associated with a particular teacher, as is common in India. They last for as long as he lives and then fade away. Two exceptions to be noted here are the Namdharis and Nirankaris of the nineteenth century, both of which still exist. Their contribution to the story of Sikhism and present-day Sikh attitudes to them will be examined in Chapter 10.

# 2
# Derived Religions?

Christianity and Sikhism are clearly derivative of Judaism and Hinduism but neither is entirely happy with this statement and even now some Christians and Sikhs will deny it. The reasons for this attitude will be considered at this point as it is something which will recur in the following pages. Fundamentally, however, Christians and Sikhs wish to defend the belief that their religions are distinct revelations rather than developments or aspects of Judaism and Hinduism respectively. It is an issue to which anyone who is likely to work in the area of Sikh studies should be alerted. Behind the apparently fact-seeking question, 'Was Guru Nanak a Hindu?' lies the anxiety that yet again a westerner is going to diminish Sikh distinctiveness and threaten its identity by suggesting that it is merely one of the many forms which that religion has taken. Behind the Punjab crisis of the late twentieth century and the demand of some Sikhs for a homeland, an independent state of Khalistan, lurks the perennial fear of absorption into Hinduism. This is also a reason why Sikhs eagerly affirm the unity of the Panth and look anxiously at any movement within Sikhism which might seem to question the authority of the scripture and the importance of the outward symbols of uncut hair and turban. It is sometimes said of Judaism, the parent of Christianity, that it thrives best under persecution. In times of ease its distinctiveness is seen as being threatened by the dominant culture wherever Jews are living and into which many become absorbed, be it religious or secular. Sikh concern is of the same kind. The practical response lies in renewed emphasis upon the Punjabi language, keeping the hair uncut, and arranged marriages, and, theologically, rejecting suggestions that the north Indian *sants*, Hinduism or Islam, had any influence upon the Sikh Gurus.[1]

A similar view of Christianity's lack of any dependence upon Judaism can be obtained from a reading of the New Testament, especially John's Gospel where the Jews, when referred to, are frequently described in such a way that it is difficult to remember that Jesus was Jewish.

## JESUS' AND GURU NANAK'S ATTITUDES TO THEIR RELIGIOUS HERITAGE

Jesus was an observant Jew. The gospels describe his presentation in the Temple at Jerusalem and tell of him being circumcised. He attended his home synagogue at Nazareth on the Sabbath, 'as was his custom' (Luke, ch. 4). On going to Jerusalem he immediately headed for the Temple as any pious Jew up from the country would. Before his arrest he shared a final Passover meal with his friends (Luke 22). Throughout the Acts of the Apostles these Jews tried to keep their new faith within Judaism. Even the most suspect of the Apostles, the provincial Jew, Paul, was finally arrested at the Temple where he had gone to keep a vow. It was only later when the Nazarenes, as Christians seem first to have been called,[2] and their co-religionists parted ways, that links with Judaism were repudiated. They remain, of course, most manifestly in the inclusion of the Hebrew scriptures, however much they are reinterpreted, in the Christian Bible.

Guru Nanak was a Hindu, a *khatri* by caste (*jati*), of the *Bedi* sub-group (*got*).[3] He was taught *sanskrit* by the local *pandit* and presented for initiation with the sacred thread at the age of nine. He was married to a girl of his own caste when he was twelve years old. Their two sons were given Hindu names, Lakhmi Das and Siri Chand. However, neither the clerical/accountancy career which his father favoured nor domesticity appealed to him. His interest lay in teachings of holy men and spiritual questioning. Here there are parallels with Jesus – found with scholars in the Temple at twelve, more interested in them than his family (Luke 2:41–52).

Both Jesus and Guru Nanak created a new family. In Jesus' case he could even speak with some hostility about family ties. He said:

> If anyone comes to me and does not hate his father and mother, wife and children, brothers and sisters, even his own life, he cannot be a disciple of mine. (Luke 14:26)

For many years Guru Nanak left his home to go on preaching tours and when it came to appointing a successor rejected both his sons as inadequate.

The next four Gurus also came from Hindu families. Guru Arjan, the fifth Guru, younger son of the fourth, was the first to have been born into Sikh household. All ten Gurus came from the *khatri jati*.

## TEACHINGS SIMILAR TO THE PARENTAL TRADITION

**Christianity**

It has already been observed that the Christian Bible includes the scriptures of Judaism. In fact they were the first scriptures of the early Christian movement. At the time of Jesus there was disagreement as to final content of the Hebrew Bible. All Jews accepted the authority of the Torah, the five books of Moses, but while one religious group, the Pharisees, would be willing to incorporate ideas found in the *Nebi'im* and *Ketubim*, and regard such books as Psalms, Esther, Job or Ruth as scripture, another group, the Sadducees would not. For them the scripture was the Torah. What books should be accepted as canonical was not to be agreed for another sixty years, at the Council of Jamnia in 90 CE.[4] The first Christians sided with the Pharisees in their view of scripture. In fact, those Jewish scholars who have studied the life and teachings of Jesus would incline to the view that he was a rabbi of the Pharisaic tradition.[5] The New Testament does not give explicit support to this position, though it occasionally describes Jesus as a *'rabbi'*. Whether it yet had its modern technical meaning is unclear. The great missionary apostle, Paul, was a Pharisee. It may be that the disputations between Jesus and the Pharisees, so frequently mentioned in the gospels, arose because of the proximity of their ideas as well as the fact that such arguments continued into the apostotic age when the gospels were written.

It has come as a surprise to Christians in recent times to discover that there is little or nothing that is new in the teachings of Jesus. His commandments to love God 'with all your heart and with all your mind and with all your strength', and 'to love your neighbour as yourself', are to be found in the Torah (Deuteronomy 6:4–5). Rabbi Hillel, living at approximately the same time as Jesus, was asked to give the essence of the Torah and after stating the same first precept as that given by Jesus, expressed the second as:

Do not do to others what you would not wish them to do to you. The rest is commentary.

This last sentence expressed the position of Jesus as much as that of Hillel. If scholars were left only with the Sermon on the Mount, the parables, and even some of the miracles of Jesus, they would not find themselves dealing with someone who stood out from his Jewish milieu. He was interpreting the Torah as other teachers did, following the example of Moses who received not only the written Torah but the oral form as well. Typically of such teachers, Jesus did not write down interpretation of the Torah but, like them, passed them on to disciples who maintained the tradition after his death.

There is scarcely a teaching of Guru Nanak's which is not found somewhere in the Hindu tradition. He accepted the cyclical concept of time together with the concepts of *karma* and *samsara* and *moksha* even though the linear interpretation was available to him through Islam. (Here, however, it must be acknowledged that his inclination was much more to teach the importance of spiritual liberation than to speculate upon the consequences of failing to achieve it.) The guru is as strongly a part of Hinduism as rabbi is of Judaism. At a popular level Hinduism may seem to be extremely polytheistic in contrast to the fierce monotheism of Sikhism, but even in the villages one may often detect a realisation that underlying the apparent diversity and multiplicity of form in the shape of many gods, there is an essential unity. This goes back as far as the Vedas, the foundation scriptures of Hinduism, which state:

> To what is One sages give many a title; they call it Agni, Yama, Matarisvan. (Rig Veda, 1,164,46)[6]

There is no need to assert that Sikh monotheism was the product of the presence of Islam in India.

## DIFFERENCES FROM THE PARENTAL TRADITION

The next part of the story to be considered is the ways in which the two religions have reacted to the parental religion. This has been mostly, and certainly most consciously, in the area of beliefs in the case of Christianity. For the Gurus the contrast is perhaps sharpest in the areas of values and ethics. Mention has already been made of the Sermon on the Mount in which Jesus adds his gloss to the teachings of the Torah as any other Jewish teacher might have done. However, Christians would argue an important difference. Jesus said:

'You have heard it said of old . . . But I tell you'. (Matthew, ch. 5, passim)

The word 'I' should be seen as a claim that the one speaking has an authority at least as great as that of Moses or even superior to it. This kind of assertion may be rare as an explicit assertion in the synoptic gospels. However, it is often implied, for example, in such event as the healing of the paralysed man in Mark 2.1–12. Here the argument turns not on whether Jesus healed the man but on the issue of who Jesus was claiming to be. Only God had the authority to forgive sins. Jesus had either been given it by God (the Christian view), or arrogated it to himself (the view of his critics). This is the challenge presented by many others of the signs of the kingdom, popularly called miracles.

It is in John, the fourth of the biblical gospels, that this teaching is most clearly expressed, and in such a way that the reader is left in no doubt as to the relationship between the status of Jesus and that of Judaism. Though perhaps the expression 'Christianity' is premature when applied to the apostolic age (as 'Sikhism' may be before the time of Guru Amar Das, or even later), it is clear that the writer of John is definitely aware that his religion and Judaism are not one and the same. So Jesus uses the phrase 'I am' in a manner intentionally reminiscent of God in the Torah (Exodus 3:14). There Moses asks God for a name which he may convey to the Israelites when they seek to know who has sent him.

'If I come to the Israelites and tell them that the God of their forefathers has sent me to them, and they ask me his name, what am I to say to them?' God answered, 'I am that I am. Tell them that I am has sent you to them'.

This famous passage would be well known to the readers of John's Gospel. They would immediately recognise the claim being made when the phrase 'I am' came from the lips of Jesus.

At the very beginning of the gospel, of course, the reader is informed that Jesus is the *Logos*, and 'the *Logos* is God' (John 1).[7]

Later, when Jesus was taunted by Jews who doubted the authority of such a young man he replied, 'Before Abraham was born, I am' (John 8:58). They took up stones to throw at him, for they recognised the claim contained in the statement and regarded it as blasphemous. The wedding at Cana episode (John 2), is no mere story of Jesus saving a nuptial feast from disaster, it is an assertion that Judaism, represented by the water for purificatory rites, has proved inadequate; the wine of the new faith has replaced it. In John's Gospel a major theme is that Judaism has had its day, it is no longer spiritually efficacious. (The other gospels do not go so far; their theme is that Jesus is the fulfilment of Judaism. This is especially the teaching of Matthew's Gospel).

Guru Nanak does not seem to have gone to anything like this extent in repudiating the claims of Hinduism in matters of belief. There are perhaps two reasons for this. One lies in the nature of the Indian tradition generally. It is, and for most of its time has been, tolerant of other teachings. Indeed it has almost become a cliche to say that Hinduism is more a matter of orthopraxis than orthodoxy, or that Hindus may believe what they like so long as they conform to certain practices. An exception to this has often been the attitude of the *brahmins* whose spiritual authority had no place for rivals. Guru Nanak was as severe on them as Jesus was on the Pharisees, and for similar reasons.

The other is to be found in the purpose of Guru Nanak's mission, which was not to create a new religion but to call men and women to a deeper or true spirituality instead of performing rituals which he considered to be meaningless and from which those who became his disciples obviously derived no satisfaction. It might be argued that he had no more wish to found a new religion than Jesus had and that his instincts were against religion if it merely resulted in religiosity. It is interesting to note that he refused to be drawn on such matters as vegetarianism (AG 1289) or whether the dead should be buried or cremated (AG 466), because what concerned him was whether or not one had come to that perception of the truth which made these issues irrelevant. If one had not the future was bleak, whether it lay in hell, as Muslims taught, or in rebirth, the doctrine of Hinduism. When he was thirty years old Guru Nanak underwent an important experience. He later described it as follows in one of his poetical compositions:

I was a minstrel out of work.
I was yoked to divine service.
The Almighty One commissioned me,
'Night and day sing my praise'.
The master summoned the minstrel
To the High Court,
and robed me with the clothes of praise, honour,
and singing God's praises.
Since then God's Name has become the comfort of my life.

Those who at the bidding of the Guru
Feast and take their fill of this food, enjoy peace.
Your minstrel spreads your glory
By singing your Word.
By praising God, Nanak has found the perfect One.

(AG 150)

Sikhs teach that he was already an enlightened being who had attained *mukti* (Punjabi for *moksha*), enjoying the eternal fellowship of God who asked him to return to the temporal world. His birth in the fifteenth century was in response to obedience to the divine *hukam*, not the *karmic* principle which determines the birth of unenlightened beings. This emphasis upon his divinely ordained birth corresponds to the virginal conception and incarnation of the *Logos* with respect to Jesus. Both are ways of asserting that they were born 'not of the will of the flesh, but of God' (John 1:13). It follows that Christians and Sikhs claim that their messages were divinely inspired and not learned from teachers. This is what is implied in the statement about Jesus that, 'unlike their scribes he taught with a note of authority' (Matthew 7:29). He was not passing on the words of another teacher. It is also the message conveyed in *Siddha Gosht*, Guru Nanak's composition in the form of a dialogue with a group of yogis (AG 937–943). The assertion made is that a distinct revelation and era of history commenced with their ministries. The baptism of Jesus, which caused problems for the synoptic writers as Jesus had no need to have the taint of sin removed, and the experience of Guru Nanak in the river Bein, are both seen as acts of commissioning, the authentification of their calling and beginning of their work. Guru Nanak is God's messenger to the *Kal Yug*,[8] something Hindus would well understand, Jesus is the Messiah, the one foretold by the Hebrew prophets. It would be rash to state that no other teacher made the same claims as Guru Nanak, that is not what is at issue. What matters is that he was conscious of being called and ordained to bring awareness of God to an age which was spiritually bereft. In doing so he clashed with religious authorities, the *brahmins* of his Hindu world who denied his right to teach the Vedas, being only a *khatri*, though the main reason for his dispute was his proclamation of liberation to men *and* women of all castes. This included those who fell outside the parameters of Hinduism completely, the so-called untouchables whose only hope lay in a better rebirth which placed them within the system and gave them the possibility of eventual liberation. There were, of course, others who taught a similar message, but none with such coherence and few who belonged to a twice-born caste. Kabir and Ravidas were two such critics of the *varnashramadharma*, the social system of Hinduism. Kabir came from a *shudra* caste of weavers which had converted sometime earlier to Islam in the hope of improving its social status; Ravidas was an untouchable *chamar*, a cobbler who dealt in polluting animal skins. Both might be expected to challenge the system which afforded their kind no hope of spiritual liberation during this cycle of life. Guru Nanak, on the other hand, was a *khatri* and of a twice-born *varna*; for him there was the immediate prospect of liberation. To draw parallels with the friend of 'tax collectors and sinners', Jesus, at this point would be tempting but we must keep to the theme of distinctive revelation. This can be demonstrated by referring to the hymns of Guru Nanak first and then his successors.

On one occasion, Guru Nanak, a prisoner of war, became aware of being inspired to utter the divine message. He turned to his companion, a Muslim, Mardana, and commanded him to play his rebeck, 'for I feel the *bani* descending'. Mardana, who was leading a soldier's horse by the reins, hesitated, fearing the consequences if the horse bolted. Guru Nanak reminded him of his priorities.[9] (Some years ago a learned speaker discussed the poetical skills of Guru Nanak in the authors' presence only to be told that his efforts had been unintentionally mischievous; the Guru did not consider what metres, which words or rhymes to use. The Guru spoke only and utterly as God commanded him.) This is a point which the Guru would seem to endorse at least to some extent. He once said:

'I have no words of my own; as I am given, so I speak'. (AG 566)

The letters just used in parentheses refer to the Adi Granth, the name given to the collection of bani made by the fifth Guru, Arjan, in 1604. *'Adi'* means first but in a cardinal not ordinal sense. It means 'primal' and is an implicit claim that the Sikh scriptures were not composed and compiled by men of the fifteenth and sixteenth centuries but are the eternal word of God. They stand over against the Vedas as inspired scripture. Sikhs do not reject the Vedas in saying this but they do dismiss Hindu claims for their unique authority.

**Historical Developments**

History has affected both children's regard for their parents. The ambivalence of the early Christians so clearly seen in the writings of St Paul, especially in the Letter to the Romans, soon gave way to a condemnation of the Jews. The seeds of anti-Semitism, a word coined as recently as 1879 by Wilhelm Marr, go back beyond Christianity to the world of Alexander the Great and his successors, at least. His vision of *oikumene,* one world, was based on a broad-minded acceptance of Greek civilisation. Few nations could have been as devoted to their own culture as the Jews were, assured that they were the elect of God, chosen to be, 'a light for peoples, a lamp for nations' (Isaiah 42:6).

Rather than let their faith be diluted or destroyed by something novel, of man not of God, they resisted the Greek innovations. Their stance made them unpopular with the Greeks and later with the Romans.

Within the gospels the theory that Christianity had displaced Judaism as the effective instrument provided by God to deliver humanity must have provided some incentive to dislike Jews, especially when it was couched in the vehement terms of John's Gospel. In one encounter with Jews Jesus says: 'You are of your father the devil, and want to carry out your father's desire. He was a murderer from the beginning . . . ' (8:44).

The Passion narratives in the gospels, those chapters describing the arrest and death of Jesus, tend to accentuate the role of the Jews in bringing about his death, and at the same time minimising that of the Roman authorities. And such a cry as, 'His blood be on us and on our children' (Matthew 27:25), alleged to have been made by the Jewish crowd to Pontius Pilate, the Roman governor of Judaea, only served to add to feelings of hostility. One of the most famous fathers of the church, John Chrysostom, living in the fourth century, accused the Jews of deicide, as well as of being gluttons and people who lived dissolutely. A Christian Council at Elvira in Spain decreed, in 305, that Christians should not marry Jews or eat with them. As the Christians gained power in the Empire Jews were deprived of holding high office.

In 1096 the first Crusade to win back the so-called Holy Land from the Muslims was preached. Crusaders, incensed against any opponents of the true faith, attacked the Jewish quarters of towns in France and Germany on their way east. The coronation of Richard I of England in 1189 was accompanied by rumours that he had ordered a massacre of Jews. His subjects carried out what they presumed to be his orders in London and many other English cities. In 1215 the Fourth Lateran council of the Catholic (western) church decreed that no Jew should hold an office which would give him authority over a Christian. Martin Luther, the famous sixteenth-century reformer wrote a tract in which he advocated the burning of synagogues and the expulsion of Jews from Germany. The anti-Jewish laws in Germany during the rule of Hitler and the Holocaust were the product of this process as was also, belatedly, the formation of groups like the Council of Christians and Jews in 1942, the state of Israel in 1948 and the document *Nostra Aetate* issued by the Second Vatican Council (1962–65). The attitude of Christians to Jews is now more positive than at any time in history, so much so that Jewish scholars now feel able to work on New Testament studies, though it would be foolish to deny that there are still some anti-Semites.

As we shall see in Chapter 12, attitudes towards Judaism are now part of the larger issue of the relationship of Christianity to other faiths.

So much attention has been paid to Jewish–Christian relations because they are important in considering the parent–child relationship, but also because they constitute the longest recorded continuing example of religious interaction in history. The story is one of warning and, more recently, hope, but not complacency, even today.

Sikhism's relationship with Hinduism has been of a rather different kind. Guru Nanak and his successors never denounced

Hinduism (or for that matter Islam) as such. True, they were strong in their condemnation of a caste system which left many people, the untouchables, without spiritual hope, of the low regard for women, and the concepts of purity and pollution which provided the rationale for these aspects of the religion. Above all they were critical of the *brahmins* who might be said to have operated the system. Yet one cannot find passages in their compositions which state explicitly or imply that Hinduism is a false path which leads nowhere, or that the Sikh way has replaced it. It was only with the third Guru, Amar Das (Guru, 1552–74), that attempts were made to wean devotees from the practices of Hinduism by establishing alternative pilgrimage centres and festivals or observing them in distinct ways. So, the harvest/new year occasions of Baisakhi and Diwali became times when Sikhs were required to assemble in the Guru's presence rather than participate in activities associated with their Hindu culture.

Throughout the period of growing Islamisation after the death of the emperor Akbar (1605), Sikhs made common cause with Hindus as they had during the rebellions of the eighteenth century and in resisting Afghan attempts to fill the vacuum left by Mughal decline. When Maharaja Ranjit Singh (1801–39) managed to establish the Sikh Empire, as it is called, no attempt was made to impose the Sikh religion or laws based on it. His state was secular in the Indian sense of the word, that is one in which all religions are respected and none given preference. He employed Muslims as well as Hindus and Sikhs in his court and administration. No doubt much of the explanation for the religious situation in his empire lies in his own indifference and eagerness to put the establishment of political unity above all else, but some place must also be given to a Sikh tradition which is respectful of all faiths.

Such antipathy as there was to Muslims was not based upon theology, in marked contrast to that of Christians towards Jews. It resulted from atrocities committed during the eighteenth century. There are rooms in many *gurdwaras* where portrayals of these incidents in all their detail can be seen, beginning with the martyrdom of Guru Arjan, continuing through the immolation of the tenth Guru's youngest sons, and into the next century. At the festivals of Baisakhi, the martyrdoms of the fifth and ninth Gurus, and the birth of Guru Gobind Singh, the stories behind the pictures will be told by speakers in the *gurdwaras*. In this way a certain element of anti-Muslim feeling is maintained though most of this has its roots in the events of the Partition period in 1947–8 which still affects community relations in Britain, more so than in the Indian Punjab where Muslims are now a minority. During the division of the subcontinent into India and Pakistan many Muslims and Sikhs lost their lives in the violence which accompanied it. Today there are no Sikhs in Pakistan other than a few who maintain historic *gurdwaras* which are sited there.

Something in the nature of a theological response to Hinduism occurred towards the end of the nineteenth century. In 1873 the Arya Samaj became active in Punjab. At first this reformist Hindu movement had Sikh support for it seemed to be aimed at thwarting the efforts of Christian missionaries who were achieving some success in the region. However, the leader of the movement, Dayananda Saraswati, made derogatory remarks about Guru Nanak and Sikhs became conscious that its purpose of revitalising a purified Hinduism might result in them being the targets of Hindu as well as Christian evangelism. The Arya Samaj threat was considered the greater as it was indigenous rather than foreign, and was being made by a group which shared many of the aspirations of the Gurus regarding caste, image worship, and the place of women, for example. In many ways it was a critique of Sikhs who had forgotten these ideals. The upshot was the Singh Sabha movement which has had a considerable impact on Sikhism as we know it today. One publication must be mentioned, however, *Hum Hindu Nahin, We Are Not Hindus*, by Kahn Singh Nabha. He wrote to admonish Sikhs who 'although they regard themselves as Sikhs of the Khalsa accept the Hindu religion'. He continued:

This book is restricted to the difference between Hindu tradition and the Khalsa because our brethren are already aware that they do not belong to other religions. This much they know, yet they mistakenly regard the Khalsa as a Hindu sect. I am confident that my erring brethren will return to their own tradition when they read this book. Realising that they are indeed the children of Guru Nanak and of all the ten Gurus they will stand forth as members of the Khalsa, firmly convinced that we are not Hindus.

Clearly the issue is one of identity and the survival of Sikhism. Bhai Kahn Singh ends eirenically, after assembling his arguments, mainly in the form of proof texts:

Our country will flourish when people of all religions are loyal
to their own traditions yet willing to accept other Indians as
members of the same family, when they recognise that harming
one means harming the nation, and when religious differences
are no longer an occasion for discord.[10]

It is anxiety about loss of identity and threat of assimilation by
Hindus in an India which has departed from the secular ideal of
Nehru, so Sikhs would say, that lies behind the unrest in Punjab
in the 1980s. This, like Partition forty years earlier, encouraged
communalism but this must be distinguished from a theological
assertion that Hindus and Muslims are fundamentally wrong. For
many Sikhs, intermarriage between Hindus and Sikhs of the same
*got* is still preferable to a Sikh marriage between different ones.
*'Roti beti da sang'* remains a popular saying, meaning 'Hindus
and Sikhs eat together and intermarry', and another commonly
heard expression is *'Hindu Sikh bhai bhai'*, 'Hindus and Sikhs are
brothers'.

Sikhs have never, except in the period of the Sikh rule (1801–49),
enjoyed the power which Christians acquired in the late Roman
Empire and the Middle Ages. Most Sikhs would deny that they
would ever use it, if they were to establish a Sikh state, to harrass
other groups. It must be admitted, however, that Sikh militants have
sometimes used force against Hindus in the Punjab in the hope of
forcing them to live elsewhere, outside its borders. By this means
they hope to create a *de facto* Sikh state.


## THE LAND

There is at once a great similarity and yet a remarkable difference between Christianity and Sikhism regarding their homeland.
Christianity began in Israel and ever since there have probably been
some Christians in that land. During the Crusades, attempts to wrest
the country from the Muslims were made. Some Christian groups
view the restoration of Israel to the Jews as a portent of the end
of the age and the return of Jesus the Messiah. Nevertheless, the
majority of Christians, though describing Israel as the Holy Land,
do not seem to attach much theological importance to it. There may
be two reasons for this. First, before the Jewish Revolt of 66 CE,

Christianity had already become a religion of the Diaspora. Those Jews who had converted tended to live outside Israel and it seems likely that many who were of Palestinian origin had left during the series of persecutions inspired by the Jewish authorities. The New Israel of the New Testament is a community based on faith, not on land. From the outset it was attached to Greek, the language of the eastern part of the Roman Empire, not to Aramaic, the tongue spoken in Israel, and certainly not the religious language of Hebrew. Some of its authors were eager to remind their readers that 'their hope was in heaven' (1 Peter 1:4) and that:

> 'here we have no lasting city but we are seekers after the city which is to come'. (Letter to the Hebrews 13:14)

Perhaps this person of unknown identity was assuring Christians that Jerusalem and its Temple, possibly recently destroyed, had no place in their future. The writer of the Book of Revelation shared his vision of a new earth and a new Jerusalem with his readers, but it had no Temple and apart from its name had nothing in common with the city of Israel. The name meant 'vision/possession of peace' and the image conjured up might well have been in intentional contrast to the by-then desolate Temple site.

In sharp contrast to this, Sikhism began as an international movement. According to Sikh tradition, Guru Nanak made journeys as far away from the Punjab as Makkah, Tibet and Sri Lanka. He spoke to all social groups and must therefore have used local languages. Yet Sikhism is now a religion which is based in the Punjab and inextricably attached to the Punjabi language if not to the culture of the region. There are a number of reasons for the Punjabi basis of Sikhism. Perhaps the most important are:

- the adoption of the regional language. This also happened in the case of many other similar teachers and obviously limited the range of their outreach;
- the linking of the language to the *gurmukhi* script in which Punjabi is written. This must have further restricted the scope of the message;
- the choice by the other Gurus to confine their activities to the Punjab for a variety of reasons, religious and political;
- the struggle for survival in part of the seventeenth and eighteenth centuries.

Perhaps the question to ask is not why Sikhism remained confined to the Punjab but rather why it acquired a coherence and strength which is not to be found among other similar groups such as the Kabir Panthis. The answer lies in the identity which was forged from a combination of religion and ethnicity. In this way its correspondence is much more with Judaism than with the offspring, Christianity. Sikhism is now developing its own diaspora. Whether, after five hundred years of being Punjab-based, the religion will be changed in any significant way by this experience remains to be seen. If there is a temptation to make comparisons with the way in which Christianity reacted to its parental religion it must be remembered that by the end of the first century most Christians were probably of non-Jewish origin. The Sikhs of the dispersion are still predominantly Punjabi in origin and outlook.

# 3
# God

Christianity and Sikhism are monotheistic religions. This statement sometimes comes as a surprise to students who have been brought up on notions of Hindu polytheism and include Sikhs in that category. (Incidentally, this view of Hinduism is itself far from accurate but to correct it is not our task here.) Christian monotheism presents some problems for Sikhs, not so much over the Trinity as such but rather the person of Jesus. This matter will be discussed fully in a later chapter, here we need only say that the Sikh religion denies that God assumes material form, be it human or of any other kind. To quote Guru Nanak:

God has no form or features. (AG 750)

Another major difference which needs to be noted because it influenced Sikh teaching, though it does not affect Sikh–Christian dialogue, is the way in which the Gurus found themselves preaching in a society where there was a wide range of speculations and beliefs. At one one extreme was the atheistic *mimamsa* school of Hinduism, at the other monotheistic Islam. In between were men like Kabir and Ramanand[1] who taught the oneness of God, the philosophical system of *samkhya*, which might be described as providing a nominal place for God, and the *bhakti* tradition, which stressed divine love and grace. Sikhism grew up in a world of many spiritual options and the Gurus were required to define the divine nature. The Christian Bible never argues God's existence, and there were certain concepts which Jesus could take for granted as being known to his Jewish listeners.

Perhaps because of the variety of Indian beliefs about God, Guru Nanak provided a terse summary of his own. It is called the *Mul Mantra*. Tradition affirms that it was Guru Nanak's first poetic utterance. Sikhs describe it as a credal statement. Like all the Guru's poetry it is extremely terse in form and is difficult to translate. The paraphrase which we offer is:

> There is One supreme eternal reality; the true one; immanent in all beings; sustainer of all things; creator of all things; immanent in creation. Without fear or enmity; not subject to time; beyond birth and death; self-manifesting; known by the Guru's grace.

These words were placed at the beginning of the Adi Granth by Guru Arjan, its compiler. They lead into Guru Nanak's most important composition, the *Japji*. Their meaning will unfold in the course of the rest of this chapter but it might be appropriate to note here that 'by the Guru's grace' is a reference to God as self-revealing, not to any human preceptor. In all Guru Nanak's utterances 'the Guru' is God, unless it is clear that he has some other human teacher like himself in mind.

## DIFFERING MONOTHEISMS

Sikhs, and many Christians, find a place for natural religion. That is, they believe that a reasonable, common-sense view of the world will lead people to the conclusion that there is a God. In fact the Gurus spoke of humanity seeking after and yearning for God. To satisfy this longing was one of the reasons that God sent them. The place that Jesus and his apostles and the ten Sikh Gurus have as revealers of the message which brings salvation/liberation will be discussed in the next chapter, but we must recognise, at this point, that what Christians and Sikhs believe about God is based firmly and ultimately on these messengers.

Time and again the Gurus proclaimed that God is 'one without a second', that means having no partner or agent through whom creation, the sustaining of the world, or liberation was effected. Guru Nanak said:

> My God is one, brothers, my God is one. (AG 350)

Guru Arjan was equally emphatic when he declared:

> Apart from God there is no other. The Lord is both creator and cause. (AG 626)

Such a view sometimes appears to be monistic:

> God is the fish and the fisherman, the water and the net, the float of the net and the bait within it. (Guru Nanak AG 23)

This is not too surprising when we remember that the Gurus were mystics and that the vision of such people is often one which finds the presence of God in every experience and object. They also shared with many Hindus the belief that the *atman*, individual soul, is one with the Primal Soul, *Brahman*. Guru Amar Das spoke of the world as the image of God:

> This whole phenomenal world that you see, O man, is the visible image of God. Yes, in it I see the face of God. (AG 622)

Guru Nanak said:

> Seeing the marvel of God in nature, the mind is convinced. Through the Guru's Word one realises that all that exists is God. (AG 1043)

Sikhs, however, should not allow the belief that God is immanent within humanity or nature to become pantheism or to say that any created being is God.

Christian monotheism is trinitarian. The Athanasian Creed states clearly:

> The Father is God, the Son is God, and the Holy Spirit is God. And yet they are not three Gods but one God.[2]

This formula was only agreed after many years of disputation. What it is saying is that God is one, that the creator and sustainer and moral controller of the universe, and the Jesus who lived two thousand years ago, and the presence which Christians are aware of as they pray, live, and worship, which they call the Holy Spirit, are the one God – not three. They are not rival powers, but essentially one. The belief also affirms a continuum of divine activity. The Christian God is not one who set the world in motion and then rested or stood back from it. He disclosed himself to humankind as a human being,

Jesus, and is present now in the world through the Holy Spirit. St Patrick, who converted the Irish, is said to have held up a shamrock with its three leaves joined together as one, to illustrate the Trinity. A human analogy might be used, the same woman is mother, wife and sister, not three people though she has three different roles, performs different functions and displays different aspects of her personality to her husband, children and sisters or brothers. The doctrine of the Trinity is difficult to explain or understand. Perhaps here it is only necessary to realise that it provided Christians with an answer to certain fundamental questions. They are:

> Q.  Is Jesus God, or just a godly man?
> A.  He is God.
> Q.  Does he differ from the God encountered in the Jewish tradition?
> A.  No.
> Q.  If the Holy Spirit seems to tell us to do something which is totally different to the kind of things Jesus taught, should we follow such guidance?
> A.  The Holy Spirit will not do that. The Holy Spirit is given to those who believe in Jesus, his presence is, in some respects, the consequence of Jesus' ministry and resurrection.

In John's Gospel (14:16–17), Jesus told his friends:

> 'I will ask my Father and he will give you another to be your advocate, who will be with you for ever – the Spirit of truth'.

Thus, he will never inspire Christians to believe or do things which contradict what Jesus did and taught, though he may lead them into a fuller understanding of them. (So, for example, Jesus and the early Christians did not condemn slavery, which had virtually disappeared from Jewish society but flourished within the Roman world in which the new religion developed. As a powerless minority, Christians were in no position to do anything about it even if they had wished to condemn the institution. But Jesus taught love for all people and that the Kingdom of God was open to everyone. Consequently, the early church numbered many slaves among its members. Eventually, it came to be recognised that slavery and Christianity were not compatible.

This, Christians, would say was the result of the Holy Spirit's activity.)

Where the Holy Spirit is leading Christians today in matters relating to the ordination of women into the Roman Catholic and Anglican priesthoods, or in relationship with other people of faith, such as Sikhs, are issues of controversy. Discerning the truth is not expected to be easy. Belief in the operation of the Holy Spirit does not, of course, relieve Christians of the task of making up their minds, nor does it directly guarantee that they will reach the right decision or act rightly. However, the dynamism of God is safeguarded by the doctrine of the Holy Spirit for Christians as is his ongoing concern for and participation in human activities.

To critics who challenged him for breaking the rules of the Sabbath, Jesus said:

'My father is still working and I work'. (John 5:17)

He did not teach a watch-maker concept of God, one who set the world going and then retired from the action. Sikhs share this view of a constantly active deity.

The One who creates all, sustains all. The Creator who has made this world also takes care of it. (AG 467)

## God as Word and Shabad

Perhaps the most interesting and important areas to explore within the two religions is that of 'Word'.[3] It is certainly of considerable significance for both Christians and Sikhs. In the Hebrew Bible, the Christian Old Testament, the reader is immediately introduced to the importance of the word in the first creation story. God began by *uttering the command*, 'Let there be light'. The word is the instrument of creation. Later God speaks to Adam and Eve, Noah, Abraham, and others, guiding and admonishing them. At Sinai he speaks to Moses. Those words are written down and become the Torah, the 'teaching' or 'instruction' which is the authoritative word of God. During subsequent centuries, and especially from the eighth to sixth centuries BCE, a class of people arose, known as prophets. Their duty was to interpret the Torah for the age in which they lived and apply it to prevailing social, economic and political conditions. They invariably began their pronouncements with some such saying as:

'These are the words of the Lord of Hosts'. (Jeremiah 23:15)

Or

'This word of the Lord came to me'. (Ezekiel 12:1)

Or

'The Lord has sent his word against Israel'. (Isaiah 9:8)

It will be seen from this last quotation that the 'word' is considered to be something more than mere invective utterance. It possesses power. Perhaps one might say that there is a sense in which it is equivalent to the Holy Spirit in the New Testament, though the Old Testament does also mention the *'ruach yahweh'*, the spirit, or breath of God. Some other words in the Book of Isaiah make this point even more clearly:

'As the rain and snow come down from the heavens, and do not return there without watering the earth, making it to produce grain for sowing and bread to eat, so it is with my word, issuing from my mouth; it will not return to me empty without accomplishing my purpose and accomplishing the task for which I sent it. (55:10 and 11)

(The application of 'Word' to Jesus must await discussion until the next chapter.)

*'Shabad'* (or *'shabda/sabda'*) is an equally rich term. It is applied by Hindus to the sacred syllable *'Om'*, a combination of the sounds A,U,M, representing both the three Vedas and the *trimurti* of Brahma, Shiva, and Vishnu. In the Bhagavad Gita, a scripture which many Hindus revere as containing the essence of the Vedas, we are told *'Om is Brahman'* (8:3), the Supreme Being, and God, Krishna, commends its liberating capability. Of the devotee he says;

'Let him utter "Om", Brahman in one syllable,
Keeping me in mind,
Then, when his time is come to leave aside the body,
He'll tread the highest way'. (8:13)

*Brahman* is the Ultimate or Supreme Reality. *'Om'*, the sacred syllable, is the form taken by Brahman in becoming manifest in the world. It becomes comprehensible as the Vedas, which have sometimes been called *Sabda Brahman* or *Vak Brahman* to distinguish them from *Para Brahman*, Ultimate Reality. *'Sabda'* is also an important term in the teaching of the nath yogis, a group who traced their origins to Gorakhnath,[4] a fourteenth-century guru, but there is no need to expand further on the use of the term outside Sikhism other than to note its significance and widespread use in the Indian religious tradition.

Sikhism shares with many religions the belief that the Ultimate Reality is beyond human comprehension and becomes known only as a result of God's self-volition. The extent of that knowledge is also self-determined, largely on the basis of what is required to make spiritual development and liberation possible, and the capacity of the recipient. In Sikhism *Parmeshur*, or *Parameshwar* to use the Sanskrit form, is the word which means the Ultimate Reality. Sikhs also use *Akal Purukh*, the Being who is beyond time, the Eternal reality, immanent in everything but beyond human discerning. Sometimes, in Punjabi, the word *jot*, meaning light, is also used. 'God' is the convenient rendering which Sikhs have adopted to refer to all these terms.

This Being becomes manifest as divine teacher and guide, the Sat Guru. Often the term 'guru' is interpreted as 'spiritual preceptor' to avoid equating it with other teachers who impart secular knowledge, but it should be realised that a guru combines the roles of spiritual guide and pastoral adviser. Deciding to marry, changing jobs, emigrating, all these are matters that one might take to one's guru. The Sikh Gurus were men who were believed themselves to be inspired by the Sat Guru. Their claim to guruship was based solely upon this belief. Their primary function was to utter the divine word, the *shabad*. As Guru Nanak said:

The true creator, is known by means of the *shabad*. (AG 688)

The act of creating is by God's will (*hukam*), but all else comes from the 'word'. Guru Nanak said:

None has encompassed your bounds, so how can I describe you using my single tongue? Whoever meditates on your true *shabad* is united with you. The Guru's (God's) word is a shining jewel which reveals the divine by its light . . . One understands oneself and merges in the Truth through the Guru's (God's) instruction. (AG 1290)

## THE NAMES OF GOD

The Jewish disciples of Jesus inherited the Hebrew proper name for God, JHWH or JHVH and the inability to pronounce it. So awesome was this name that it was never spoken. By the time of Jesus it could be expressed only in written form. Even now there are Jews who will write G-D rather than utter the word God. There were other terms in use, such as Lord, Lord of Hosts or Almighty. These passed into the vocabulary of the Christian Church. In addition Christians adopted the word Father or the phrase Heavenly Father, which were the names preferred by Jesus. Father, as ascribed to God, was not new upon his lips. It is to be found in the books of Isaiah and Hosea especially, but less extensively. Creator, God of Peace, Lord of Hope, are among many other names used in Christian prayers to remind believers of his attributes.

Likewise, many expressions are used by Sikhs. Interestingly, they include Hindu names such as *Hari, Gopal, Jagdish, Prabhu, Ram,* and *Vasudev* as well as *Allah* and *Khuda* from Islam. These, however, are simply names. It is not helpful to analyse their Hindu or Islamic significance. The Gurus seldom if ever employed them with such concepts in mind. In fact, the Gurus probably used them for convenience when addressing those who used them in their devotions. Other expressions which are more specifically Sikh are *Akal Purukh*, the Being Beyond Time or the Timeless One, *Parmeshur* (or *Parmeshwar* in its *Sanskrit* form), which is used in much the same sense, *Karta Purukh*, Creator, and *Vahiguru*. This is the popular name applied to God in conversation. Literally translated it means, 'Praise to the Guru' but more usually the phrase 'Wonderful Lord' is used. It became popular sometime after the days of Guru Nanak. Bhai Gurdas wrote:

*Vahiguru* is the *Gur-mantra*: by meditating on it, the filth of self (*haumai*) is removed. (*Var* 13:2)

The word which the Gurus used to describe God's essence was *Nam*, Name.

*Nam* has various meanings. It is rather like the Greek term *logos*. Sometimes it is synonymous with 'God', as in the verse:

*Nam* sustains animal life; *Nam* supports the whole universe and all its parts. (AG 284)

Or

I thank the True Guru who has revealed the Name that was hidden to me. (AG 697)

To be more precise, however, *Nam* is God as revealed:

Wherever God is manifest there is God's Name. Whatever is, that is the manifestation of God's Name. There is no place where the Name is not. (AG 4)

*Nam* is also synonymous with Word (*shabad*), as in this passage composed by Guru Angad:

Without the Word how can one cross the ocean of fear? Without the Name the disease of duality has spread throughout the world. People have sunk in the ocean and perished. (AG 1125)

There is, however, the possibility of distinction, the Word being the means of communication and the Name the object to which it points or leads:

One enshrines the Name in one's heart through the Word. (AG 1242)

It may be tempting to compare the use of *Nam* in Sikh teaching with the insistence upon the Name of Jesus in Christianity, but it is not helpful. *Nam* is far less restricted in interpretation, perhaps intentionally. *Ram nam* was and is used by devotees of *Rama* as a *mantra*. They were assured of his help whenever they used it. So those who carry a corpse for cremation will chant:

'*Ram nam satya hai*'. (Ram's is the true name).

Sikhs will chant '*Satnam Vahiguru*' which conveys a similar belief. *Nam* can be given broader meaning, including Islamic, through the *Sufi* tradition.

Where there may be similarities is between the practice of *nam*

*simram* and prayer or worship in the Name of Jesus. Both are ways
of realising the goal of being God-realised. This idea is explored in
Chapter 8.


## THE NATURE OF GOD

Ultimately God is ineffable. That is a statement upon which Christians and Sikhs, as well as members of many other religions would
agree. Job, in the Old Testament, affirmed this belief (e.g. Book of
Job, chaps 38–42). So did Guru Nanak:

> The Lord is contained high up in the sky and down below in
> the nether regions too. How can I tell of the Lord? Make me
> understand this thing. Some rare people know what is the Name
> that is uttered in the mind, without the tongue. Without a doubt,
> words cease in such a state. That one alone understands on whom
> God's grace rests. (AG 1256)

Believers would affirm that it is only as a result of divine volition
that God's nature may be known. Otherwise human beings will
create God in their own image, making a portrait which coincides
with their changing moods or their own personalities rather than
with reality.

That God is formless is another shared affirmation of the two
faiths. In neither a church nor a *gurdwara* will one find represen-
tations of the divine form. Sikhs may regard pictures of Jesus as
of the same kind as the Hindu *murtis* which the Gurus denounced
so vehemently. Certainly they would not find it easy to persuade a
Sikh companion that Jesus is not being revered as Krishna would
be in a Hindu mandir. A Hindu, overhearing the discussion, might
also wish to correct the Sikh and suggest that Hinduism was being
misunderstood, but the popular practices of Guru Nanak's day have
left their mark upon present-day Sikhs, just as medieval Catholic
practices have affected Protestant Christians. A Christian might
suggest that the attitude of many Sikhs towards their scripture, the
Guru Granth Sahib, is idolatrous and something which the Gurus
would deprecate if they were alive today. Some Sikhs might accept
the criticism. Sikhs describe God as *nirguna* and *saguna*, without
form and with form, or without qualities and with them. Guru
Arjan said:

The Absolute Lord is formless (*nirguna*). (AG 387)

But also:

God is without qualities (*nirguna*), but also with qualities (*saguna*): God's manifest power has over-awed the entire world. (AG 287)

As *Parmeshur/Parmeshwara*, the Being beyond time, God is *nirguna*, but being present in creation, God also possesses form. God is also personal but care must be taken in using this statement with Sikhs. Again Hindu beliefs and practices have significantly influenced their attitudes. The stories of Gods who are born and die and possess human foibles, as are found in Hindu mythology, make suspect suggestions that God is personal. However, God is loving and possesses many other attributes as well as a stern insistence upon social justice and high moral living. So Guru Nanak could say:

Nanak seeks God's protection, that of his friend, sweet as *amrit*. (Guru Nanak, AG 784)

And:

Why do you doubt that the Creator will protect you? The One who gave you birth will also provide for your maintenance. The Creator of the world also takes care of it. (AG 724)

Guru Arjan wrote:

Whatever God does is righteous and just. (AG 541)

And:

No one need be afraid of God, God is just. (AG 90)

In other words the God of the Gurus is not quixotic and unpredictable. On the contrary, dependability is a quality of the divine which the Gurus stressed, aware, no doubt of the uncertain behaviour which characterised Hindu beliefs about God at the village level. Thus Guru Angad could say:

The One who creates and fashions the world keeps it in its place. The Omnipotent and bounteous Creator gives sustenance to all beings. Mortals do the work which has been assigned to them from the beginning. Nanak says, other than the One there is no one else. (AG 475)

Of course, God is also one who speaks to human beings, as Guru. Christianity inherited a Jewish teaching which accepted God as personal but had already explicitly rejected the worship of idols. The Book of Isaiah scathingly rejects them as manifestations of divinity:

> A man plants a cedar and the rain makes it grow, so that later on he will have a tree to cut down; or he picks out of the forest an ilex or an oak which he will raise into a stout tree for himself. It becomes fuel for his fire; some of it he uses to warm himself, some he kindles and bakes bread on it. Some he even makes into a god, and prostrates himself; he shapes it into an idol and bows before it. One half of the wood he burns in the fire and on this he roasts meat, so that he may eat this and be satisfied; he also warms himself and says, 'Good! I can feel the heat as I watch the flames.' Then what is left of the wood he makes into a god, an image to which he bows down and prostrates himself; he prays to it and says; 'Save me; for you are my God.'
>
> Such people neither know nor understand, their eyes made too blind to see, their minds too narrow to discern. Such a one will not use his reason; he has neither the wit nor the sense to say, 'Half of it I have burnt, and even used as embers to make bread; I have roasted meat on them and eaten it; but the rest of it I turned into an abominable object; really I am worshipping a block of wood.' He feeds on the ashes indeed! His deluded mind has led him astray, and he cannot recover his senses so far as to say, 'This thing I am holding is a sham.' (Isaiah 44:14–20)

Guru Nanak condemned idolatry in a similar manner, and spoke with sarcasm against those who worshipped idols. He said:

> Pandit, you install the image alongside its lesser godlings. You wash it, worship it, offer it saffron, sandalwood and flowers. You fall at its feet seeking to propitiate it. But you beg men for what you wear and eat! (AG 1240)

Unlike Isaiah's smith, who made the idol and then bowed to it, the pandit (the word can mean wise man) did not seem to believe in the idol to the point of taking its ability to sustain him seriously!

Moses, Aaron, and the prophets condemned any tendencies towards the making of idols which they encountered. One of the most important commandments in the Torah is:

> You must not make a carved image for yourself, nor the likeness of anything in the heavens above, or on the earth below, or in the waters under the earth. You must not bow to them in worship. (Exodus 20:4–5)

When Christians say that God is personal they, like the Sikhs, mean that he is loving, just and righteous. Love is the key concept of God for the Christian as truth is for the Sikh:

> Everyone who loves is a child of God and knows God, for God is love. (1 John 4:7)

This is the verse that sums this up, though God's love runs through the Old Testament, as well as the writings of the early Church, being an especially strong theme in the book of Hosea, for example.

As for caring and compassionate, perhaps the most poignant verse in the New Testament is that which records Jesus' words to Jerusalem:

> How often have I longed to gather your children, as a hen gathers her brood under her wing; but you would not let me. (Matthew 23:37)

Justice is also an attribute of God in Christian teaching. St Peter described God as the 'holy and righteous one' (Acts 3:14), and the emphasis upon forgiveness and love in the New Testament should not allowed this aspect to be overlooked. However, Christians want to say that in the life of Jesus, the full personhood of God became manifest. As Jesus said:

> He who has seen me has seen the father. (John 14:9)

The whole Bible is shot through with statements and narratives which affirm the trustworthiness of the God about whom it is written. Christians would also find in the post-Resurrection appearances of Jesus to the disciples who had proved so fickle in their allegiance to him, the ultimate proof that God's dependability is beyond doubt.

The Jesus who lived a life of compassion and died upon the Cross, suffering, as Christians believe, on behalf of others, demonstrates the limitless nature of divine love. As they look at the Cross, especially on Good Friday, they say, 'God loves like that', but despite their belief in the Incarnation they hold as fundamental the belief that God is a formless spiritual being.

**Transcendence and Immanence**

Christianity emphasises the transcendence of God. Humanity may be born in his likeness and image (Genesis 1:26), and, in the person of Jesus, God came to live among them as a man, but the language of most of the Bible is about the otherness of God, of him being 'out there', the creator. Traditionally, the Church has been wary of mystics who find Him in nature or within themselves. Older books on (western) philosophy of religion, though they may not be explicitly Christian, share this caution.

The Creation accounts of the Book of Genesis implicitly convey the impression of God as transcendent, as do many psalms and the visions of the prophets. When they spoke of the Spirit of God being within them their words often really indicated temporary possession, infusion, rather than immanence. The utterances of prophets are often preceded by such a phrase as 'the word of the Lord came upon . . . ' or 'the spirit of God came on . . . '. Promises such as, 'I will put my spirit within you' (Ezekiel 36:27), and 'I shall pour out my spirit upon all mankind' (Joel 2:28), by using the words 'put' and 'pour', share this idea of possession, as do references to Christians being filled with the Holy Spirit. Christians believe that the promise contained in the words of Joel quoted above were fulfilled at the festival of Pentecost following Jesus' Resurrection (Acts 2), but in John 20 the Holy Spirit is given to the apostles on the day of Resurrection (verse 22), and the author of Revelation, rather like a prophet in the Old Testament, can say, 'On the Lord's day, the Spirit came upon me' (1:10). There is the verse in John's Gospel which speaks of the light which is in everyone:

> The true light which gives light to everyone was even then coming into the world. (John 1:9)

Most Christians would interpret it as the light which is the source of enlightenment was coming into the world. Members of the Society of Friends (Quakers), however, believe that it refers to that of God in every human being, and that it is, therefore, a statement of immanence.

The Sikh would give priority to immanence. Examples abound in the Guru Granth Sahib, in a similar proportion to those emphasising God's transcendence in the Bible. A few examples from the words of Guru Nanak must suffice:

God pervades all created beings; God creates all and assigns to all their tasks. (AG 434)

God created nature and pervades it. (AG 84)

God is hidden in and enlightens every heart. (AG 597)

There is also a strong belief in the transcendence of God, however, as is indicated by such a verse as the following:

The one who creates all and whose love yokes all, oversees it all, detached and alone. (AG 722)

But the concept of immanence is seldom far away:

The one who permeates all hearts is transcendent too. (AG 294)

**God as Creator**

That God is *Karta Purukh*, Creator, as well as *Akal Purukh*, the Being who is beyond Time, the Eternal, is an affirmation as important to the Sikh as to the Christian. Why, according to Sikh belief, God should have wished to create the universe is not easy to discover. The Gurus said:

For countless aeons there was undivided darkness. There was neither earth nor sky, only the pervasive infinite Order of God (*hukam*) . . . .

There was no Brahma, Vishnu, or Shiva. No one else but the one. No female or male, no caste or birth, no suffering of pain or pleasure. . . . . .

There was no *devata*, temple, sacred cow or *gayatri mantra* . . .
No Muslim scholar or judge, no *sheikhs*, no pilgrims to Mak-
kah. . . . .
When that one wished the world was created. Without support
God created the firmament. . . . .
By God's will the one created the creation and watches over all.
(AG 1035/6)

This passage is quoted extensively because it makes the point
very strongly, as one reads the catalogue, that in the beginning
was unity. Duality was not the divine intention but has been the
consequence of creation. There was no caste, there were no *sheikhs* or
*hajjis* who divided the unity of spiritual reality in the Guru's view.
But with creation the potential for division came into existence.
That consciousness which distinguishes humanity from the rest of
creation and enables it to be aware of and obey the command of
God (*hukam*), was used for self-assertion so that the orderliness of
creation was spoilt by *haumai*, self-centredness or egoism. (These
two terms are discussed later.)

Christianity is equally emphatic that the world is the creation of
God. It takes hold of the Jewish creation myths of Genesis chapters
1 and 2 interpreting them in its own way, as it does the rest of the
Jewish Bible, or Old Testament.

'In the beginning God created the heavens and the earth' are the
opening words of the Bible. The creation accounts which follow are
taken literally by some Christians and understood in a variety of
ways by others, but all affirm the truth enshrined in these first
words. For the Christian as for the Sikh, the world is no accident,
nor is it explicable only in scientific terms of natural evolution.
Though a large number of Christians will turn to science to explain
the 'how' of existence they find the reason 'why' in the purposes of
God. Sikhs, however, have been spared the science versus scripture
controversy which some Christians have been engaged in since the
mid-nineteenth century. One reason for this may be the fact that
the theory of evolution was propounded and developed in the
west by scientists and philosophers whose religious background
was Christian. A second may be that Sikh accounts like the one just
quoted do not conflict so obviously with evolutionary theories. This
is not deny that there are scientists whose background is Sikh who
find it impossible to reconcile their scientific knowledge and understanding with belief in the existence of God. It is simply to say that it

is not texts in the Guru Granth Sahib which cause them difficulties, it is the problem of belief in the kind of divinity described in these pages – one who creates, sustains, and is all-powerful.

Why God decided to create the universe is a question which the Bible and the Guru Granth Sahib answer by asserting, implicitly or explicitly, that it is the result of God's will.

One of the hymns of Guru Nanak makes this point:

> God, self-created, assumed the Name (*Nam*). Secondly, God created nature and, seated within it, looked upon it with delight.
>
> You are the Giver and the Creator. As is your pleasure so you bestow and show mercy. You, knower of all, give and take life with a word. Abiding within your creation, you behold it with delight. (AG 463)

Many passages support the notion of God as the Being responsible for all aspects of creation. There is no place for a dualism which regards evil as in some way caused by some other force or power. For the Sikh no such being exists:

> Whatever God wills has happened; there is no other doer. (AG 154)
>
> Pain and pleasure are part of God's order and will. (AG 223)

## The Problem of Evil and the Nature of God

If God is omnipotent and the source of truth and love the question of the existence of evil, especially in the form of undeserved or so-called innocent suffering is one to which believers in such a God must address themselves. As we have seen, Christians and Sikhs both believe in such a God.

## Christianity

Christians have often tended towards dualism. There is a being in the Bible who is called Satan. He is often identified with the serpent who tempted Eve in Genesis chapter 3 of the Bible, and with the Devil. In the last book of the Bible, Revelation, the author describes an angel who 'seized the dragon, that ancient serpent who is the Devil or Satan' (20:2).

Both Satan and the Devil are referred to frequently by Jesus and, for this reason, many Christians believe in the Devil or Satan as an actual supernatural being. In Mark 1:13 is the statement that Jesus was tempted by Satan in the desert for forty days. In the same gospel, Peter took issue with Jesus who had just prepared the disciples for his death and resurrection. Jesus replied:

'Out of my sight, Satan'. You think as man thinks, not as God thinks. (Mark 8:32)

In other words, Peter was tempting Jesus to disobey the will of his father. A central feature of the Book of Revelation is a cosmic battle waged between celestial forces led by the archangel Michael and the dragon. With the defeat of evil the reign of God is established.

Dualism, despite a belief in the Devil, is not an acceptable Christian belief. The power of the Devil is limited and Christian teaching leaves no room for doubt that evil has potentially been overcome by the sacrificial death of Jesus which was, to use military language, the decisive battle of the war. What remains is simply a mopping-up operation. Through faith in Jesus the Christian may already participate in the benefits of his victory, especially the defeat of evil in one's personal life, through grace, and the gift of eternal life through faith in Jesus Christ. The concept of a personal Devil is not one which all Christians find acceptable. They perceive a tendency to dualism despite the denials of theologians through the centuries. They prefer to interpret the biblical passages symbolically, including those in which Jesus seems to accept the Devil's real existence. Their critics would say that the origin of evil is something which they fail to explain and its effect a matter which they do not take sufficiently seriously. Why, they might ask, was it necessary for Jesus to die unless evil were a potent and real force? This issue is one to which we shall return in the next chapter.

## Sikhism

For Sikhs evil and suffering are the consequences of misinterpreting the world. The word *maya* is an important one in Indian philosophical thought. Sikhs use it to describe the state of delusion suffered by those who commit the error of believing that the world is permanent. It is real, it is not an illusion, as classical Hindu *Vedanta* teaches. It is God's creation. However, if one becomes attached to it rather than to its creator, the consequence is the disaster of rebirth. This is *maya*. Guru Nanak described the condition as being like that of a merchant whose mind is fully occupied with wealth creation:

> In the third watch of the night [i.e. human adulthood] you fix your attention on wealth and the bloom of human beauty. You do not remember the Name of God which brings release. Forgetting the Name of God, the soul is lead astray through keeping the company of *maya*. Absorbed in wealth, intoxicated by bodily beauty, it fritters its opportunity away. You neither adhered to your duty nor performed good deeds. Nanak says: the third watch is the soul's attachment to money and carnal beauty. (AG 75. Translation McLeod, 1968, p. 185)

*Maya* is a term rich with meaning throughout Indian philosophy. For Guru Nanak it means delusion rather than the illusion of *vedanta* philosophy.[5] The world is real, it is the creation of God, but it is not permanent any more than the other worldly goals and achievements to which human beings aspire. This does not mean that they are evil in themselves. Wealth, for example, can bring benefits to others if it is responsibly used; the tragedy lies in making it an end in itself so that people are exploited by those who pursue it and the only permanent goal is lost sight of, namely spiritual liberation.

To illustrate this Sikhs tell the story of Guru Nanak's meeting with two men – Bhai Lalo, a poor but good person of low caste, and Malik Bhago, rich, important, and of high birth. In the story the Guru takes a piece of bread from each of them. When he squeezes that of Bhai Lalo milk comes from it, the symbol of purity; blood comes from Malik Bhago's!

Attachment to *maya* must inevitably lead to a rejection of Truth and the pursuit of lies:

> *Maya*'s disciple is false; abhoring the Truth, bound up in duality, he transmigrates. (AG 109)

The consequence is death:

> Amassing *maya* kings become proud, but the *maya* to which they are attached does not go with them (after death). (AG 1342)

This *maya* is as much God's creation as the tree from which Adam and Eve were forbidden to eat in the Judaeo-Christian story of the Fall to which we shall soon turn. Guru Nanak says, in the *Japji*:

> The creator is and shall be, not departing when creation disappears. Having created the various kinds, colours and aspects of *maya*, the manifestation of divine greatness, God watches over it. (AG 6)

The usual forms ascribed to *maya* are *kam, lobh, moh, krodh, and ahankar*; lust, covetousness, attachment, wrath, and pride. Properly used these are the virtues of love or compassion, desire for the well-being of others, commitment to God's service, commitment to justice, and self-respect. In other words, human beings have the freedom to respond to the world as they wish. Evil or suffering are the result of wrong choice.

At a human level it is likely that both Christians and Sikhs respond to the suffering or evil which comes their way, and for which they are apparently innocent victims, in similar ways. They may regard it as a reminder that this present life is only part of the story and that they are being warned not to be over-attached to it. They may find God's presence and love to be more real as they go through what might be called the suffering barrier. They may find no rational or theological answers sufficient, but hang on to a conviction that God *is*, and remain hopeful, leaving people who seem to possess greater intellects and a deeper faith to handle the theology!

## God as Male/Female

In recent years the feminist movement has become active in some parts of the Christian church. One concern it has turned its attention to is the use of sexist language to describe God. It asserts that for as long as God is addressed as 'Father', 'Lord' or 'he' attitudes to women will continue to be of the kind which lack respect for their spirituality and consider them to be inferior members of God's creation and the church as well as society at large.[6] Their views are eminently justified. In large sections of the church the role of women is one of subordination to men. In Roman Catholic Christianity, and the Orthodox Church to some extent, celibacy is preferred to marriage as a Christian virtue, often with the implication that woman has inherited the mantle which the Genesis chapter 3 story of the Fall of humanity gives to Eve, that of temptress. Men have rarely been able to cope with women who threaten them by being their equals, as the story of St Joan of Arc in the history of England and France amply demonstrates, and the experience of women theologians in much more recent times endorses. What Christian women are doing is attempting to establish a status for themselves in the church by challenging the patriarchal nature of godhead which is derived from Judaism and apparently validated by the fact that in Jesus God became man, not woman, and the choice by Jesus of twelve men to be his closest disciples. (That they were also Jews and that he had female disciples too, unlike many similar teachers of his day, are facts conveniently overlooked by those denominations which would exclude women from the ministry.)

Sikh women have none of these theological problems to contend with. True, the Gurus were men but that is seen to be a cultural matter. If it is difficult for female gurus to achieve credibility in the late twentieth century how much more so five hundred years ago!

God, according to Sikh teaching, is beyond the categories of male and female. They are attributes of the creation, not the creator:

The wise and beauteous Being (*purukh*) is neither a man nor a woman nor a bird. (Guru Nanak, AG 1010)

Like wealth they are *maya* in the sense that they have their place. God chose to decide that human beings and other creatures should reproduce through the union of male and female and gave them to one another for support and companionship, but lust or excessive attachment can separate the devotee from God to whom, ultimately, the only true attachment should be. Thus, of God, Sikhs can say:

God, the one, dwells within all but is revealed only to those who receive grace. (AG 931)

The emphasis on the one and on the divine presence within every human being would be seen as preventing the conclusion being drawn that God is seen to possess characteristcs of gender.

Sikhs will frequently utter the words: You are my mother and father, we are your children (AG 268), as they occur in a verse by Guru Arjan used at the close of congregational worship, and,

You are my father, you are my mother,
You are my kinsman, you are my brother. (AG 103)

In these passages it is the love, care, and protection of God which is being referred to, not gender. In the same way, when devotees are described as God's brides (AG 763), or brides whom God enjoys (AG 21), we are invited to think of spiritual union, not sexual.

When the Guru Granth Sahib is translated into English, or other languages, there is a temptation and a need to amplify its terse poetical verses. So, where the personal pronoun may be missing in the *gurmukhi* original 'he' or 'him' is often inserted. This custom, together with the inclination of the Gurus to use such names as Hari, Gobind, and others taken from Hindu mythology and relating to male forms of deity, can easily lead writers into presenting a male concept of God as being Sikh.

The case of Sikh women is not improved by the fact that, despite the message of the verse quoted above (AG 1010), in two of the English translations the word 'he' is used of God (*purukh*). In the third 'Lord' is preferred! If influential scholars persist in the use of sexist language there is little hope of a general change in attitude back to the stance of the Gurus.[7]

## God as Ruler of History

Individuals generally manage to find purpose in their lives through family, career goals, sporting achievement or other forms of material success. Christians and Sikhs are also sustained by these but they find a reason for living through the relationship to God whose will they seek to do daily in their lives. This, however, is not the whole story, for they also believe that history, as well as the lives of individuals, has a purpose.

This is the underlying message of the Old Testament. It is taken up in the revelation given to the authors of the New Testament, especially in the last book, but also in many other places. Revelation, which ends the Bible, is permeated with surreal and fantastic imagery, most of it used to describe seven visions. It may be the product of a period of savage persecution and be intended to reassure Christians who were threatened with torture and even death. Its message is that despite appearances which often seem to convey a contrary message, evil will be defeated and the rule of God will be established. The sixth vision, in chapters 17 to chapter

20, verse 10, is of the defeat of the whore of Babylon, the Roman Empire, and the return of the victorious Christ. The final vision, in the last chapter, ends with the consummation of history in the establishment of the new Jerusalem.

> Every accursed thing shall disappear. The throne of God and of the Lamb will be there, and his servants shall worship him; they shall see him face to face and bear his name on their foreheads. There shall be no more night, nor will they need the light of lamp or sun, for the Lord will ever give them light; and they shall reign for ever. (Revelation 22:3–5)

The picture provided in 2 Peter 3:13 is one of the destruction of the existing order:

> The day of the Lord will come like a thief. On that day the heavens will disappear with a great rushing sound, the elements will be dissolved in flames, and the earth with all that is in it will be brought to judgement . . . .
> Relying on his (Christ's) promise we look forward to new heavens and a new earth, in which justice will be established.

'May your kingdom come' is part of the prayer which Jesus taught his disciples (Matthew 6:10 and Luke 11:2). His mission was not only to preach the coming of that kingdom but also to inaugurate it. Christians speak of a *parousia*, the return of Jesus Christ as the recognised and acknowledged Lord. 'Second coming' is the popular phrase used to describe this dynamic intervention. Whether it is to be seen as an historical event or not, and that is something about which Christians hold a variety of views, the beliefs have one aspect in common, namely that the sovereignty of God will be established for all to see.

The *Babur bani* are four brief verses in the Guru Granth Sahib which were composed by Guru Nanak and which refer to the Mughal Babur's invasion of northern India between 1520 and 1526. The first in order in the Guru Granth Sahib reads:

> You have protected Khurasan [Babur failed to conquer it in 1505] and spread terror in India. You did this, but, to avoid the blame you sent the Mughal as the messenger of death. So many blows were inflicted that men cried out, 'O God, do you feel no

compassion?' O God, you are the Maker you are impartially the master of all. Even if one mighty man smote another your mind is not affected by anger. If a powerful tiger falls upon a herd and destroys it, its master is asked why he did not protect it. Dogs have spoilt and devastated the priceless country, no one will mourn their passing. Lord, you join and separate. In this your greatness lies. (AG 360)

The second verse reads:

The wealth and sensual beauty which had intoxicated them became their enemies. The command was given to the messengers of Death to strip them of their honour and carry them off. If it seems good to you you give glory, if it pleases you you give punishment. If they had taken time to think would they have received the punishment? But the rulers paid no heed, instead they passed their time in merry making. Now Babur's authority has been established the princes starve. (AG 417)

The message of the third verse is similar:

The Mughals and Pathans fought each other, wielding swords on the battle field. One side took aim and fired guns, the other urged on its elephants. Those whose letters had been torn in God's court had to die . . . .
The Creator acts and causes others to act. To whom should we complain? Weal and woe are according to your will. (AG 417)

These may be eye-witness comments upon Babur's invasion. There are many distinctive features about them but their relevance for us lies in the emphasis which they place upon the activity of God in history and the stress upon God as its ruler. This is fairly unusual in the Indian religious context where time is cyclical not linear and the historical process does not appear to have much significance. Here, however, Babur is clearly God's instrument. In this book it might be appropriate to suggest a parallel with the Assyrians, who are thus described in the Old Testament:

The Assyrian! He is the rod I wield in my anger, the staff in the hand of my wrath. I send him against a godless nation, I bid him march against a people who rouse my fury. (Isaiah 10:5-6)

The fourth *bani* once again describes Babur's invasion but continues:

> The Lord is true, his decisions and commands are based upon justice. But only when the body's garment is torn to shreds will Hindustan remember my words; 'He comes in seventy eight and goes in ninety seven, when another disciple of a warrior will arise (to uproot them). (AG 723)

In the first three verses there is no suggestion that Babur will be brought to book in the way that the prophet speaks of the future punishment of the king of Assyria (verse 12). However, Sikhs interpret the fourth as a prediction that Babur's empire, which began in the Indian year *Samvat* 1578 (1521–22 CE), would be overthrown in 1597 (1540 CE), when Humayun was defeated by Sher Shah Sur.

Sikh congregational worship ends with a prayer known as *Ardas*. It contains another statement of belief in God's sovereignty over history as well as the implied recognition that the present order is not as it should be and will be eventually. It reads:

> May the kingdom of justice come.

# 4
# Jesus and the Gurus

Some comparisons between the role of Jesus and the Gurus in the religious context of the times in which they lived has already been made in Chapter 2. Here they will be considered as mediators of divine revelation.

The focus of revelation for Christians is Jesus through whom, they believe, God to be supremely revealed. Jesus both proclaimed and was the Word of God. For Sikhs the Gurus were messengers through whom the Word was revealed. This is why neither Jesus nor Guru Nanak needed any human teacher. Their followers have always believed their inspiration to come directly from God. John's Gospel asserts that Jesus:

> was born not of human stock, by the physical desire of a human father, but of God. (1:13)

Guru Nanak said:

> Nanak has obtained the infinite, transcendent Supreme God as his Guru. (AG 599)

Sikhs would demur, however, at the point where Christianity affirms the divinity as well as humanity of Jesus.

## THE PROBLEM OF INCARNATION

Within the Hinduism with which Guru Nanak was familiar was a belief in *avatar*, the idea that God enters history by taking a physical form which may be animal or human. The best known and most worshipped *avatars* are Rama and Krishna, manifestations of Vishnu. The purpose of *avatar* is probably best summed up in the words of Krishna in the Hindu Bhagavad Gita, chapter 4:7:

Whenever the law of righteousness (*dharma*) withers away and
lawlessness (*adharma*) raises its head, then do I generate myself
on earth.

For the protection of the good, for the destruction of evil-doers,
for the setting up of righteousness, I come into being age after
age.

Sikhs deny this concept. God is, as we have seen, essentially
*nirguna*, without qualities including physical form, they argue.
'Form' is assumed in such divine manifestations as *Nam*, Truth,
Word, or righteousness (*dharma*), but these operate through the
spirit of God which is latently present in all human beings.

For the Sikh, the concept of *avatar* contains within it several
problems, if, with Geoffrey Parrinder, 'It is regarded as a divine
action, undertaken to destroy evil in the world and redress the
balance of right' (*dharma*).[1] If God is the creator and sustainer of
all, and omnipotent, man is by definition powerless before him.
There can be no imbalance of right and wrong, or if there is it is
due to the all-pervading deity. How can *dharma* 'wither away' if
God is omnipotent? If *dharma* is threatened and in such danger it
must be the work of the omnipotent God. No one else is capable
of acting with such power. Certainly not human beings who are
God's creation and subject to the divine will. If one replies that they
have free will, one is immediately confronted with the question of
whether God has a right to interfere with their choice? Should not
the God of the Gita have resisted the temptation to take sides in
the Kaurava-Pandava war and let the human participants settle the
dispute among themselves? The issues become two fundamentally:
what need has God to intervene; what right has God to intervene.[2]

The Sikh Gurus never quoted the Gita in their teachings, though
Guru Gobind Singh may refer to it in the following verses:

If you maintain that Rama is not born and is invincible, how do
you explain his coming from the womb of Kaushalya?

How is it that Krishna whom you call Master of Death was
helpless in death's hands?

How is it that the same Krishna who is called all-goodness and
devoid of enmity is seen driving the chariot of Arjuna (against his
enemies)?

Regard only that One as God whose mysteries none has been
or will be able to unravel. (Swayya 13, Dasam Granth, p. 713)

It is the Krishna of the Puranas who features most in the Guru Granth Sahib and the Dasam Granth, a compilation of Guru Gobind Singh's compositions made some years after his death. The Gurus may well have found distasteful the concept of a child, Krishna, who stole the milk and played in the mud, a man who flirted with cow girls and eventually died, being God. Such a being could not liberate others, being himself subject to death.

The symbolic meaning of Krishna mythology which Hindus would point to in response to Sikh criticisms is one which the Sikh Gurus did not appreciate.

The concept of *avatar*, Sikhs would say, also suggests that God is irresponsible or careless, allowing history to run out of control to the extent that particular intervention is necessary. God is omnipotent and permanently active. The divine *hukam*, God's command, is eternally supreme. Thus Guru Nanak can say:

> All are subject to God's *hukam*. Nothing is outside its sway. (AG 1)

> Telling, seeing, speaking, moving, living and dying – all are transitory. The True Lord, having established the divine order (*hukam*), has placed them all under it. (AG 145)

This leads Sikhs to reject belief in miracles. These seem to suggest that God is capable of being manipulated and to question the sway of the divine *hukam*. Furthermore, as Guru Nanak said:

> The desire to possess miraculous powers is a false attachment. It keeps out the love of *Nam* from the heart. (AG 593)

Christianity does not, of course, teach that Jesus should be regarded as a sudden intervention into history. He came 'in the fullness of time' (Galatians 4:4) and was 'the lamb of God slain from the foundation of the world' (Revelation 13:8). The Incarnation is part of the eternal plan of God for the redemption of humanity, not an after thought or a desperate rescue bid. Jesus once said:

> 'My Father continues to work, and I must work too'. (John 5:17)

These words are to be understood in conjunction with his statement, 'The Father and I are one' (John 10:30).

## MIRACLES

Miracles are another matter upon which Christian and Sikh might seem to disagree. Christians would assert that miracles are evidence of God's power at work in the world, not necessarily or primarily extraordinary happenings which conflict with supposed laws of nature. In fact, of course, the word 'miracle' is an incorrect translation of the Greek words used in the New Testament Gospels. The three Greek words most commonly used in the New Testament for 'miracle' are *terata* (wonders), *dunameis* (mighty acts) and *semeia* (signs). The miracles of Jesus are never merely wonders, they are always signs. But they are significant only to those who perceive their meaning. To the rest of the people who beheld them they were acts beyond the commonplace but not unique. They might provoke awesome respect but often the result was hostility. They were intended to be signs of Jesus' Messiahship and the coming of the Kingdom of God. When John the Baptist needed reassuring that Jesus was the Messiah, the disciples whom he sent to ask the question received the reply:

'Go and report to John what you hear and see; the blind recover their sight, the lame walk, lepers are made clean, the deaf hear, the dead are raised to life, the poor are brought good news – and blessed are those who do not find me an obstacle to faith'. (Matthew 11:4–5 and Luke 7:22–25)

Of all the powerful signs of the New Testament the supreme one, of course, is the Resurrection of Jesus. The Christian religion stands or falls on whether it is believed to be true or not. The other signs are of minor importance compared with this. Indeed Jesus readily conceded that he was not unique in possessing the ability to perform such deeds. To critics who alleged that his power came from evil sources, he answered:

'If it is by Beelzebul that I drive out devils, by whom do your own people drive them out?' (Matthew 12:27 and Luke 11:19)

The miracles to which Sikhs object are of the wonder-working kind, those which cause problems to philosophers of religion and to theologians because they seem to imply a potentially disorderly universe in which God operates as a *Deus ex machina*, stepping in at whim, when things are reaching the point of chaos or are going badly for his favourites, or an attempt to induce belief through demonstrating the ability to manipulate the natural order.

Professor Kartar Singh outlined the Sikh critique of miracle in his *Life of Guru Nanak*:

> Since long ago there have been two views or rather explantions of miracles. One, chiefly current in the west and associated with Christianity, regards miracles as supernatural phenomena due to divine interference in the course of nature . . . This definition, first adopted by Hume's school in the last century, has been tacitly accepted by the Church and has now filtered down to the general public by whom it is still believed to be correct . . .
>
> The other view about miracles, generally current in the east, is that they are manifestations of special powers which are in varying degrees latent in every man and are capable of development by discipline, practice, and cultivation. It is believed that some are, from their very birth, endowed with highly developed spiritual powers so that they can perform acts which, to ordinary people, appear wonderful.
>
> Having stated the two views regarding miracles it may be said at once that miracles in the first sense are not associated with the name of Guru Nanak or his successors and constitute no element or basis of their message. Guru Nanak's appeal was always addressed to the heart and mind of his listeners. He convinced them of the truth and soundness of his message *not by miraculous evidence* but by his sweet humility, profound reasonableness, soul stirring songs and discourses, and by his personal example.[3]

When Guru Nanak was challenged to prove the divine authority of his mission by performing miracles he replied to the yogis, the group of men who questioned him:

> I have nothing to exhibit, no supernatural powers to display, for I depend on nothing but the holy congregation (sangat), and the Word (*shabad*). (Bhai Gurdas, Var I, pauri 42)

He added:

The Divine Master (Guru Nanak) said; 'Listen, dear Nath, listen to my word. I am telling you the truth, I have no miracle to exhibit except the miracle of the True Name'. (Var I, pauri 43)

The third Sikh Guru, Guru Amar Das, contrasted the approach of the yogis who tried to obtain *Nam* by occult practices and austerities with those who were actually given it by God:

> Yogis seek to acquire the Name (*Nam*). They concentrate to the point of exhausting themselves. *Nam* can only be obtained by God's guidance. Without devotion to *Nam* all effort is futile. Such use of supernatural and miraculous power is accursed. Supernatural powers are conferred (by God).
> Nanak, *Nam* abides in the mind through the Guru.
> This alone is the miraculous might and the psychic power. (AG 650)

What yogis actually acquired, according to Guru Amar Das, was *haumai*, the self-centredness and pride which came from boasting of their efforts and austerities. This effort is called *sadhana*. Guru Amar Das contrasted it with *karimat*, acts of God's grace.

The miracles of Jesus would be seen by Sikhs as akin to the 'miracle' of the *shabad* which the Gurus uttered.


## THE INCARNATION

Before going on to present the Christian doctrine of the Incarnation more fully it must be made clear, of course, that Sikhs were reacting against a particular Hindu concept, that of *avatar*, and that it is not easy for them to set it on one side when they are presented with the Christian belief that Jesus is the Son of God!

The phrase 'Son of God' is often a stumbling block in interfaith discussions. With Muslims, far more than Sikhs, it presents an immediate barrier when Christians are trying to explain the Incarnation.

It was only in 451 CE that the church agreed a formula to express the nature of Jesus as God and man. Explaining the formula is one which theologians have attempted ever since. In 451, at the Council of Chalcedon, the church declared that Jesus was truly human and truly divine; that he was God, not *like* God, and that he was as human as anyone who had ever lived, differing from the rest of humanity only in that he was without sin.

To go further than this would be to try to explain a mystery, that is, something known only to God which has not been disclosed to humankind.

The purpose of the Incarnation was seen from different points of view by various New Testament writers. Some, like Mark, for example, saw it as the triumph of good and divine power over the destructive forces of evil through suffering. Jesus suffered not because he claimed to be the Messiah but because he *was* the Messiah and the way of the Cross was divinely ordained. This was not a concept which Judaism accepted but the gospel writers as a whole provided a basis for it in a reinterpretation of the Jewish scriptures. This began with Jesus' sermon in the synagogue of his village of Nazareth when he read the words from the Isaiah scroll, chapter 61:1–2, and commenced his address with the words:

'Today, in your hearing these words have come true'. (Luke 4:21)

The last resurrection narrative of Luke's Gospel describes Jesus opening the minds of the disciples to 'understand the scriptures'. He ended his exegesis by saying:

'So you see that scripture foretells the sufferings of the Messiah and his rising again from the dead on the third day'. (Luke 24:45–47)

St Paul explicitly linked the Incarnation with Adam, the ancestor of the human race. He wrote:

As in Adam all died, so in Christ shall all be made alive. (1 Corinthians 15:22)

One of the great arguments in his letter to Christians in Rome is that Jesus by his obedience even to the point of being willing to die, undid the consequences of Adam's disobedience and that those who identify through faith with that obedience would enjoy eternal life.

John's Gospel speaks of Jesus as the *logos*, the eternal Word, a term which has already been encountered:

In the beginning the Word already was. The Word was in God's presence, and what God was, the Word was. He was with God at the beginning, and through him all created things came to be; without him no created thing came into being. In him was life, and that life was the light of mankind. The light shines in the darkness, and the darkness has never mastered it. (John 1:1–5)

Jesus is the Messiah, God's Chosen One (John 1:34), the Lamb of God (John 1:36), symbolising the removal of sin, but above all Jesus is the *logos*, God's self-expression, whose purpose is to manifest the nature and glory of God.

This is probably the meaning of the Incarnation which Sikhs can best appreciate. 'Messiah' is a concept whose meaning is confined to the Judaeo-Christian tradition. Though it is used in the Qur'an as a title of Jesus (*Sura* 5:72–75), one does not feel that it has any more significance than it had for non-Jewish Christians. Once the cultural milieu of Christianity came to be Gentile, especially in regions where there was no Jewish population, its impact, potency and challenge was lost.

'Saviour', as we shall see (Chapter 5), is really foreign to the Sikh religion in which the concept of regeneration is more appropriate. However, it will already have been realised that Word, *shabad*, is one of the key terms of Sikh theology, and that God, as Guru, is linked with *shabad*. They occur together many times in the Sikh scriptures.

Here are a few passages which might come to the mind of a Sikh who reads the first chapter of John's Gospel.

> The *gurbani* (Word) is the Guru and the Guru is the *gurbani*. (AG 982, Guru Ram Das)

> The Guru's Word abides with my soul. (AG 679, Guru Arjan)

> The *gurbani* (word) is the divine light in this world.
> Through grace it comes to abide in the mind of mortals. (AG 67, Guru Amar Das)

> O disciples of the True Guru, know that the Word of the Guru is perfectly true; God, the Creator, causes it to be uttered. (AG 308, Guru Ram Das)

In placing the emphasis upon the Word as the means of divine revelation another aspect should not be neglected, one which Sikhs and Christians both consider of great importance. The second verse of the Johannine Prologue contains the assertion:

He was with God in the beginning, and through him all things came to be; without him no created thing came into being. (John 1:2)

The *Logos* is the agent of God in the creation of the world. Guru Nanak said:

One word and the universe throbbed into being, hundreds of thousands of rivers began to flow. (AG 3)

The term used here for 'word' is *kavau* meaning 'command', so the verse might be expanded to read 'At a single word of command the universe throbbed into being'.


## A SIKH VIEW OF JESUS

Perhaps the Sikh response to Jesus is best presented in a poem, *The Man Who Never Died*, by the late Dr Gopal Singh, who served India as MP, ambassador to Bulgaria and governor of Goa, and represented the Sikhs as an observer at the World Council of Churches Assembly in Vancouver. Among these many duties he also managed to find time to produce the first complete English translation of the Guru Granth Sahib and a *History of the Sikh People*. The poem which is now quoted selectively deserves to be read in full by anyone interested in Sikh–Christian relations. Only a few quotations can be provided here. It begins:

> This is the story of the Man
> Who never died:
> and Who proclaimed
> that he who's born
> must be reborn;
> and he who's dead
> must rise from the state
> of death. (p. 9)

> I am the eternal spring, that comes to man,
> again and over again,
> when the hour is come.

> For my God is not the God of the dead, but

of the living.
He who loses his life like
a drop into the ocean, becomes
the ocean himself.
but, whosoever saves his life from the sea
shall lose it in the dust.

I have sown with blood
that you may reap with honour! (p. 61)

Others have talked of God. I have come
to make gods of you all. (p. 63)
And so they resolved
‑‑ ‚‥ ⸱‥  ᴐe nailed to the Cross
along with
two thieves
one on each side, to mock
His claim to godliness,
and meet Him
with the fate of a mere man!

For, they thought
the felon and the martyr to be
the same! (p. 68)

Dr Gopal Singh's poem demonstrates a sound knowledge of the
gospels but the Jesus who emerges from their pages and becomes
the subject of his poem seems more like a guru in the Indian
tradition than a Jewish sage. He is certainly not the Jesus worshipped by Christians. He suffers, but not vicariously. This is a
concept foreign to the Indian tradition. Jesus was a martyr. That
is something that Sikhs understand well. The fifth and ninth Gurus
died for the faith as did many thousands of men and women in the
eighteenth century. The Cross showed human cruelty and divine
love but not vicarious sacrifice. Here is a great difference between
what Christians believe about the purpose of the Incarnation and
Sikh teachings about the Gurus.

## BELIEFS ABOUT THE SIKH GURUS

Dr Gopal Singh's view is quite naturally reminiscent of Sikh beliefs
about the human Gurus. They had already achieved enlightenment

and were enjoying existence in the eternal presence of God in a state of eternal bliss, *sahaj*, when God asked them to return to live on the earth. In his poem, Vachitar Natak, Guru Gobind Singh wrote:

> When God gave me the order I assumed birth in the *kalyug*,
> I did not desire to come as my attention was on God's feet.
> God remonstrated with me and sent me into the world.
> (Macauliffe, vol. V, p. 296)

Here we are apparently presented with something which at the least appears to be very close to the concept of *avatar*. In earlier verses of the poem he has even traced his descent to Rama and beyond him to the king Raghu and Kesain (Kalsain), the sage of the Vedas (pp. 290–1).

However, the purpose of the Guru's birth is to proclaim *Nam*, to call men and women to the worship of the One God which had been neglected and forgotten even though God had sent many messengers. The list catalogued by Guru Gobind Singh included Vishnu and Brahma, Mahadev (Shiva), Goraknath, Ramanand, and ended with Muhammad, of whom he wrote:

> I then created Muhammad, king of Arabia. He too established a religion of his own, cut off the foreskins of his followers, and made everyone repeat his name.

He ends his comments upon these messengers by denouncing them all, in words attributed to God, for attempting to turn people to themselves and not to the one who sent them:

> No one fixed the True Name in man's heart. All these were wrapped up in themselves and none of them has recognised me, the Supreme Being.

God continues:

> I have glorified you as my son, I have created you to proclaim the Panth. Go spread the faith there and restrain the people from senseless acts. (p. 299)

To this the Guru responded:

I stood up, clasped my hands, bowed my head, and replied: 'Thy religion shall prevail in the world when thou providest assistance'.

He then explains his birth and his relationship to God:

> For this reason the Lord sent me. Then I took birth in the world.
> What he spoke, that I speak, and I bear no enmity against anyone.
> Those who call me Supreme Being shall all fall into the pit of Hell.
> Recognise me as God's servant only: have no doubt of this. I am the slave of the Supreme Being. (pp. 299–300)

Both Guru Nanak and Guru Gobind Singh explicitly stated that they were rare, extraordinary human beings in the sense that their birth was the result of God's will (*hukam*), not previous *karma*. They belonged to the category of human beings who had achieved liberation but returned to earth at God's bidding. In the words of Guru Arjan:

> Above birth and death are your holy ones, for they come into the world to do good to others. They bless all with gift of spiritual life, lead all to your worship and unite all with you. (AG 749)

In the Sikh–Christian context one cannot help thinking of the words which were written about Jesus in John's Gospel:

> Born not of the will of the flesh, nor of the will of man, but of God. (John 1:13)

However, it would be wrong to infer that the Guru was divine. The parallel, if one is sought, is much more closely with Jeremiah, both in predestination and mission, of whom God said:

> Before I formed you in the womb I chose you, and before you were born I consecrated you; I appointed you a prophet to the nations. (Jeremiah 1:5)

The concept of the prophet as one who proclaims the eternal word of God, being infused with the divine spirit (the *ruach Yahweh*, to use the Hebrew phrase), is consistent with the important Sikh doctrine that the ten Gurus were one in the doctrine they taught and also in a mystical sense. Two bards at the *dehra* of the fifth Guru expressed it thus:

> The same is the divine light, the same is the life form. The king has merely changed the body. (Satta and Balwand, AG 966)

Bhai Gurdas, a distant relative of the same Guru, expressed the idea in more detail:

> Before he (Nanak) died, he installed Lehna and set the Guru's canopy over his head. Merging (his) light in (Lehna's) light, the *Sat Guru* changed his form. None could comprehend (this mystery): a wonder of wonders he revealed! Changing his body he made (Guru Angad's) body his own. (Var 1:45)

On page 150 of the Guru Granth Sahib there are a couple of auto-biographical verses where Guru Nanak described his calling. They have been quoted on p. 16. This was a commissioning experience. Guru Nanak was an enlightened being before birth.

Hence the inability of his Hindu *brahmin* mentor, in the *janam sakhis*, to impart anything that he did not already know. The purpose of the anecdote was not merely to pour scorn upon the belief that knowledge of the Vedas could provide spiritual enlightenment, it was also to emphasise the already enlightened status of the child. In fact the *janam sakhis* call him Baba Nanak throughout, an honorific and respectfully affectionate way of referring to a guru. This is reminiscent of the gospels of Matthew, Mark, and John beginning with the affirmation that Jesus is the Christ. In books about their religion, therefore, Sikhs expect the word 'Guru' always to be given a capital 'G', in the way that Christians often use the phrase 'Lord Jesus'.

Guru Nanak's birth was non-karmic, as Sikhs would consider that of Jesus to be. Guru Nanak's river Bein experience has a number of similarities to the baptism of Jesus by John the Baptist (see Matthew 3, Mark 1, Luke 3). They occurred when each man was about thirty years old. They both happened to men who were already perfect and had, in one sense, no need of this outward sign. The experience prepared the way for a period of itinerant ministry.

Of course there are differences too. Jesus was publicly identifying with the work of John the Baptist to the extent that his acceptance of baptism (for repentance and the forgiveness of sins) seems to have presented the author of Matthew's Gospel with the need to explain why Jesus should submit to it and theologians since to discuss what the descent of the Holy Spirit on Jesus actually signified. The Story of Guru Nanak's commissioning contains none of this sort of ambiguity, though Sikhs may discuss what actually happened during the three-day period when the Guru went missing. This is something to which the account in the Guru Granth Sahib does not refer, rightly putting the emphasis where it belongs, on the divine authority of his ministry. This stress is also made in Matthew's account, where the heavenly voice affirms that 'This is my Son' (3:17), the other evangelists use 'You are'! However, these were written by reporters of the event and not by Jesus himself, though Christians would say that the experience was narrated to the disciples by Jesus, just as the river Bein incident was communicated to his followers by Guru Nanak.

Ultimately, however, the distinction between Christian beliefs about Jesus and those of Sikhs about the Gurus has to do with the concept of revelation. For Christians, Jesus is God and as the incarnate deity reveals God in a way that human beings can most fully understand. The Gurus convey the revelation but are not themselves the revelation. Sikhs treat them with obvious and deserved respect, but in a human sense they were just like other men. In fact, Guru Nanak once said:

The truth of revelation dawns upon whoever contemplates the celestial Word. (AG 946)

In other words, it is open to any Sikh to attain to the level enjoyed by the Gurus. The concept of *jivan mukt*, that is, liberation, while still in this earthly existence, means that this is not something which must await death though Sikhs would admit that it is rare to meet those who reach this state.

Those who heard the Gurus speak and believed in them heard the voice of God and were transformed by it. Those who met Jesus and believed in him met God in him, that is the distinction, but Sikhs would blur it by insisting that the Word is one.

## THE PROBLEM OF SUFFERING

### The Christian Understanding and Solution

As God incarnate, Jesus must hold the key to understanding the problem of suffering as far as Christians are concerned. Regarding its origin and purpose they may disagree. Some will link it with the Fall and explain it as a consequence of the sin of Adam and Eve in the Garden of Eden (Genesis 3). Others may speak of a personal devil, the personification of evil, who is engaged in a battle for the hearts, minds, and souls of humanity. There are those who will try to explain evil and suffering in evolutionary terms so that genetic disorders, for example, are part of the process of the natural development of human and other life forms. Ultimately only God knows why the innocent suffer but Christians believe that when Jesus died on the Cross he was the perfect example of one who did not deserve what befell him. and that his suffering provides the key to human deliverance. He had done no wrong. It was the Roman Governor, Pontius Pilate, who told Jesus' accusers:

'I find no case for this man to answer'. (Luke 23:4)

This statement is so important that it is found with slight variations twice in Luke's Gospel (23:4 and 14) and three times in the Gospel of John (18:38, 19:4 and 6). Jesus is also described as being sinless. Many New Testament verses make this point because the Christian Gospel depends upon it. Only one who was without sin could bear the sins of others. In 1 Peter 2:22 innocency of the criminal charges of blasphemy and plotting an insurrection, which Jesus denied, and sinlessness, are combined in a statement which some versions of the Bible put in quotation marks. The suggestion being made may be that this was part of the explicit teaching of the apostles. The sentence reads:

'He committed no sin, he was guilty of no falsehood'.

His suffering was part of God's plan, not just an example of human inhumanity and his Resurrection demonstrated the power of love to overcome evil, sin, and death. Faced with suffering the Christian must be prepared to tread the same path assured that the kind of hope expressed in Paul's First Letter to Corinth is not vain. The whole of chapter 15 stresses that Christian hope is based upon the reality of Jesus' death 'for our sins' (verse 3) and his Resurrection. The last verses sum up the chapter's message:

'Death is swallowed up; victory is won!' O Death where is your sting? The sting of death is sin, and sin gains its power from the law. But thanks be to God! He gives us the victory through our Lord, Jesus Christ. Therefore, my dear friends, stand firm and immovable, and work for the Lord always, work without limit, since you know that your labour cannot be lost. (Verses 54–58)

## The Sikh View

Sikhism accepts the reality of suffering. Guru Nanak said:

From the beginning of time, pain and pleasure are written in men's fate by the Creator. (AG 1054)

Much suffering is the result of false attachment, that is, being deluded by *maya*:

Man is afflicted by ego and *maya* so he suffers. (AG 412)

The strong monotheist doctrine of the Gurus leaves no place for evil as an independent entity or force, so Guru Nanak explained it as a fact of life, as real as joy but not as welcome, and like pleasure, something which can lead one from the only way of overcoming it, obedience to the will of God:

It is absurd to ask for the gift of joy and the withdrawal of sorrow. Pleasure and pain are the two garments given to man from the divine court. Where one is bound to lose by speech it is best to keep silent. (AG 149)

It is better to pursue the path which provides a remedy for pain rather than debate its origins. As Guru Arjan advised:

Do not delay in practising righteousness, but think before committing evil. Hold fast to God, and forsake greed. Seek the protection of God's holy people to wash away impurity so that you may become righteous. (AG 1354)

But this does not mean that suffering exists to draw people to God as a last resort. That would be immoral. The role of the Gurus, however, was to alert them to the reality of suffering as something more than pain which could be alleviated by such remedies as monetary wealth or physical pleasure, and offer them the solution of making real their potential and latent unity with God.

## Eschatology

'He will come again to judge the living and the dead' is one of the important statements of the Christian creeds. The Bible is clear and united in expressing the view that this will be an historical event undertaken by a physical Jesus (e.g. Revelation 1:7, 'Lo, he is coming with the clouds'), though contemporary theologians may sometimes interpret it existentially as the experience of believers when Jesus comes into their lives. Sikhs do not have a similar belief about the Gurus, though they have beliefs of a kind in eschatology. The concept that history is in God's control and that one day justice will be established is part of Sikh belief (see Chapter 3). The Gurus were, of course, messengers. God would not put all things under their feet any more than entrust them to any other members of the human race. In any case, they were nowhere claimed to be the last of God's messengers, nor did the divine purpose envisage the earthly rule of the saints. The establishment of the kingly rule of God is not a Sikh concept. It was certainly not the mission of the Gurus to be the creation of a Sikh state. Significantly, it was transformation of heart and mind that they laboured to produce. Even Guru Gobind Singh made no effort to establish a political empire.

Intermittently there have been efforts to create Christian states and during the Middle Ages the concept of Christendom was popular. With the Protestant Reformation the hope of establishing such a superstate receded and many Christians today would oppose the idea. Not only would they point to practical problems of rulership and organisation but to the belief that the only way in which Jesus can reign is through the Holy Spirit changing hearts and minds and inspiring men and women to obey the will of God. It may be that severance from the land of Israel and three centuries of political weakness forced Christians to think of a 'kingdom which is not of this world', but the words are those of Jesus himself (John 18:36) and when they have been ignored and Christians have acquired and used political power, the consequences for Christianity have, in the long term, been unhappy.

However, for Christian and Sikh alike there is the question to be considered of how they should use any power which they might possess in the sphere of temporal politics and life.

# 5

# Spiritual Liberation
# and Salvation

## HUMAN NATURE: CHRISTIANITY

In Genesis chapter 2 of the Bible, Adam and Eve eat the fruit of the
tree of knowledge (3:6) which they were forbidden to eat (2:17).
They were told that the consequence would be the end of their
idyllic existence; life would be one of toil and suffering culminating
in death. 'Dust you are, to dust you will return' (3:19) was the
punishment declared to them by God. They were expelled from the
Garden of Eden which God had created for them. The world, which
had been created 'good' (God saw all that he had made, and it was
very good, Genesis 1:31), had been spoiled by the disobedience of
Adam and Eve, the first humans.

Judaism has never interpreted Adam's and Eve's sin as affecting
the whole of humanity and creation. On the contrary the prophets
Jeremiah and Ezekiel placed the responsibility for sin firmly upon
each individual, stating that:

Everyone will die for his own wrongdoings. (Jeremiah 31: 29–30)

And

It is the person who sins that will die. (Ezekiel 18:4)

The remedy for sin was the Torah, which human beings have
the ability to keep, but if by accident or even design they fall
short of its standards they can repent and, if they are sincere,
receive forgiveness. Certain rituals, associated especially with the
Day of Atonement, symbolise the process of seeking and receiving

forgiveness, especially those committed against God, such as a breach of religious observance. But always repentance is expected. As the prophet Micah expressed it in words which are among the best known of Old Testament verses:

> What shall I bring when I come before the Lord, when I bow before God on high? Am I to come before him with whole offerings, with yearling calves? . . .
> Shall I offer my eldest son for my wrong-doing, my child for the sin I have committed?
> The Lord has told you mortals what is good, and what it is that the Lord requires of you: only to act justly, to love loyalty, and to walk humbly with your God. (Micah 6:6–8)

If one committed a sin against another human being, theft or slander, for example, forgiveness should be sought from the offended person, not from God.[1]

Before the Day of Atonement Jews are still expected to ask forgiveness from anyone they have wronged. Jewish teaching, then, is that each person holds his or her eternal destiny in their own hands. By living according to the Torah salvation can be achieved. Each man is his own Adam, each woman her own Eve.

Christian teaching, on the other hand, states that Adam's sin affected the whole of humankind, and more. St Paul, who might be called the first Christian theologian, wrote:

> The whole created universe groans as if in the pangs of childbirth. (Romans 8:22)

These are not natural evolutionary growing pains but are the result of Adam's fall from the bliss of Eden. This fall is also given as the reason for the Incarnation. Again we turn to St Paul, who expressed the idea very succinctly:

> For since it was a man who brought death into the world, so it was a man who brought the resurrection of the dead. As in Adam all die, so in Christ all will be brought to life. (1 Corinthians 15:21, 22)

Some Christian thinkers have taken this further, teaching that the whole of the life of Jesus recapitulated obediently the sinful life

of Adam and so restored those who believe in Jesus to the full
humanity which God intended Adam to enjoy. Notable among these
was St Irenaeus in about 180 CE. He wrote:

> As through a disobedient virgin man was stricken down and fell
> into death, so through the Virgin who was obedient to the Word
> of God man was reanimated and received life. It was necessary
> that Adam should be summed up in Christ, that mortality
> might be swallowed up and overwhelmed by immortality; and
> Eve summed up in Mary, that a virgin should be a virgin's
> intercesssor, and by a virgin's obedience undo and put away
> the disobedience of a virgin. And the trespass which came by
> the tree was undone by the tree of obedience, when, hearkening
> unto God, the Son of man was nailed to the tree; thereby putting
> away the knowledge of evil and bringing in and establishing
> the knowledge of good. By the obedience whereby he (Jesus)
> obeyed even unto death, hanging on the tree, he put away the
> old disobedience which was wrought by the tree. (*Demonstration
> of the Apostolic Preaching*, 32–34 amended)

In the above extract the contrast between the disobedient Adam
and the perfectly obedient Christ is extended to include Eve and
Mary, Jesus' mother. This finds a place for woman in the story of the
redemption of humanity as well as in the Fall. It also demonstrates
that the whole process of the Incarnation from the time that Mary
accepted her role as Christ's mother to the obedience with which
Jesus accepted his calling to suffering and death, recapitulated the
tragedy of Eden but with obedience replacing sin. It was left then
only for humanity, the descendants of Adam and Eve, to share in
the benefits of Jesus and Mary through faith.

The Eastern Orthodox regard for the bread and wine in the
Eucharist as the 'medicine of immortality' which enables the
believer to become more Christ-like, owes much to this Recapitu-
lation Theory of the Atonement.

For all Christians, the death of Jesus is not merely another of the
many examples of human injustice and innocent suffering that are
chronicled in history. It was, in some way or other, the divinely
chosen remedy for Adam's sin and its cosmic consequences.

What the phrase 'fallen humanity', which Christians often use
means is that the sin of Adam and Eve in disobeying God by eating
fruit which had been forbidden them brought disaster upon not

only themselves and their descendants but the whole of creation. Suffering and death become part of their experience. Jesus spoke of his need to suffer on behalf of others:

> The Son of Man did not come to be served but to serve, and to give his life as a ransom for many. (Mark 10:45)

This sentence encapsulates much of Jesus' teaching. Earlier in the gospel is mention of his warning to the disciples that he, the Son of Man,

> had to endure great suffering, and to be rejected by the elders, chief priests, and scribes; to be put to death, and to rise again three days afterwards. (Mark 8:31)

Political and religious motives for the execution of Jesus have been provided by scholars over the centuries but the primary concern of the New Testament writers was to provide theological explanations. After all, no one expected the 'Lord's anointed', the Messiah, to suffer and die. This concept of Messiah seems to have had no place in the Judaism of Jesus' day. It must be considered a Christian teaching. Scholars are divided upon its origins, whether it is to be attributed to Jesus or to the apostolic writers. Traditionalists would say that it was Jesus who proclaimed his Messiahship, citing his response to Peter's affirmation: 'You are the Messiah' (Mark 8:29).

Jesus is said to have given them strict orders to tell no one about him (verse 30), and many similar remarks. They would particularly point to words attributed to Jesus in John's Gospel, where Messiahship may be said to be understood but subsumed in the more comprehensive title, Son of God. This would seem to be the message of the second Prologue to the Gospel (John 1:19–51) which begins with John the Baptist's denial that he is the Messiah and ends with Jesus accepting the titles rabbi, Son of God and King of Israel from a previously sceptical Jew, Nathaniel. Jesus responds to his outburst of acclaim with the enigmatic statement:

> In very truth I tell you all: you will see heaven open and God's angels ascending and descending upon the Son of Man. (John 1:51)

Against this is the uncertainty of John the Baptist, the failure
of Peter and the other eleven disciples to come to terms with
Jesus' teaching, even up to his Ascension, when the apostles asked
Jesus:

'Lord, is this the time when you are going to restore sovereignty
to Israel?' (Acts 1:6)

An added problem is the obvious difference between the Jesus of
John's Gospel and the Jesus of the other three, synoptic gospels, so
described by Christian scholars because of their overall similarity of
stance. In them there is the possibility of doubt on the part of Jesus
that he is the Messiah. There is none of this in John. Any uncertainty
is in the minds of the Jews and is usually culpable for they should
have recognised Jesus to be the promised Messiah.

He came to his own and his own would not accept him (1:11)
is a major charge with which the Jews stand indicted, or even
condemned. The Jesus of this gospel leaves the reader in no doubt
of their guilt. Concerning the statements of identity in which Jesus'
Messiahship and divinity are explicitly made, James Dunn has
written:

There is nothing like them in the Synoptics. If they were historical,
their omission by the Synoptic Evangelists is absolutely astonish-
ing and inexplicable.[2]

The proclamation of the church from early times has been that
Jesus was more than a martyr. He died innocently, voluntarily
and in obedience to God's will. His death was necessary, part of
God's eternal plan for the salvation of humanity. His suffering was
vicarious. He had done nothing to deserve it.

The Resurrection is the event which, according to the gospels,
convinced the disciples, but for other Jews Jesus' death as a criminal
was a stumbling block to accepting him as Messiah. St Paul, presumably drawing on his experience as a missionary, wrote:

We proclaim Christ (the Messiah) nailed to the Cross; and though
this is an offence to Jews and folly to Gentiles, yet to those who
are called, Jews and Gentiles alike, he is the power of God and
the wisdom of God. (Romans 1:23–24)

New Testament writers frequently explained the necessity of Jesus' death in terms of sacrifice. The question of why it was needed was answered in two ways; first it was the method which God chose to demonstrate his love. Perhaps the most famous verse in the whole Bible for Christians is John 3:16:

> God loved the world so much that he gave his son, so that all who believe in him shall not perish but have eternal life.

Secondly, as noted above, it was a re-enactment of human experience. Adam had been tempted and he succumbed. He sinned, that is, he rebelled against God. Jesus was tempted many times but overcame temptation and the consequence of Adam's failure, death, by rising from the dead. All this is worked out in St Paul's Letter to the Romans. Fundamental to his thesis is the belief that:

> All have sinned and come short of the glory of God. (Romans 3:23, 5:12)

The Torah, unsatisfactorily translated as 'law' in many English versions of the New Testament ('teaching' is a better rendering), was incapable of providing a remedy because it proved impossible to keep. Even worse, by specifying misdemeanours such as covetousness it reminded Paul that he was covetous. It confronted him with inadequacies and failings which he was unable to overcome because of a radical deficiency in his nature. He discovered that the good he desired to do he could not; the evil that he sincerely wanted to shun, he committed. Nothing, he felt, could deliver him from this condition, until he found salvation in Jesus and, through the power of the Holy spirit and his grace, freedom from the bondage of sin.

Some Christians have felt that the portrait of human nature which St Paul painted was one of utter depravity. There was nothing at all commendable in fallen humanity. We need not discuss this here but it must be considered later in the chapter, in the section on grace. By now what matters should have been made clear, namely the Christian belief in the inability of humanity to find favour with God, either by keeping the Torah or, as non-Jews, to live according to standards of decent morality. The Jewish scriptures and the general story of human weakness and wickedness provided sufficient evidence for those who wished to be convinced.

One other theory of the atonement deserves mention, which stresses the effect on humanity of what Christ did. Seeing his suffering, the believer responds to his love by living a transformed life.

Supporters of this view would point to the many places in the gospels where Jesus suggested that people had a 'better nature' which enabled them to respond to his appeal to repent and follow him. There are also teachings, like the Sermon on the Mount, which assumed a capacity on the part of his listeners to respond. Perhaps, above all, there is the parable of the Prodigal or Lost Son who came to his senses after leaving home and living a disastrous life. His father (God) reinstated him into the family without demanding any sacrifice or payment.

Critics of this theory claim that it does not take sin seriously. Jesus is no more than an example of how his followers should live. It is too naive in its view of human nature as well as giving no satisfactory explanation of the necessity of Jesus' death.[3]

## HUMAN NATURE: SIKHISM

Sikhism does not explain the origins of the human condition but certainly presents a very different view from that of St Paul. The word which is often translated 'sin' in Punjabi is *pap*, which can mean performing an unworthy act, the stress being upon action. Christian teaching, especially as seen in the Sermon on the Mount (Matthew 5 and 6), is about the spirit of rebellion against God. 'Sin' for members of Indian religions means going against the established *dharma*. Sikhism, in keeping with the Indian tradition in general, teaches that human beings are unenlightend but capable of enlightenment. The divine light is diffused in each one of them. In Guru Nanak's words:

> God is hidden in every heart; the Lord illumines every heart. (AG 579)

Even the most dissolute of human beings is capable of regeneration. This is the significance of a number of *janam sakhi* narratives, for example, the conversion of the robber-murderer Sajjan Thag who built a mosque and a temple to provide hospitality for travellers and murdered them as they rested in them overnight! Hearing the *bani* which Guru Nanak sang, he was moved to become a changed man.[4]

Here it might be noted that those Christians who favour the Moral Theory of the Atonement would be sympathetic to this Sikh teaching. They would draw attention to examples in the gospels of sinners who came to Jesus in a spirit of penitence and were forgiven, especially the 'woman who was living an immoral life' (Luke 7:36–50). He once described his mission as 'not to call the righteous but sinners to repentance' (Mark 2:17). The very ability of such sinners to respond must indicate some ability to hear the call and respond to it. Nevertheless, most Christians would acknowledge that the basis of the Christian doctrine of humanity is that 'all have sinned and come short of the glory of God' (Romans 3:23, cf. 5:12).

Unregenerate humanity is characterised and bedevilled by wrong attachment. Those things which are transitory, like wealth and status, even family, become goals to be desired. One is deluded into thinking that these things have ultimate worth and permanence. The one thing that matters, attachment to God, is neglected, even despised. Thus Sajjan Thag built places of worship, but to trap the pious, not to glorify God. This is the snare of *maya*.

For the Sikh Gurus the problem was *man*, not sin. This Punjabi word is very difficult to translate as there is no concept in western thought which is really similar to it and in any case Guru Nanak uses it in a number of different ways which correspond to such terms as 'mind', 'soul', or 'heart'. In the unenlightened the *man* is unstable, unreliable, and a bad guide. Guru Nanak warned against trusting it:

> The *man* is unsteady, it does not know the way. One who puts his trust in his own *man* is as one befouled; he does not recognise the Word (*shabad*). (AG 415)

The difference between the ideal, of which human beings have some inkling of awareness, and actual human achievement, is caused by self-reliance, *haumai*, which distorted human perception and led to unity being distorted by the illusion of duality *maya*.

*Maya*, then, is an incorrect interpretation of creation. It is the error of treating as having an independent and lasting existence things which exist because God willed them to, partly for the benefit of humanity. (Though Sikhism sees humankind as distinct from other species in that it can enter into a conscious, voluntary relationship

with God, it does not teach that we are stewards, far less those who
have been given lordship over creation, as in the Genesis accounts
where Adam names the animals (Genesis 2:19–20) and is given
dominion (1:26) over them.)

If creation is seen for what it is, a revelation of God's glory, it
can lead the viewer to spiritual liberation. All too often it simply
provides the means for self-indulgence, the exercise of *haumai*.
Theoretically, each person coming into the world is free to obey
the Creator and live according to God's will (*hukam*). There is
no doctrine of a universal Fall. Though surrounded by men and
women who have succumbed to self-centredness and a materialistic
interpretation of reality, it is unlikely that anyone can escape the
snares of selfishness. The hope which Guru Nanak preached lies in
the grace of God as Guru and the company of enlightened men and
women, the *sangat*. The *man* of the natural, unregenerate person is
dominated by *haumai*.

*Haumai* has been referred to on a number of occasions. Its meaning
has been given as self-reliance or pride. It is one of the most
important words in Guru Nanak's religious vocabulary. The literal
meaning is 'I-I' (*hau-main*). *Haumai* is part of God's creation, for
nothing exists unless God wills it. So Guru Nanak taught:

> God created the world and also invested it with *Haumai*.
> One's mind is purged only if one enshrines the Word in the
> mind. (AG 1010)

*Haumai* is not without some value and purpose:

> Under the compulsion of *haumai* one comes and goes, is born
> and dies, gives and takes, earns and loses, speaks truth and lies,
> smears one's self with evil and washes one's self of it. (Guru
> Nanak, AG 466)

But the motive is one of self-interest and more often than not the
result is immoral conduct.

The worst consequence of *haumai* and its connection with such
other key words such as *maya* and *hukam* is indicated in another
verse of the Guru's:

> (In *haumai*) one fails to perceive the true nature of liberation. In
> *haumai* there is *maya* and its shadow (doubt). *Haumai* directed

actions cause birth again and again. When *haumai* is banished access to the door (of liberation) is gained. Without knowledge of God there is only argument and wrangling; destiny is written by God's Order (*hukam*).

The great Punjabi poet Bhai Vir Singh described *haumai* as a veil of falsehood which prevents the attainment of truth.

Self-reliance is not far from the mark when one tries to translate *haumai* into English. Egoism, self-centredness, even self-conceit may also be used. It is really that attribute or attitude which prevents one from acknowledging and obeying God. The unenlightened person is without hope, being deluded into thinking that spiritual liberation, whatever that phrase may mean to them, if it has any significance at all, is something that can be earned. It can be gained, won, or deserved by self-effort. *Manmukh* is the term used to describe such a human being. Such a man or woman may seem to be deserving of respect and even adulation. Their lives may be self-disciplined and highly moral. But, in Sikh eyes, he or she is caught up in delusion, *maya*.

Those who are self-reliant cannot, by definition, obey God's will, and they implicitly reject the gift of grace. Their destiny, be they ascetics or those who indulge in worldly pleasures (both are *manmukh*), is interminable wandering; that perhaps is not surprising for one whose condition is essentially unstable. To quote Guru Nanak again:

Within them is neither wisdom nor contemplation, and they do not love God. They transmigrate endlessly. (AG 1418)

*Samsara*, transmigration or wandering, is equivalent to hell in the Semitic traditions to the extent that it is characterised by suffering. This need not be physical and hell is not a place. Guru Arjan taught that:

In the midst of a myriad joys, if one does not cherish the Name, one lives as if in the depths of hell. (AG 707)

*Narak* is the word for hell which is used here. 'City of Death', *Yamadwara*, is the phrase which is commonly used by Guru Nanak but it means more than dying. It is the state of those who in earthly terms are dead but spiritually have not achieved liberation.

These are the 'lost' of the New Testament, those who do not pass immediately into the Lord's presence at death as believers do (Luke 23:43, 2 Corinthians 5:8, Philippians 1:23).

While Sikhs will say that the spirits of such people are doomed to come and go they recognise that this is not a final state. The process offers opportunity for spiritual liberation. This is not to say that the prospect of rebirth is an enjoyable one and should deflect a person from concern for regeneration. The uncertainty of the samsaric journey is hellish! The present life might be tolerable and even more, very enjoyable, but that is not the purpose of life – and there is no guarantee that the next birth will be as good even in material benefits. However, Guru Nanak did not concentrate on the nature of *samsara* or whether it, or the Muslim linear view of time, was correct. His concern was to persuade his listeners to avoid the pain of an afterlife in which their present separation from God persisted. This is what Guru Arjan had in mind when he gave the warning which is quoted above. He also said:

My heaven is wherever God's praises are sung. (AG 749)

Christians, because of an insistence on belief in Jesus Christ as being necessary for salvation, as well as a linear concept of time, find the state of those who die lacking faith in Jesus a problem. The plight of those who have come within the sound of the gospel and have wilfully rejected it may result in eternal damnation. Some Christians would see this as just. Others would plead that there may well have been mitigating circumstances leading to rejection of the gospel. For example, God may be blamed for some tragic personal experience with the consequence that the message of the gospel is rejected almost unheard. Or again, European colonialism's link with Christianity has led to some people of other ethnic groups, especially blacks, turning to Islam and rejecting Christianity. There is also the difficulty which arises from the belief that Jesus is the saviour of all humanity, namely the plight of those who have never had an opportunity to hear of him, people perhaps living in some isolated part of the planet. There is also the condition of those who lived before the time of Jesus. The condition of the former has inspired many generations of Christian missionaries, especially those whose theology teaches that eternal damnation faces those who have not become Christians even though they may never have heard the gospel. For the second group the credal statement 'He descended into hell' offers a solution. The clause refers to two passages in 1 Peter (3:18–20 and 4:6) where it says that Christ:

> In the spirit also went and made his proclamation to the imprisoned spirits, those who had refused to obey in the past, while God waited patiently in the days when Noah was building the ark.

In the second, the writer refers to the way in which converts have given up their immoral practices, to the bewilderment of their former companions. He then goes on to promise that these immoral people will not escape judgement:

> . . . but they will have to give account of themselves to him who is ready to pass judgement on the living and the dead. That is why the gospel was preached even to the dead: in order that, although in the body they were condemned to die as everyone dies, yet in the spirit they might live as God lives.

The passages are somewhat obscure. However, taken together with the belief that Jesus like any other person went to Hades when he died, they may suggest that his visit had a purpose, to preach the gospel to the dead. This has been the traditional interpretation of the above sentences. The purpose of his mission was to give those who were in the state of death an opportunity to be saved.

These verses present a number of problems. For example, hell is depicted as a location where the dead continue to exist. Some Christians take the words literally and share this belief. However, our concern in this section is to draw attention to the implication of the passage which is that God wishes everyone to have eternal life. This is the destiny which God intends for humanity. The story of the Garden of Eden which has already been mentioned, explains how death came into the world. Humanity, as embodied in Adam and Eve, were created to enjoy life and not to suffer death. Sikhs too believe that this life of spiritual liberation is the destiny which God has planned for the whole human race.

## The Way of Deliverance

It has already been implied that Christianity teaches that salvation is through faith in the work of Jesus. The believer shares in the benefits of his passion, his suffering upon the Cross. With Jesus they rise to eternal life. As we have seen, this presents the difficulty of what happens to those who do not believe through lack of opportunity. Sikhism has no such problem to solve. The chance to encounter God and so become enlightened does not exist only through the message of Sikhism. The Christian may be given it while reading the Bible, attending church, or going about the daily routines of work. So may the Jew or Hindu, Jain, and the rest. Who is to say that the transforming influence of God, the Guru, does not reach those who follow tribal religions? As for those who do not respond, their failure can be explained by *karma*. They may not yet be ready for enlightenment. Perhaps in the next human birth they will receive it. It is God's will that all humanity should eventually achieve enlightenment and spiritual liberation.

Christians also hold the belief that God wishes all humanity to be saved (Acts 2:21, Romans 10:9) and the question has often been asked by them whether ultimately all will actually experience salvation. At this point there is a tension between the divine characteristics of love and justice. God's love, as Christians regard it, never gives up. This is the message of the parable of the forgiving father or prodigal son (Luke 15) to which attention has already been drawn. Whatever the son does and however long it takes him to come to his senses, the father (God), is waiting, looking for him, and longing for the opportunity to forgive him and restore him to his place in the family. This teaching is reinforced in the Cross. There Jesus demonstrated the limitlessness of God's love (John 13:1). James Denney, a Christian theologian, used to say, when he looked at a cross in a church, 'God loves like that'. However, other Christians would have to argue that if God is just and human beings possess free will, the possibility of them being allowed to reject the offer of salvation must exist.

The way of deliverance for the Christian is faith in Jesus resulting in Jesus becoming their saviour and lord. This entails on the one hand recognition that human effort cannot achieve this, Jesus must 'save', and on the other hand a commitment to obey God's will. The Sikh similarly believes that enlightenment leading to spiritual liberation, *mukti*, comes from God and that once it has been received the regenerated person must live a life committed to God, obedient to the divine *hukam*.

Sometimes the emphasis upon God's love has resulted in believers continuing to live according to their former nature. The writer of the Letter to the Ephesians, perhaps St Paul, warned against presuming upon God's indulgence:

> Renouncing your former way of life, you must lay aside the old human nature which, deluded by its desires, is in process of decay: you must be renewed in mind and spirit, and put on the new nature created in God's likeness, which shows itself in the upright and devout life called for by the truth. (Ephesians 4:22–24)

*Seva*, community service, has always characterised the Sikh who has become *gurmukh*. It has long been considered the antidote for a feeling of self-importance. Bhai Gurdas described their way of life in the following way:

> The hands of the *gurmukh* are blessed, for they toil in the service of the Guru and the sangat. They fetch water, grind corn, fan the people, and perform any service that is required of them. They copy the compositions of the Gurus and prepare hymn books, and sing to the accompaniment of musical instruments. They bow low to the Guru and embrace their fellow devotees with joy. They labour to earn an honest living, and distribute part of their income for the benefit of others. Having touched the perfect Guru, their hands have become holy, they will not touch the body of another woman or the property of others. Ego and pride have been lost through serving others. (Var 6:12)

### Grace

God's grace is essential for salvation or regeneration to be realised. Christianity and Sikhism seem to be equally emphatic in this respect. The word 'grace' occurs many times in the scriptures of both religions, with the meaning of an undeserved gift from God. Deliverance from suffering and death is by grace. St Paul boldly said:

> It is by grace you are saved through faith; it is not your own doing. It is God's gift, not a reward for work done. (Letter to the Ephesians 2:8–9)

Guru Nanak said:

Liberation comes only through grace. (AG 2)

And

Without (God's) grace, Nanak says, no one is liberated;  .
If God is gracious God is called to mind, the soul is softened
and one becomes absorbed in love of God.
The soul is made one with the Supreme Soul. (AG 661)

Interestingly, both writers were reacting against teaching which
affirmed that liberation or salvation could be obtained by good
works, following one's *dharma* in Hinduism, and keeping the precepts of the Torah if one were a Jew.

Broadly speaking, Christian and Sikh agree that grace is characteristic of God, that it derives from the heart of God one might say. It is
a divine activity, the purpose of which is to enlighten, redeem, trans-
form, recreate or regenerate human beings. The nuances of usage
depend very largely on theologies of the nature of unregenerate or
fallen humanity and the method of deliverance, the means of grace.
However, most certainly Christianity and Sikhism are religions of
grace.

God's grace can easily be taken for granted, the result being
a *laissez-faire* attitude to moral conduct. Hence the insistence of
Christian and Sikh teachers upon the need for a changed way of life.
Effort, either to lead a renewed life or to seek grace, may be rejected.
We find, therefore, St Paul writing to Christians at Philippi:

You must work out your own salvation with fear and trembling
for it is God who works in you inspiring both the will and the
deed, for his own chosen purpose. (2:12)

Join together, my friends, in following my example. You have
us for a model; imitate those whose way of life conforms to it.
(3:17)

Guru Nanak's pithy words 'Truth is the highest of all virtues, but
higher still is truthful living' (AG 62) are to be found displayed in
many homes and *gurdwaras*. They sum up the belief that God is
Truth, so honesty should characterise the godly, just as the Christian
teaching is that God is love, so love should dictate the conduct of
the Christian.

The Christian view of the church as the mystical body of Christ has led to some Christians asserting that it is the means of grace *par excellence* even, perhaps, to the point of stating that only through it is salvation possible. 'Outside the church there is no salvation', was a declaration by a fourth-century bishop (354–430) St Augustine, in opposition to the growth of heretical groups, but for some Christians it has become more than that. It has turned into a concept of the church as the successor of Jesus, his body, membership of which is essential to salvation and the receipt of grace through its sacraments. This affects the attitude of Christians to other faiths, a matter which will be taken up in the final chapter.

This view is not echoed in the Sikh concept of the Panth, though the *Rahit Maryada* warns Khalsa Sikhs to have no dealings with *minas*, *masands*, *dhirmalias*, and Ram Raias (p. 22;1). These were groups or, in the case of *masands*, leaders, who would take members away from their exclusive commitment to the Panth.

'Truth is attained through God's grace' (AG 62), is a Sikh precept which has never been interpreted in a restrictive sense as applying only to the truth as revealed to the Gurus. However, grace must naturally permeate the company of those who are regenerated by God's grace, so the Panth or *sangat* can become a vehicle of grace:

> Just as the castor oil plant imbibes the scent of the nearby sandal-wood, so the fallen become emancipated through the company of the faithful. (Guru Ram Das, AG 861)

Regarding the destination of the saved or liberated soul, both Christian and Sikh speak of living in God's eternal presence and remain silent if asked for more detail.

## God as Present in Church and Panth

That the presence of God may be experienced through private prayer and in public worship is a belief which both faiths share. They also believe in the necessity of corporate worship and fellowship, as the above verse indicates with regard to Sikh teaching. Christians can give this no greater importance than when they describe the church as the 'body of Christ' (see St Paul on this, for example 1 Corinthians, chapter 12).

There is more to this notion than wisdom and good sense. There is an underpinning of theology in both cases. A key verse, treasured by all Christians, is Jesus' statement:

Wherever two or three are gathered together in my name I am present in their midst. (Matthew 18:20)

The final words of the Gospel of St Matthew end with the assurance:

'I will be with you always, to the end of time'. (Matthew 28:20)

Countless Christians have claimed that to be true in their experience. Another important affirmation is:

'He who dwells in love is dwelling in God and God in him'. (1 John 4:13)

It is not surprising, therefore, to find the Christian church described as the body of Christ, as has been mentioned, and its members using the Greek word *ecclesia* to describe themselves. It means those who have been summoned or chosen, the elect, though not in the sense of called to enjoy privileges. Often the calling has been to suffering and martyrdom. In the English language *ecclesia* lives on in the word 'ecclesiastical' but the word for *ecclesia* in English is 'church'. For many people in the English-speaking world, and those who belong to other faiths, 'church' is the name given to a building. Really it refers to the people who meet in it to worship. The place is unimportant and ultimately unnecessary. Christians would say that it is the believing community, called by the Holy Spirit to witness to God and continue the work of Jesus as the body of Christ, which matters.

This teaching has a strong parallel in Sikh doctrine. The Panth is the embodiment of the Guru. The famous relative of Guru Ram Das, Bhai Gurdas, expressed it this way:

'One is a Sikh, two a *sangat* (a congregation), where there are five *Parmeshur* is with them'. (Var 13;19)

Guru Nanak said:

'Through praising the Lord the bond is established with his court'. (AG 143)

Here the implication seems to be that worship, a congregational act, as opposed to private meditation, *nam simran* transcends the gathering of human devotees. Sikhs believe that they become one with those who sing God's praises in the divine court, that is, in the eternal presence of God. Consequently:

'God's essence is obtained in the congregation of the holy (*sat sangat*). (AG 598)

It is in later writings, those of Guru Gobind Singh relating to the Khalsa, and in statements attributed to him, that the doctrine of the Guru Panth is most fully expressed. When he instituted the Khalsa on Baisakhi Day, 1699, the Guru declared:

I am the son of the Immortal God. It is by his order that I have been born and have established this form of initiation. They who accept it shall henceforth be known as the Khalsa. The Khalsa is the Guru and the Guru is the Khalsa. There is no difference between you and me.[5]

There is no need to dwell on 'son', which Sikhs would regard rather in the way that Jews understand the words of Psalm 2 where God says to King David, 'You are my son'. It refers to honour and being chosen, not to divinity, which the Gurus always repudiated (see Chapter 4). The significant sentence is the one which reads: 'The Khalsa is the Guru and the Guru is the Khalsa'. Bearing in mind the Indian view that *Brahman*, the Divine, exists within human beings as the *atman*, a belief which Sikhs share with Hindus, these words relate to much more than a social unity and human fellowship. The Khalsa participates in guruship. Thus:

'Where there are five there am I,
Where the five meet they are the holiest of the holy',[6]

is a statement of Panthic election of the same kind as that of Guru Gobind Singh's own belief, and that of his predecessors, that their birth was divinely ordained. The Khalsa, ultimately, was not a merely a device invented by the tenth Guru to overturn the power of the *masands*. These were administrative officials who were appointed to deputise for the Gurus in the time of Guru Amar Das, and had arrogated to themselves such power that Panthic unity was threatened. It was divinely inspired.

Despite this view of the Khalsa, Sikhs have never equated it with the Panth in such a way as to exclude those who have not been initiated into the Khalsa from membership of the Panth. The question of Sikh identity, 'Who is a Sikh?' is one which we must turn to later when we also ask, 'Who is a Christian?' (Chapter 10), but at this point we must note that Panth, the equivalent to church, is a more all-embracing and less precise word than Khalsa, which defines a section of the Sikh community and which has no parallel within Christianity. For this reason a Sikh addressing a *sangat*, might begin by saying:

Guru Panth, Khalsaji; 'Guru-and Khalsa Panth' – an all-embracing phrase.

In practice the use of Guru Panth and Khalsa Panth seem to be synonymous.

# 6

# The Scriptures

Christianity and Sikhism have in common the fact that they are religions which attach great importance to scripture. The liturgical centrality of the Bible, however, varies between different denominations and is nowhere quite as noticeable as it is in Sikhism, where the Guru Granth Sahib provides the essential physical focus of worship and all other ceremonies with the exception of funerals. (Even here scriptural material is used even though the book itself may not be present.)

Both religions also came from traditions which were scriptural, though in different ways. Judaism placed great emphasis upon the Torah which was given to Moses by God on Mount Sinai. This provided the Hebrew people with spiritual guidance and a code of conduct, the articles of their covenant with God. (It still plays a central role in Jewish worship.) In later times a series of prophets arose who were men commissioned by God to summon his people back to observing the Torah covenant which they were neglecting. Many of their teachings were written down. These, together with such liturgical material as the Psalms which were used in Temple worship and other writings, came to be regarded by many Jews of Jesus' day as scripture almost on a par with the Torah, though there was one strong body of opinion, the Sadducees, who refused to accept this view. Among its main proponents were the religious group known as Pharisees.

The scriptures of Hinduism are complex and varied but for our purpose we need only make a few observations about them. The most sacred and authoritative are the four Vedas which should be studied by the three twice-born castes but may only be taught by the *brahmins*, that from which the priests come. The duties of the four classes of society were later amplified in another scripture, The Laws of Manu which may date from about the beginning of the Common Era. They are set out in a few brief but important sentences:

For the sake of the preservation of this entire creation (*Purusha*), the extremely resplendent one, assigned separate duties to the classes which had sprung from his mouth, arms, thighs, and feet.

Teaching, studying, so too making others perform sacrificial rites, and giving away and receiving gifts – these he assigned to the *brahmins*.

Protection of the people, giving away of wealth, performance of sacrificial rites, study, and non-attachment to sensual pleasures-these are, in short, the duties of a *kshatriya*. Tending of cattle, giving away of wealth, performance of sacrificial rites, study, trade and commerce, usury, and agriculture – these are the occupations of a *vaishya*.

The Lord has prescribed only one occupation for a *shudra*, namely service without malice of these other three classes. (Laws of Manu 1:87)[1]

These were very influential upon Hindu society in Guru Nanak's day, even if their impact in the late twentieth century is somewhat less. For spiritual sustenance the *shudras* and those who lie outside the Hindu system altogether, the scheduled classes, the Ramayana in its various forms and translations, especially the version produced by Tulsi Das (a near contemporary of Guru Nanak), and the compositions of *bhakti sants*, were the main sources, together with the Puranas. These cover a number of topics, especially the creation and dissolution of the universe, often in easily comprehensible stories.

For our discussion we need to note that early Christianity and the Gurus had to address themselves to the question of how to respond to existing scriptures and their authority.

Christianity adopted its parent scripture but interpreted it so that its chief purpose came to be seen as preparing the Jews for the coming of Jesus the Messiah. St Paul referred to the Torah as 'our school master, to bring us to Christ' (Galatians 3:24). The prophets were no longer seen to be spokesmen of God recalling their co-religionists to the Covenant, but foretellers of the Messiah's birth and ministry. So, for example, a promise of imminent deliverance from the threat of an Assyrian army besieging Jerusalem becomes a prediction of the Nativity in the words:

A virgin shall conceive and bear a son. (Isaiah 7:14)

Modern translations, based on the Hebrew text rather than the Greek translation (the *Septuagint*) favoured by non-Hebrew reading the early church, render the words as:

> A young woman is with child, and she will give birth to a son . . . .

The crucial passage for Christians is the so-called Servant Song, Isaiah 52:13–53:12, especially verses 3 to 12 of the latter chapter. They read:

> He was despised, shunned by all, pain-racked and afflicted by disease; he had no beauty, no majesty to catch our eyes, no grace to attract us to him. Yet it was our afflictions he was bearing, our pain he endured, while we thought of him smitten by God, struck down by disease and misery. But he was pierced for our transgressions, crushed for our iniquities; the chastisement he bore restored us to health and by his wounds we are healed. We had all gone astray like sheep, each of us going his own way, but the Lord laid on him the guilt of us all. He was maltreated, yet he was submissive and did not open his mouth; like a sheep led to the slaughter, like a ewe that is dumb before the shearers, he did not open his mouth. He was arrested and sentenced and taken away, and who gave thought to his fate – how he was cut off from the world of the living, stricken to death for my people's transgression? He was assigned a grave with the wicked, a burial-place among the felons, though he had done no violence, had spoken no word of treachery. Yet the Lord took thought for his oppressed servant and healed him who had given himself a sacrifice for sin. He will enjoy long life and see his children's children, and in his hand the Lord's purpose will prosper. By his humiliation, my servant will justify many; after his suffering he will see light and be satisfied; it is their guilt he bears. Therefore I shall allot him a portion with the great, and he will share the spoil with the mighty, because he exposed himself to death and was reckoned among the transgressors, for he bore the sin of many and interceded for transgressors.

These words were recorded many centuries before the ministry of Jesus, of course, but his followers argued that they referred to him. They saw many parallels between the 'servant's' fate and his. Jesus' death, they concluded, was not a tragic accident, the unfortunate end of a good man, much less the deserved punishment of a blasphemer; it was divinely ordained, being foretold by one of Israel's greatest prophets.

This kind of biblical exegesis is Jewish; there was nothing novel about the method, what is remarkable is the thoroughgoing nature of the reinterpretation. So complete has it been that Christian students often find it impossible to understand the Hebrew scriptures in any other context than that of their Christian faith, as the 'Old Testament'. (Anyone wishing to pursue this approach further might read the Gospel of Matthew in a modern translation and then examine the Old Testament passages which he quotes in their original context).

It would seem that Jesus himself was responsible for using the scriptures of his Jewish heritage to demonstrate his Messiahship (Luke 24:27) as well as the decision to regard the prophetic and other writings as scripture as well as the Torah. He often quoted from these books. Some Jewish scholars consider Jesus to have been one of those teachers who later came to be called *rabbis* of the liberal Pharisaic tradition.[2] It was their influence which led to Judaism accepting this broad definition of scripture. Certainly St Paul was a Pharisee (Acts 23:6). When the author of the Second Letter to Timothy in the New Testament affirmed the belief that 'all scripture is inspired by God' (3:16) he was expressing that attitude of the early church based on the views of Jesus himself, that the prophetic writings and the Psalms constitute the Torah in the fullest sense of the word. The church was also endorsing the pharisaic position as opposed to that of the saduccees which said that only the first five books of Moses were authoritative. The consequence of this belief is the inclusion of the whole corpus of Hebrew scripture in the Christian Bible, though under the name Old Testament, first used by Melito of Sardis somewhere around 180 CE, to distinguish it from the explicit Christian books and define its status relative to them.

Sikhism took a very different attitude to the scriptures of Hinduism. Guru Nanak, as a *khatri vaishya* by caste, had a right and duty to study the Vedas but not to teach them because, as has already been noted, this was the prerogative of the *brahmins*. He could not, therefore, be a guru in the Sanskritic tradition. This may have been one reason for his repudiation of Vedic authority but undoubtedly the two major ones were his rejection of the belief in a priestly caste and his refusal to accept the concept of scripture as a closed corpus of revealed truth. The third Guru, Guru Amar Das, expressed this view of revelation in these words:

> Namdev, the calico printer (*chimba*), and the weaver (*julaha*) Kabir, attained liberation through the True Guru. Deeply spiritual men chant their words, none can efface them, brother. They were freed from *haumai* and caste. (AG 67)

He contrasted them with the religious, including *brahmin* priests and philosophers who, not knowing the Guru, remained bound:

> The followers of the six philosophical schools, *yogis* and *sannyasis*, lacking the Guru, have gone astray in doubt. (AG 67)

In this respect the Sikh Gurus represented the strong Indian tradition which is traceable at least to the times of the Buddha and Mahavira, the Jain, which affirms the continuity of revelation and refuses to limit it to a special, exclusive group of people, usually men. In a sense the doctrine which underlies the Indian concept of guru is one which says that God's self-disclosure is on-going. Of course, there has been and still is an attempt to confine guruship to the *brahmin* caste and for such gurus to base their teachings on the Vedas. In fact during the time of the ten Sikh Gurus a *smarta* reaction was taking place in Hinduism which led to disciples of non-brahmin gurus, including those of Kabir, seeking to legitimise their *sadhana* by attributing their origins to a *brahmin* guru.[3] Thus, for example, the famous *brahmin* guru Ramananda is said to have been Kabir's guru, though Kabir himself, like Guru Nanak, strongly denied that he had any guru but God. Significantly, there has never been any attempt among Sikhs to establish this kind of pedigree. Not surprisingly, therefore, Guru Nanak never quoted the Vedas or referred to them to justify his teachings. No passages from the Vedas or the Qur'an find a place in the Guru Granth Sahib.

However, it should not be concluded that the Sikh Gurus rejected the Vedas as scripture. Guru Nanak wrote:

> *Nam* is the support of the worlds and universes,
> *Nam* is the support of the smritis, vedas and puranas. (AG 284)

Guru Arjan affirmed that:

The vedas and smritis sing the Creator's praises. (AG 785)

It was probably the claim to their exclusive authority made by their *brahmin* interpreters that he was rejecting.

Nothing as explicit is to be found in the Guru Granth Sahib by way of commendation of the Qur'an, but Guru Nanak advised Muslims:

> Wise is he who cleanses the mind. A Muslim is one who removes impurity by reading and acting upon what he reads. Thus he becomes acceptable (to God). (AG 662)

There is a verse in the B40 Janam Sakhi which is quite explicit in its acceptance of the Qur'an, but it is not found in the Adi Granth. It reads:

> Strive to make firm your faith in the Qur'an; let it be laid upon the foundation of mercy.[4]

There are, on the other hand, almost nine hundred compositions of non-Sikhs to be found in its pages, five hundred and forty-one of them being by Kabir, nearly ten per cent of the total which is put at about five thousand, nine hundred hymns.

## THE EMERGENCE OF THE SCRIPTURES

Christianity, at its birth, as has been stated, already possessed a body of scripture. The apostles would not dispute its integrity whenever and wherever they preached. Instead they would provide interpretations and emphases which demonstrated the claims which they were making for Jesus as God's Messiah and Son. An example of their method may be read in Acts 8:25–40 where an evangelist, Philip, hears an Ethiopian Jew reading the passage from Isaiah, 52–53, which was quoted earlier. Philip explained that the words referred to Jesus; the Ethiopian was convinced and became baptised.

The apostles probably had no intention to add to the existing scriptures. After all, Jesus, their leader, had not written a book. He had remained steadfast to his tradition by teaching orally. It might be remembered that Judaism believed that at Sinai Moses was given the written Torah and also the Oral Torah which was transmitted verbally by the religious teachers to their disciples who in turn handed it on to the next generation. It was only committed to writing with much misgiving in the second century CE when there was a danger of this rabbinical voice being silenced and the message lost. In 135 CE the famous 85-year-old Rabbi Akiba was tortured to death in the presence of his own disciples. With his demise went a considerable body of knowledge. Perhaps this event, or at least the Hadrianic persecution of which it was a part, triggered off the decision to write down the Oral Torah.[5] Jesus used the same method of transmission. There is plenty of evidence in the gospels of him teaching disciples and sending them out in twos to support and corroborate one another. The letters of Paul presuppose a knowledge of the message Jesus preached, for Paul himself writes:

I handed on to you the tradition I had received. (1 Corinthians 15:3)

Another reason why Jesus and his followers did not embark upon producing a scripture of their own may have been their belief that Jesus' ministry inaugurated the new and final age mentioned in books like Isaiah. There was an urgency about it which resulted in the itinerant method of the apostles delivering the good news rather than sitting down to write books. When each copy had to be made by hand it was a laborious process and one with limited value in a world where few people could afford books even though most Jews were literate to a greater degree than other communities in the Empire. As rare eye-witnesses of the events of the gospel from Jesus' baptism to his Ascension, the apostles' task was to bear witness to what they had seen as well as to what they believed (Acts 1:21–22).

The apostle Paul would not have had the arrogance to consider his letters to be scripture yet they were the first of the Christian church. Not all of them have been preserved. His correspondence with the Christians of Corinth, for example, has probably been conflated from four letters to the two which are found in the New Testament. It is certainly possible to conjecture from this example, that the recipients of Paul's letters, as well as Paul, did not consider that what they received from him was scripture. Otherwise every word would have been carefully preserved.

In 64 CE an event took place which was as traumatic for Christians as the death of Rabbi Akiba was to be for Jews seventy years later. It is generally accepted by scholars that the apostles Peter and Paul were executed during the Emperor Nero's Rome persecution. This may well have prompted Mark to write down a form of the gospel which Peter preached, and some individuals or groups of Christians to take deliberate steps to preserve the letters of Paul. Soon the written word was taking the place of the eye-witnesses as they died out. Christianity was on its way to having a scripture, one combining the Jewish with their own. It was not until the fourth century, however, that the contents were finalised. In the meantime books moved in and out of the accepted *corpus* depending on such things as supposed authorship. (Accreditation to an apostle counted for much. This may well have led to the decision to include the Letter to the Hebrews which was attributed to Paul, and the exclusion of a popular work, The Epistle of Barnabas). Value in countering ideas which were considered as doubtful was another criterion. Gnosticism, a belief that the material world was evil and that Jesus was really a spiritual, not physical, being, was one of the main ideas of this kind, hence the emphasis in the gospels which were recognised as orthodox, of the real humanity of Jesus.

Sikhism's scriptures begin with the compositions of Guru Nanak which were believed from the first, by Guru Nanak himself, to be divinely inspired. The story is told of Guru Nanak and Mardana, his rebeck-playing companion, walking along a road as part of a convoy of prisoners after the Mughal capture of the town of Saidpur. Guru Nanak told Mardana to prepare to play. 'I feel the *bani* descending', he said. Mardana was hesitant to let go the lead of a horse he had been told to look after. The Guru sharply reminded Mardana of his priorities. 'Let the horse go, the *bani* is descending'!

There is a statement in the Sikh scriptures themselves that Guru Nanak uttered the *bani* only when inspired. He said:

'I speak, O God, only when you inspire me to speak'. (AG 566)

And

'As you inspire me, so I praise you, for I an ignorant man can say nothing myself'. (AG 795)

This belief in inspiration meant that Guru Nanak's hymns were soon written down by his disciple and later successor, Lehna, better known as Guru Angad. However, it was not until the time of the fifth Guru, Arjan, that a conscious decision was taken to collect his compositions and those of the four earlier Gurus. The impetus to do so came from two directions. One was similar to that which prompted the compilation of the Christian canon, namely the need for orthodoxy. By the time of Guru Arjan the prize of leadership of the Sikh community was a rich one in power and material wealth. Rival claimants, especially the Guru's elder brother, were not hard to find. One way in which they attempted to establish their credentials was by producing spurious hymns or altering authentic ones in conformity with their heterodox teachings. There was a need for an authorised version. The second reason for making such a compilation was to provide the now widespread communities with the *bani* which has always been the basis of Sikh spiritual nurture. In 1604 Guru Arjan gave his approval to the compilation which he had supervised, and it was installed as scripture. (The original still exists, at Kartarpur, near Jullunder.)

This collection was known as the Adi Granth. *Granth* means collection. *Adi* means first in an ordinal sense. It affirms that the Adi Granth is the original revelation rather than, by implication, the Vedas. Here there is a parallel with the assertion made by the author of the fourth Christian gospel that Jesus is the *logos*, co-eternal with the Father, who can say:

'Before Abraham was I am'. (John 8:58)

Theologically, the Sikh scriptures are not a seventeenth-century document. They are the eternal word of God, the *shabad*.

It was Guru Nanak who began to collect the compositions of the non-Sikh *sants* which have already been mentioned. There is one important piece of evidence to support this assertion, and there may be a second. The first is a verse from Sheikh Farid which occurs in the Guru Granth Sahib and is cited elsewhere by Guru Nanak himself. Farid's verse reads;

You could not make a raft at the time you should have made it. When the sea is full and overflowing it is hard to cross. Do not touch the saffron flower with your hand. Its colour will fade my dear.

First the bride herself is weak and in addition, her husband's command is hard to bear. As the milk does not return to her breast so the soul doesn not enter the same body again. Says Farid, O my friends, when the spouse calls, the soul departs crestfallen and this body becomes a heap of ashes. (AG 794)

Guru Nanak's rejoinder is:

Make meditation and self-control the raft by which you cross the flowing stream. Your path shall be as comfortable as if there were no ocean or overflowing stream. You name alone is the unfading madder with which my cloak is dyed. My beloved, this colour is everlasting. The dear friends have departed how shall they meet you? If they are united in virtue they will, and once united mortals never suffer separation again. The True One puts an end to coming and going. (AG 729)

The fact that they are not adjacent to one another in the Guru Granth Sahib is to be explained by the fact that Guru Arjan had his own reasons for placing passages where he did when he compiled the collection. His reason for separating the verses is unknown. He also responded to Farid who wrote, 'Only those who keep awake are blessed with God's bounties' (AG 1384). Guru Arjan adds:

The bounties are all from God. None can take them as a matter of right. Even some who are awake do not receive them, while others are awakened from their sleep and blessed. (AG 1384)

Another example is from the poet Pipa (AG 695):

That which is in the part is also in the whole, the one who seeks finds. Says Pipa: God is the quintessence of all and is revealed to us through the Guru.

Guru Nanak states more tersely:

Know the one who is the entire universe and all its parts.
Know the one through the Guru and the Guru's Word.
                                                              (AG 1041)

In the original there are linguisitic similarities. Guru Nanak seems eager to emphasise the need for the Guru more than Pipa does and perhaps stresses the immanence of God more through the terseness of his words.

A third is a saying of Kabir's (AG 331):

> Impurity attaches to whatever we do. Even our kitchen is impure. All devices for avoiding it only increase the bondage. Rare are those who realise the way of liberation. Says Kabir: impurity does not attach itself to those who contemplate the Lord in their hearts.

Guru Nanak's allusion to it reads:

> How may impurity be removed when even our kitchen is impure? Says Nanak: such impurity is only washed away by enlightenment. (AG 472)

The phrase 'even our kitchen is impure' is identical in both passages apart from the fact that Kabir uses Hindi.

The Farid–Nanak link is certainly convincing. The others, it must be conceded, are somewhat less so but cumulatively they are sufficient to persuade Sikhs that Guru Nanak was aware of compositions by these three teachers.

The other reason for asserting that the collection of compositions of the *sants* was not made by Guru Arjan but may be the work of Guru Nanak is that some of them are to be found in the two extant Mohan Pothis, collections of some of the *bani* of Guru Nanak and his successor made on the instructions of Guru Amar Das.[6] Dhanna, Parmanand, Bhikan, Sadhana, Surdas, and Ramanand's works are also included, as well as those of Kabir and Namdev. It has to be admitted, however, that the verses of Farid and Pippa which have been quoted do not occur in the extant Mohan Pothis, but neither does the important Asa-di-Var by Guru Nanak and many compositions by Guru Angad and Guru Amar Das. Clearly not all of Guru Arjan's source material has survived. Professor Teja Singh suggested that Guru Amar Das may have collected the *bhagat bani* but gives no reasons to support the claim.[7]

There may be a number of reasons for the inclusion of this material in the Sikh scriptures but the one to which Sikhs draw attention is to affirm that the Word has never been revealed exclusively to a particular people or through a particular scripture. It is the nature of God as Guru not to be confined. The voice proclaims the message of liberation whether anyone listens or not. In the Indian religious tradition from which Sikhism comes, the *anahad shabad*, the unstruck music, the sound *OM* is the source of the creative power which made the universe. The presence of non-Sikh material in the Guru Granth Sahib is a constant reminder that God's revelation is inclusive not exclusive. God has spoken through the Gurus; the Sikh scripture is the word of God, but most Sikhs would say that so too are the Vedas, the Qur'an and the Bible.

Here we have to acknowledge the danger of a sectarian tendency within Sikhism. During the nineteenth century, the Panth's existence came under a new threat. It had responded successfully to outward force in the form of Mughal and Afghan armies in the eighteenth century but now came an intellectual challenge from Christian missionaries and the Hindu reformist Arya Samaj. In many ways the perceived menace was beneficial. It drew from Sikhs a response which resulted in the creation of educational institutions and a Sikh renaissance. It also led to a process of self-definition which eventually took the form of the Rahit Maryada, the Sikh Code of Conduct, which lays down rules of personal conduct, provides instructions for performing worship and other ceremonies, asserts that a Sikh should not be a member of any other religion, and that no other scriptures may be used in the *gurdwara*, though they may be quoted and referred to.[8] This development parallels that in the Christian tradition where on the one hand the Spirit of God is said to blow where it will (John 3:8), but on the other is conferred by baptism and is sometimes denied being found within other traditions. This kind of development had been anticipated by some of the Gurus themselves. For example, Guru Amar Das had a deep well, which was reached by a steep flight of steps, dug at his village of Goindwal. It became an alternative bathing place to Hardwar and was presumably constructed to accommodate the needs of Sikhs, some of them second-generation members by now and not zealous converts. The purpose may have been to draw them to the Guru's *dehra* where they could be weaned from beliefs about the efficacy of bathing at holy places, rather than letting them go to centres like Hardwar where they would come under the influence of the *brahmins*. The Guru also established the practice of summoning Sikhs to attend him personally at Baisakhi and Diwali, north Indian Hindu festival times, presumably again to refocus their attentions. At a scriptural level the hymns of the Gurus were superseding the Puranas and other texts as the *shabad*. If Guru Amar Das was responsible for deciding to include some *bhagat bani* in his Mohan Pothi it could well have been a device for enlarging the Panth. Devotees of teachers whose works were included would be inclined to look favourably upon the Panth and, perhaps, join it. Nevertheless, seeking to attract outsiders was not undertaken at the expense of their message. Only compositions congenial to Sikh teaching were admitted into collections of the *bani*. The third Guru's son, Guru Ram Das (AG 773), extended the process of encouraging Sikhs to develop their own distinct identity by composing the wedding hymn, Lavan, which came to be used at marriages instead of Vedic *mantras* spoken by *brahmins*.

In 1708 Guru Gobind Singh declared that there would be no human Gurus after him. His place would be taken by the scripture which he had completed in 1706 by adding his father's hymns but none of his own. He installed it as Guru just before he died. From this time it has therefore been called the Guru Granth Sahib (though the name Adi Granth is still used).

The compositions of the tenth Guru were compiled some years after his death in a book which was given the name Dasam Granth, the collection of the Tenth Guru. As it comprises the hymns of a Guru it is theoretically regarded as having the same authority as the Guru Granth Sahib but Sikh scholars, unlike some western commentators, do not regard all its contents as having equal worth. There are poems such as the autobiographical epic Vichitar Natak ('The Wonderful Dream'), in which the Guru traces his family's descent and that of the Bedi clan of Guru Nanak from Rama, which should not be taken literally. Sikhs read it with the awareness that he himself regarded Rama as an heroic human figure not an incarnation of God. Other sections are purely spiritual and abstract in content, resembling much more the contents of the Guru Granth Sahib. The Dasam Granth lacks the liturgical status of the Guru Granth Sahib. It is not installed in *gurdwaras* or carried in processions. Even though the Jap and ten Swayyas (couplets) by Guru Gobind Singh are recited during the *amrit* initiation ceremony only the Guru Granth Sahib is present in the room where it is held.

It should be remembered that the Dasam Granth as such post-dates Guru Gobind Singh by some thirty years and that some of its contents may be posthumously attributed to him. The complex language of its compositions (in Persian, Sanskrit, and Hindi, as well as Punjabi), make it a closed book for all but the ablest of scholars.

These are other reasons for its popularity and liturgical use never equalling that of the Guru Granth Sahib.


## CONTENT AND ARRANGEMENT OF THE SCRIPTURES

Some idea of the content of the Bible and Guru Granth Sahib will have already been formed. The Bible comprises two sections, referred to by Christians as the Old Testament, the Jewish part, and the New Testament, the writings of Christians. The Old Testament is suffused with historical material but none of this, any more than the narratives of the New Testament, should be regarded as straightforward, objective, factual story. Like the *janam sakhis*, the hagiographies of the life of Guru Nanak which the Sikh community produced after his death, they are accounts of God's presence and participation in the historical process.[9] Judaism has a great sense of God's activity in history and of him as the Lord of history. Something of that is present in the New Testament but something that a Christian is likely to be aware of when they talk with Jews today is the extent to which that part of the Jewish heritage is often missing from Christian thinking.

The New Testament begins with four gospels. 'Good news' is the usual rendering of the Anglo-Saxon term. These are not biographies in the modern sense of the word. They have more to say about who Jesus is for those who believe in him, and the purpose of his ministry, than about his daily life. In fact, about a quarter of their content is taken up with the last week of his ministry and the account of his death and Resurrection. Their variety in content and the fact that there are four and not one is probably indicative of the different circumstances and community needs which led to them being written. Though some Christians have attempted to deny that any divergence exists between the accounts, others would accept them and say that it is indicative of a diversity which lies at the heart of Christianity.

After the gospels comes the Acts of the Apostles, written by a man named Luke. He was a companion of St Paul's but was not an apostle. In part this book is the story of the spread of Christianity but it is very selective in content (no mention is made of the likely mission of St Thomas to India, for example, or the evangelical activity of most of the other apostles). It should probably be linked with the imprisonment and martyrdoms of Peter and Paul in Rome in 64 CE.

It may have been an *apologia* as one of its concerns is to show how they, its chief characters, were often unjustly persecuted by Jewish and Roman authorities. It seeks to exonerate them from the charges of treason and blasphemy which had been brought against them, just as Luke, in his gospel, affirmed the goodness and innocence of Jesus.

Next come a series of letters, many of them attributed to St Paul, as well as others under the names of such men as Peter and John who feature prominently in the gospels. Finally, there is Revelation, a book which was probably intended to reassure and comfort Christians facing persecution in the time of the Emperor Domitian (c. 96 CE). Some Christians have used it throughout subsequent centuries to predict historical events and especially a second coming or return of Jesus and the end of history.

The Guru Granth Sahib consists entirely of poetry which is divided into thirty-one sections or *ragas*. These are based on Indian musical *rags* equivalent to such things as *aubades* or nocturnes in western music. This does not mean, however, that a *shabad* set to an evening *rag* will necessarily be sung at that time of day. Printed copies of the Guru Granth Sahib were first produced towards the end of the nineteenth century. They are now identical to one another in page length and numbering, being 1430 pages long. Hence the ability simply to use page numbers in references to the Guru Granth Sahib given in this book. Sometimes Sikh scholars provide only *Rag* location, but there is an increasing tendency to use pagination. The opening thirteen pages of the scripture are not set to *ragas*. These are the hymns which Sikhs use in their daily devotions.

Printed copies of the Dasam Granth are 1428 pages long in the Shromani Gurdwara Parbandhak Committee's edition. This is an anthology of compositions listed by name and not arranged in any particular, discernible order.

## ATTITUDES TO THE SCRIPTURES AS SEEN IN LITURGIES

The importance of the Guru Granth Sahib cannot be lost on anyone who enters a *gurdwara*. There it is before them, enthroned, over-arched by a canopy, symbolising respect in Indian culture (as an umbrella may still be held over the head of a dignitary even on a dull but not wet or sunny day). Here there is probably a parallel to be noted with the canopy held over the Blessed Sacrament, when it is carried in Roman Catholic processions or placed over it on the altar. The Guru Granth Sahib will be attended constantly by a Sikh who waves another symbol of respect and authority over it, a *chauri*. This is a fan made of yak hair or nylon thread, or peacock feathers. It is the obvious focal point of attention.

In Christian churches the place of the Bible may not be as apparent though it may stand on a lectern from which it is read during the service. In some Protestant churches it may precede the minister into the pulpit. Its arrival may be acknowledged by the congregation standing to receive it. Elsewhere it will be placed upon the altar and carried into the congregation during Mass. Sometimes only a portion of it, a copy of the gospels, will be used for this purpose. The congregation will turn towards the book to listen to the reading in the way that Sikhs will face the Guru Granth Sahib as it is brought from or taken to its overnight resting place to be installed in the *gurdwara* daily. Some Christians may bow slightly, all Sikhs will make a low bow, some might prostrate themselves completely.

At home Sikhs may keep a copy of the Guru Granth Sahib in a place set apart for it, known as 'Babaji's room'. Housholds which do possess a Guru Granth Sahib should provide it with its own room. Often, because it cannot be given the proper respect through lack of space, Sikhs will choose not to possess one. Instead they will have a *gutka*, a small book containing the hymns used in daily devotion, including those found on pages one to thirteen of the Guru Granth Sahib. This they are likely to keep wrapped in cloth. They will uncover it and handle it only when they have washed their hands. Few Christians nowadays seem to accord their holy book the kind of physical respect which Sikhs give to theirs, though in past times the Bible was often kept in a special box when not in use and taken out for family prayers each morning and evening. The Bible is likely to stand on a shelf beside other books of a religious or secular kind. Among Protestants a justification for this for this may be their wish to emphasise that it should be like other books in the sense that it should be available for everyone to read and not the preserve of a priestly group. Honour should properly be paid to Jesus, the Word of God, rather than to the book in which the word is written.

(Perhaps the contrast may be reinforced by an experience of the Christian author of this book. When he wished to obtain a bilingual copy of the Guru Granth Sahib he approached the committee of the *gurdwara* in Leeds. They agreed to comply with his request knowing that he did not smoke and would respect their stipulation that the eight volumes should be placed on the highest shelf in his study. There they now stand, and his mother's family Bible has been moved to the same shelf!)

## THE SCRIPTURES AND PRIVATE DEVOTION

Private devotion is discussed in Chapter 8 but the use of the scriptures in the activity needs to be mentioned here. Each day millions of Christians face what it brings with prayer. Part of this act of devotion is likely to be a reading of some verses of the Bible. Often a lectionary or book of Bible notes may be used to help them discipline their reading and interpret the passages read. Sikhs have certain prescribed hymns, for example the Japji of Guru Nanak, which they should meditate upon daily. The scripture provides both Christians and Sikhs the means for focusing attention upon God.

## SCRIPTURE AND DOCTRINE

Authority is dealt with in Chapter 10 but it must be referred to here. Faced with an issue of doctrine or morality both Christians and Sikhs will consult the scripture. When they do so they find certain principles firmly established, for example, the need to love God and to serve one's fellow human beings, the commands to obey God and to honour parents. Obviously the scriptures are earthed in the cultures to which they were revealed but devotees believe that they contain a spirituality and morality which is universal. There are places where the texts may go further than this and give fairly explicit and precise doctrinal teaching. In the New Testament there is St Paul's Letter to the Romans. In this he set out the principles of the gospel which he preached. Siddha Gosht and Dakhani Oankar might be said to serve a similar function within the Sikh tradition. However, for the most part, when it comes to matters such as peace and war, genetic engineering, or euthanasia, the religions have to take into account general principles enshrined in tradition as well as trying to search the scriptures where no specific guidance can be found. There can be a difficulty for Christian and Sikh in allowing new insights to emerge from them. One is reminded here of the episode in the film 'Gandhi' where the Mahatma and his Christian friend C. F. Andrews faced the possibility of physical attack. When they were discussing what they should do Gandhi referred to Jesus' words in the Sermon on the Mount about 'turning the other cheek' (Matthew 5:39), to which the missionary replied, 'I never thought that those words were to be taken literally'. The sixteenth-century Reformation in Europe had, in part, the effect of liberating the scripture from traditional interpretation. That is a Protestant viewpoint, which some Roman Catholics now share, but some might point to the resulting profusion or confusion of so-called biblical doctrines of the church, for example, and to a literalism that often killed the spirit of the Word. There is always a danger, faced by any 'book religion', of deciding upon a teaching and making the scripture endorse it. This threat faces both the religions which are the subject of this book.

## SCRIPTURAL CRITICISM

The nineteenth century saw the beginning of attempts to get behind the Bible to the communities and situations which gave birth to it. This was inspired by a recognition that the Bible is a far more complex compilation of documents than it may appear to be at a superficial reading. Also important was the influence of an evolutionary approach to all studies, sometimes accompanied by an insistence on rationalism, a willingness to discount the divine, revelatory element and a tendency, consequently, to regard the Bible like folk literature as a purely human product. This was especially true of approaches to the Old Testament. There were necessary reasons for this textual analysis (perhaps a happier word than criticism), to be undertaken. For example, there are two creation and two flood narratives in the Book of Genesis. There are places where one episode in the life of Jesus seems to differ from the account in another gospel. Christians had always been aware of these things but had found ways of harmonising the texts. The newly offered solutions to these and other issues seemed blasphemous. It cost men like Julius Wellhausen, one of the earliest proponents of the new approach, his post at the University of Griefswald (1872). This is not the place to tell the story of modern biblical criticism but it must be said that Christians have employed methods developed over the last century in an attempt better to understand the first Christian communities which produced the gospels. After all there is a gap between the ministry of Jesus and the first gospel of at least thirty years.

Such an approach to scripture is generally inimical to Sikhs. The purpose of scripture study is devotional rather than analytical, to allow God's voice to be heard from the pages. Here they are at one with many other members and scholars of eastern religions. Thus, for example, westerners who look for the kind of commentary on the Bhagavad Gita which they are accustomed to reading on books of the Bible, will be disappointed in their search. Probably the only one of that kind is that written by the late R. C. Zaehner, a western Roman Catholic.[10]

Such a method of analysis is also unlikely to be very productive when applied to the Sikh scriptures. The hymns of Guru Nanak, for example, are poetry. They disclose some details of the communities which were challenged or comforted by them but there is no disputing the authenticity of the compositions of the Guru which are contained in the Guru Granth Sahib. Textual variations might be assumed to exist in a few cases in the collections such as the Mohan Pothis which pre-date Guru Arjan's compilation of the Adi Granth, but these would be scribal errors. The original copy which Guru Arjan scrutinised, and which bears corrections in his hand, survives at Kartarpur in Punjab and Sikhs scholars who have examined it affirm that there are no discrepancies. The efforts which Christian and Jewish scholars have found it necessary to undertake to arrive at an agreed text of the Bible has not been a task which has had to concern their Sikh counterparts working on the Guru Granth Sahib.

A textual analytical approach has, however, been used on the *janam sakhis*, accounts of the life of Guru Nanak. Frequently this *genre* of Sikh literature is described as hagiography but a better word is 'Testimony', which is the literal meaning of the word *sakhi*. In 1968 Professor W. H. McLeod published *Guru Nanak and the Sikh Religion* which employed the tools used for over a century by western historians and textual experts upon documents ranging from the Anglo-Saxon Chronicles to the Bible. This book and subsequent historical studies of the Sikh tradition by the same scholar have disturbed many Sikhs who regard such work as a thinly disguised attempt to undermine the Sikh religion. It is not easy to account to western readers for the reaction of Sikhs to this scholar's work which certainly does not have that motive. Real solutions to the issue of Sikh reaction must lie in such things as the difference between western and eastern approaches to the study of religion. The western approach seems to many Sikhs to be purposeless at best and at worst maliciously destructive, part of a plot devised by Christians to undermine the foundations of the religions of the east. Christianity, though eastern in origin, of course, is regarded as a basic ingredient of western culture and even the inspirer of some attempts to denigrate eastern culture.

Dr Darshan Singh, in his recent analytical survey of western studies of Sikhism (*Western Perspective on the Sikh Religion*, Delhi, 1991), has drawn attention to Edward Said's important study of western approaches to eastern cultures, *Orientalism* (London, 1978). In this Said defines orientalism as many things; a doctrine and an influential academic tradition (p. 203), a mode of discourse and style of thought (p. 2), 'a western style for dominating, restructuring and having authority over the Orient' (p. 3). Finally he writes, 'To speak of Orientalism therefore is to speak mainly, though not exclusively, of a British and French cultural enterprise, a project whose dimensions take in such disparate realism as the imagination itself, the whole of India and the Levant, the Biblical texts and Biblical lands, the spice trade, colonial armies, and a long tradition of colonial administrators, innumerable Oriental "experts" and "hands", an Oriental professorate, a complex army of "Oriental" ideas (Oriental despotism, Oriental splendor, cruelty, sensuality), many Eastern sects, philosophies, and wisdoms, domesticated for local European use – the list can be extended more or less indefinitely' (p. 4). The extent to which the charges that Said makes are sustainable must be left for those who read his book to decide for themselves. However, westerners who engage in Sikh studies should at least be aware of the suspicion with which their work is likely to be regarded by some members of the Panth. What Darshan Singh seems to wish to point out is the tendency of western writers to create the Sikh religion in their own image. Critics of McLeod may be concerned about the danger that his approach presents to the Panth. They would argue that it has severely injured if not mortally wounded Christianity and will, if it is not checked, damage Sikhism irrevocably, in a way that Islam in the form of the Mughal, Christianity with its missionaries and the British Empire, and the present Hindu resurgence have not managed.

Darshan Singh does not explicitly link McLeod, whose quality of scholarship he appreciates, with the orientalist thesis but it is clear that he sees most western studies of the Sikhs to be influenced, consciously or unconsciously, by a wish to formulate his religion in western categories. It is no accident that in the title of his study 'Perspective' is written in the singular!

It may be surprising to western readers that it was textual and historical criticism of the *janam sakhis* which sparked off Sikh objections to the work of Professor McLeod. After all, the earliest of them was written in the century after the events which they describe and their purpose was religious, not biographical. For Sikhs, however, the issue was not ultimately the historical reliabilty of the documents, the criticism of the *janam sakhis* was a direct attack upon Guru Nanak himself and through him upon the authenticity of the Sikh religion. The author or compiler of the *janam sakhis* expresses its purpose in these words:

> He who reads or hears this *sakhi* shall find his highest joy fulfilled, for through it he shall meet Guru Baba Nanak. He who with love sings of the glory of Baba Nanak or gives ear to it shall obtain joy ineffable in all that he does in this life, and in the life to come salvation.[11]

Plainly, from an examination of this passage, Guru Nanak had become for seventeenth-century Sikhs, at the popular level, not only a messenger but an embodiment of the message and, therefore, one through whose *darshan* or vision spiritual liberation could be achieved. Although this view may conflict with that of Guru Nanak himself and the orthodox position stated in an earlier chapter, nevertheless it expresses the emotional and spiritual relationship which Sikhs have today with the Gurus, especially with Guru Nanak. Consequently, those who question the Sikh tradition are likely to find themselves accused of attempting to undermine Sikhism itself. Lest anyone should think that only western scholars are subject to Sikh suspicion one might mention the late Professor Fauja Singh, a highly respected historian. In 1974 he published a reassessment of the reasons for execution of the martyr Guru Tegh Bahadur. This naturally brought a strong academic response from other Sikh scholars but it also resulted in a popular outcry which eventually forced Fauja Singh publicly to retract his view.[12]

There are parallels in the current Sikh experience with the story of biblical criticism in the west during the nineteenth century. This is well described in *The Quest of the Historical Jesus* by Albert Schweitzer. The attempts which were made to distinguish between the Jesus of history and the Jesus of faith were often regarded by ecclesiastical authorities, both Protestant and Roman Catholic, as scarcely veiled endeavours to destroy the credibility of Christianity and often resulted in scholars being deprived of academic posts if they were in the gift of religious bodies, as they usually were. The present Sikh situation has parellels with this but a number of distinct factors must be noted. First, biblical criticism was the result of the Enlightenment. Few Sikh scholars have, as yet, studied in the west and acquired an understanding of the methodology. It is not part of their academic tradition. Secondly, the power of popular Sikhism is far greater than that of popular Christianity. The Panth is not a synod or council of bishops, much less the voice of scholars, it is in a very real sense the Sikh people concentrated in Punjab. No Sikh professor can afford to ignore this fact. Thirdly, a religion which considers itself to be under threat – from Hindu fundamentalism in political guise in the case of Sikhism – is not welcoming to the kinds of attentions which seem to provide yet another danger by gnawing at its very foundations. Finally, suspicion of orientalism, even if the term is not known or used, is not confined to the work of western scholars; it extends, as we have noted, to Sikhs who are perceived to be using western methodology. To those who ask, in a manner which would seem extremely orientalist, 'When is Sikh scholarship going to catch up by embracing these western approaches to the study of religion?' the Sikh might well reply 'Never'. They might argue that the present challenge to Sikhs is to disengage themselves from the academic influences of the west in the way that they have freed themselves from political slavery. Some might even suggest that the profit which Christianity has gained from a century of self-criticism appears too limited for Sikhs to be encouraged to tread the same path.

Christian scholars might well point to benefits which can be derived from the use of textual analysis. Professor Donald G. Dawe attempted to do this in a paper which was really intended to persuade Sikhs of the value of the approach employed by Professor McLeod.[13] It was presented at an international conference in 1969 convened to mark the five-hundredth anniversary of the life of Guru Nanak. McLeod was not physically present at the conference but was seldom out of mind as the many allusions to him in the papers bear witness.

Dawe argues that 'by knowing history we are no longer victims of historical contingency and its vagaries' (p. 363). In other words, the discovery of the historical Guru Nanak can free the Panth from the accretions of subsequent years. The Sikh struggle against syncretism, very important in 1969 when innumerable commentators, Sikh and non-Sikh, were describing Guru Nanak as a Gandhi before Gandhi, seeking to reconcile Hinduism and Islam.[14] Twenty years later Dawe might be seen to be indicating the way that awareness of the Nanak of history might enable Sikhs to detach themselves from the acceptance of caste and the inferior status of women which are still part of the reality of Sikhism in the 1990s. Drawing on the distinction between Historie, the 'basic factual data of time and place' and Geschichte, 'the meaning and value of past events in the life of the community', Dawe attempted to show that the work of such scholars as McLeod could be liberating and thus positive rather than destructive. He ended his paper with these words:

> The history of religion often belies its beginnings. Forms now emptied of meaning, usurp the place of the immediate experiences of God. The ceremonial routine, the administrative organisation, the long tradition, although formed to preserve truth, often obscure it. Religious communities must constantly seek renewal by a return to the vitalities around which they were once formed. No religious community can live out of its religious dogmas and traditions for long, no matter how passionately held. It is only as we look through these traditions and teachings to the reality to which they point that there can be return to charisma. In this, historical analysis has a part to play. By understanding our history we avoid being the victims of a particular moment in history. By understanding the growth of tradition and institutions we can perceive afresh the truth around which they grew. In this way, reformulations and interpretations will be possible that can keep religion alive in every age of man, modern as well as ancient. (p. 371)

It cannot be said that Dawe's contribution to the debate has been mentioned by subsequent Sikh writers. For them liberation lies in the inspiration which is received from listening to the Guru's Word in the Guru Granth Sahib, and that seems to be under threat from western scholarship. The Panth, for Sikhs is the embodiment of the living *Sat Guru*, God, not merely an institution.

As Sikhism comes increasingly to the attention of the world's scholars and students of religion, it will find its history, beliefs, practices, and values coming under growing scrutiny from outsiders. Some scholars, Sikhs among them, perhaps, will take the western approach. The Panth, meanwhile, will have to consider seriously those from within its numbers and those outside it who return to the original documents upon which the tradition is based and question some of the non-Sikh aspects which have been absorbed into it over the centuries; for example, its acceptance of caste and gender inequality. But change, if it happens, will come from within, probably as a result of the experiences of Sikhs living in the Diaspora.

Writing about the effect of Christian mission in Punjab, Darshan Singh wrote:

> It provided a very strong impetus for reform and interpretation – reform in the religious practices and religious organisations, and reinterpretation of the belief systems, philosophies, in the light of new challenges. It gave rise to a number of religious reform movements among all religious groups. Sikhism did not remain unaffected by this new powerful challenge'. (pp. 86–7)

These words might relate prophetically to the impact of western academic studies upon the Sikh tradition. They might also refer to the possible consequence for Christianity as well as Sikhism of both religions being linked in constructive and sympathetic dialogue.

## TAKING GUIDANCE FROM THE SCRIPTURE

At the close of a Sikh service the person who is acting as custodian of the Guru Granth Sahib at that moment, will close it and then open it at random. The first line of the first complete hymn on the left-hand page will be read to the congregation. It constitutes the Guru's command or advice for the day. The practice is called *'vak laina'*, seeking advice. Sikh families or individuals will do the same each morning, using a *gutka* if they do not possess a copy of the scripture. This practice may remind Christians of the conversion story of St Augustine of Hippo, which reads as follows.

29. So was I speaking, and weeping in the most bitter contrition of my heart, when, lo! I heard from a neighboring house a voice,

as of boy or girl, I know not, chanting, and oft repeating, 'Take up and read; Take up and read.' Instantly, my countenance altered, I began to think most intently, whether children were wont in any kind of play to sing such words: nor could I remember ever to have heard the like. So checking the torrent of my tears, I arose; interpreting it to be no other than a command from God, to open the book, and read the first chapter I should find. For I had heard of Anthony, that coming in during the reading of the Gospel, he received the admonition, as if what was being read, was spoken to him; *Go, sell all that thou hast, and give to the poor, and thou shalt have treasure in heaven, and come and follow me.* And by such oracle he was forthwith converted unto Thee. Eagerly then I returned to the place where Alypius was sitting; for there had I laid the volume of the Apostle, when I arose thence. I seized, opened, and in silence read that section, on which my eyes first fell: *Not in rioting and drunkenness, not in chambering and wantonness, not in strife and envying: but put ye on the Lord Jesus Christ, and make not provision for the flesh,* in concupiscence. No further would I read; nor needed I: for instantly at the end of this sentence, by a light as it were of serenity infused into my heart, all the darkness of doubt vanished away.[15]

The practice of opening the Christian scriptures at random in order to receive divine guidance is not often heard of or encouraged today except, perhaps, at a popular devotional level, but in this passage we see that it has the authority of two of Christianity's greatest saints to commend it. Augustine of Hippo (354–430), was one of the greatest Fathers of the Church, and St Anthony (251–356), the pioneer of monasticism.

The Guru Granth Sahib, like the Bible which is likely to form the basis for the preacher's sermon, is seen to be the repository of wisdom. Sikh and Christian can echo the words of the Jewish psalmist:

Your word is a lamp to my feet, a light to my path. (Psalm 119;105)

Each, as an individual and as a member of their respective communities, hopes to be able to say that the promise made by the psalmist has been kept:

I have bound myself by oath and solemn vows to keep your just decrees. (v. 106)

The words of Guru Arjan when he had completed the compilation of the Adi Granth, sum up the similar Sikh belief:

> In the platter are placed three things, truth, contentment and wisdom, as well as the nectar of the Lord's Name, the support of all. Whoever eats their food and relishes it is emancipated. This cannot be forsaken, so keep it always enshrined in your mind. (AG 1429)

## TRANSLATIONS OF THE SCRIPTURES

Bible translations have existed since earliest times, in fact the Jewish scriptures had been translated from Hebrew into Greek almost two hundred years before the birth of Jesus so that Jews living in Egypt, or Syria, as well as Greece, who had no Hebrew could read their scriptures and keep alive their faith. It was this version which was used by the early Church.

Greek was the language of the New Testament. Arguments have been put forward to suggest that Matthew's Gospel was originally written in Aramaic, the spoken language of Jesus and Judaean and Galilean Jews of his day.[16] These, however, have not won general acceptance among scholars and the earliest fragments of the New Testament which exist are all written in Greek.

Greek was chosen not because it was the language of the intelligentsia but because it was the universal written language of the Mediterranean world, at least from Rome westwards.

It is claimed, probably correctly, that a puzzling acrostic found at Pompeii reads 'Pater Noster', the first words of the Lord's Prayer. If this is true it is evidence that Latin was being used by some Italian Christians before 79 CE, the date of the town's disappearance under the ash of the volcano Vesuvius.[17] Be that as it may, surviving texts of the New Testament from the fourth century onwards testify to it being translated into Latin, and several African and Slavonic languages. During the European Middle Ages Latin became the official language of the Catholic Church and translations into the language of the common people was discouraged. This meant, in English terms, for example, that although Bede of Jarrow in northern England was working on an English version of the gospels when he died in 735 and other sections of the Bible were translated in later centuries, such activity was virtually halted between about 1100 and 1526. A notable exception was the English Bible of 1384 attributed to John Wycliffe, but this and a few similar attempts led to the *Constitutions of Oxford* of 1408 which forbade the production or use of English versions without the permission of a diocesan bishop – who would not give it! In 1526 William Tyndale published an English New Testament, inspired by the German Reformation and the German New Testament of Martin Luther of 1522. Tyndale had to work in Germany and even there he was not safe. In 1536 he was arrested near Brussels, strangled to death and his body burnt. The Reformation restored the Bible to the people and the recent development of the printing press made it possible for cheap copies to be circulated in large quantities. The Bible is now available in almost every written language.

The Sikh scriptures, for all their terse poetical form, were composed in the language used by spiritual teachers in the Punjab five hundred years ago and would have easily been understood by everyone. The Punjabi alphabet was given its present form by Guru Angad, probably working in conjunction with Guru Nanak whom he eventually succeeded as Guru. Written Punjabi, known as *gurmukhi*, literally 'from the Guru's mouth', owes much of its development to the Sikh movement. From 1604, when the Adi Granth was compiled, partly to protect the Panth against fraudulent compositions intended to promote rival, non-Sikh teachings, care has been taken to ensure that copies of the scripture are accurate. The seventh Guru, Har Rai, even repudiated his son, Ram Rai, for altering one word of the text. Ram Rai went to the Mughal court in place of his father. There he was asked to explain a verse which, the Emperor had been told, was defamatory to Islam. It read:

> The dust of a Muslim is kneaded into clay by a potter and made into bricks which cry out as they burn. (AG 466)

Ram Rai blamed a scribal error for the word 'Muslim', saying that insted it should have read *beiman*, 'faithless'. When news of Ram Rai's failure to stand by the words of Guru Nanak and the text of the Adi Granth reached Guru Har Rai he said:

> The guruship is like tiger's milk which can only be contained in a golden cup. Only he who is ready to devote his life thereto is worthy of it. Let Ram Rai not look upon my face again.[18]

Printing reached the Punjab in the nineteenth century and caused some anxiety among the Sikhs, who were concerned that the proliferation of copies of the Guru Granth Sahib would result in it being treated with lack of respect. When a five-volume printed version was eventually published *gurdwaras* were instructed not to bind them together and install them. Only handwritten copies were to be used. At least three printed editions of different lengths co-existed for some time but by the first decade of the twentieth century uniformity had been achieved with the one-volume text of 1430 pages published by the Shromani Gurdwara Parbandhak Committee being accepted and used in *gurdwaras*. This is now the version which is used world-wide.

Transliterations in the Urdu or Devanagri script were published in the first quarter of the twentieth century but it was only in 1961 that a complete translation into a foreign tongue appeared. This was the achievement of Dr Gopal Singh. It comprises four volumes. In 1969 Dr Man Mohan Singh completed his eight-volume translation which had been commissioned by the Shromani Gurdwara Parbandhak Committee. Professor Gurbachan Singh Talib completed his translation shortly before his death. The fourth and last volume was published in 1990. Dr Jarnail Singh, living in Canada, has made a French translation but as yet the funds have not been found to publish it.

The need for translations into what are becoming the mother tongues of the Sikh dispersion will increase with the passage of time. Already American converts to Sikhism, members of the 3HO organisation (Healthy, Holy and Happy), are using Man Mohan Singh's translation in conjunction with the installed *gurmukhi* text, though its archaic English and uncalled-for use of the male pronoun 'he' and 'Lord' often mean it is of limited help for readers in the late twentieth century. An example of this can be read in this extract from Dr Man Mohan Singh's work:

> Highest of the high and unrivalled is thy dignity, O Lord
> Various are thine colours and super colours.
> Thy wondrous deeds, one can realise not.
> Thou alone art the inner life of the living beings and
>     knowest everything.
> Everything is under thy sway and beauteous is thy mansion.
> In thy home is bliss and it is thy home where
>     congratulations ever pour in.

Thine celebrity, magnificeance and glory behove thee alone.
Thou art brimful of all the potencies and art seen
everywhere.
Nanak, the slave of thy slaves, O Lord, makes supplication
before thee.

Dr Gopal Singh provides the following translation:

Highest of the high is they station, O Lord. Yea, wondrous art thy wonders: one cannot realise their mystery. It is thy light that sustains all life and thou knowest our inmost state. Everything is under thy sway. Blessed, blessed is thy home; it ever rings with wedding songs. Yea, thou alone containest thyself with thy majesty and glory. All powerful art thou; yea, thou art here and there also. Nanak is the slave of thy slaves, O God, and his praise is to thee alone. (AG 965)

From a study of these two passages it can be seen that archaic language is likely to create problems for readers. Though both translations may be said to capture the essence of the message they fail to make it easily accessible.

At present Sikhs tend to deny that the need for reliable, fluent modern translations is an urgent priority. Many of those living in the Punjab can see no necessity for it. Those who recognise that translations are important go on to express two concerns. First, they are anxious that the poetic nature of the original should be respected by it being rendered into poetry. This has caused problems for all the Sikhs who have produced translations into English. They have been greatly influenced by their deep knowledge of Shakespeare and the King James version which they may well have been brought up to respect in missionary or English-medium colleges where they studied. Secondly, they doubt whether a translation can retain the meaning of the original, especially when the Gurus used poetry, a form which can never be translated perfectly. Against this is the fact that many young people growing up in the Diaspora have no access to their scripture any more than increasing numbers of young English-speaking Christians can understand the King James version of the Bible. To be frank, many adult Sikhs have for a long time depended on interpretations provided by commentaries written in modern Punjabi to help them understand the meaning of the original text. There is no sign, as yet, of the Shromani Gurdwara

Parbandhak Committee in Amritsar, or some other wealthy body, financing the kind of project which has resulted in modern translations of the Bible, such as that used in this book. This monumental task is still left to the skills of individual scholars, few of whom can combine energy, intellectual ability, grasp of the original tongue and the nuances of the language into which the translation is being made, with the dedication of several years of their lives, even if they can obtain financial support. Meanwhile, because the scripture is essential to the development of Sikh spirituality, there are young Sikhs who feel deprived of that heritage.[19]

# 7

# Worship

## THE NATURE OF WORSHIP

Honouring and praising God is the purpose of worship for both
Christian and Sikh. It is the necessary response which the believer
makes to a consciousness of God's love and grace. It is no more
possible for the believer to withhold it than it is to deny food or
help to a needy loved one. Guru Nanak said:

> What should I ask and what should I be heard uttering except
> that I hunger and thirst for your sight! (AG 762)

The psalmist wrote:

> I pine and faint with longing for the courts of the Lord's Temple;
> my whole being cries out with joy for the living God. (Psalm
> 84:2)

Both were expressing the craving which Christians and Sikhs
hope to satisfy in congregational worship. The response is often
articulated in the form of poetry set to music. The classic statements
upon which much Christian hymnody is based are the psalms
of its Jewish parent, like the one quoted above. These were the
means by which Jesus and his disciples praised the Lord as they
ascended to Jerusalem, worshipped in the Temple there, or attended
a synagogue service on the Sabbath. Sikhs rejected explicit Hindu
songs of praise, *bhajans*, composed in praise of Krishna or some other
deity. Instead they used the *'bhajans'* composed by Guru Nanak and
his successors for this purpose. These also educated their followers
theologically in the easiest and most memorable way possible.
    (Here Sikhism and Methodist Christianity have much in common;
both were born in song and use hymns to praise God and instruct
the faithful.)

There may be a readiness among Christians and Sikhs to regard worship as a natural human activity, the acknowledgement of worth brought on by a beautiful sunrise, a majestic waterfall, or a painting, but the worship which we are concerned with has an extra dimension. It is characterised by a recognition of God, from whom the impulse to worship derives, an affirmation of belief, even though the worshipper may feel inadequate, and a desire for communion despite a possible sense of awe bordering on fear as one contemplates the eternal reality, God. Each of these attitudes is conveyed in the following examples:

> Holy, holy, holy! Lord God Almighty!
> Early in the morning our song shall rise to thee;
> Holy, holy, holy, merciful and mighty!
> God in three persons, blessed trinity!

In this popular Christian hymn composed by Reginald Heber, Bishop of Calcutta there is awe as well as trinitarian orthodoxy. The hymn is based on some words in the Book of Isaiah, chapter 6 Christian worship is offered to God through his Son, Jesus Christ and is inspired by the Holy Spirit. This is not to say that the Christian does not approach God direct, after all Jesus is God. It is a way of saying that Jesus is the focus, the one through whom and in whom God is understood. The use of 'in the name of Jesus', or 'for Jesus' sake', at the end of a prayer, or such words as

> Praise, praise the Father, praise the Son,
> And praise the Spirit, Three in One,

at the end of a hymn are reminders of this and of orthodox belief. For some Christians it is a statement that Jesus is the only way that God may be approached. They might have in mind some sentences in the Letter to the Hebrews where the author makes use of ideas related to the Temple worship with which they were familiar:

> the blood of Jesus makes us free to enter the sanctuary with confidence by the new and living way which he has opened to us . . . . We have a great high priest set over the household of God; so let us make our approach in sincerity of heart and full assurance of faith, inwardly cleansed from a guilty conscience, and outwardly washed with pure water. (Hebrews 10:19–22)

Perhaps a similar idea is contained in some words of Guru Arjan:

> We are defiled. You purify us. We are without merit. You bestow merit. We are ignorant. You are wise, enlightened and skilful.
>    Lord, such we are, such you are. We are sinful; you are the remover of impurities
>    . . . You are the ever gracious bestower of blessings; deliver us, your children. (AG 613)

The casual observer might conclude that Sikh worship is similarly channelled through the Gurus in the form of their hymns but there are notable differences between Sikh beliefs about the Gurus and Christian beliefs about Jesus. These have been dealt with elsewhere (Chapter 4) and need not be repeated here. Two reminders must be made, however. First, the Guru Granth Sahib does contain non-Sikh material. Secondly, the Gurus are not worshipped. Sikhs do not permit the use of non-Sikh material in worship in the *gurdwara* because it is obviously not in the Guru Granth Sahib and therefore cannot have the approval of the Gurus. However, they do not have the reservations that some Christians have who question the validity of worship which is not expressly offered in the name of Jesus. Christians seem to find shared worship in interreligious services more of a problem than Sikhs do – but this is a matter to be taken up later (Chapter 12) rather than here.

## THE FORM OF WORSHIP

Sikh worship is called *diwan*. This is literally, attendance at God's court. The term was used of audiences given by Mughal emperors to hear the pleas of their subjects. It is straightforward and uncomplicated and must very nearly reflect the worship of those Sikhs who gathered around Guru Nanak some five hundred years ago. They would sit on the ground facing the Guru's seat (*gaddi*), listen to his instruction and sing his hymns to the accompaniment of Mardana's rebeck. (After Mardana's death his son Shahzada acted as accompanist). Today, in the *gurdwara*, the Sikhs continue to sit on the floor but add to the original practical reason a stress upon equality. No one of whatever rank should be seated in a way which suggests some kind of honour or distinction (though a chair would be provided for a disabled person, of course). The focus is now the Guru Granth Sahib, usually placed on a platform, or perhaps enthroned upon a *manji*. This is a low stool covered with a cushion. Invariably there will be a *chanini* or canopy over the *manji* on which the scripture sits. The reader or some other Sikh will hold a *chauri* and wave it over the Guru Granth Sahib from time to time. The *chauri* is fan used as a symbol of authority and sovereignty. It may be made of peacock feathers tied together in a bundle about three quarters of a metre long or it may be more elaborate and ornate, yak hairs or nylon embedded in a silver or wooden holder. Men and women usually sit separately, as they do in Christian churches in some parts of the world, but all worship together and all aspects of *diwan* may be conducted equally by women or men.

These two illustrations demonstrate Sikh insistence upon a basic similarity between worship in the time of Guru Nanak and today. Sikh worship is a combination of *kirtan* and *katha*, that is, of singing hymns from the scripture to musical accompaniment, and delivering homilies based on the Guru Granth Sahib. Sometimes a *katha* may be delivered by one of the *ragis*, the musicians who lead the worship, or by another member of the *sangat*, or a visitor may be invited to give an address. During each act of worship several hymns will be sung and a number of addresses given. To be more precise than this is not really possible. In major *gurdwaras* in India the daily singing of *kirtan* may begin before dawn and continue until after sunset. Devotees, who will have taken a bath first thing in the morning, will come to the *gurdwara* to pay their respects to the Guru Granth Sahib as opportunity permits.

It is in the evening when the work demands of the day are less intense that men and women will sit in the *gurdwara* and someone will give a *katha*.

At the beginning and end of Sikh worship there is a recognisable order. First, the Guru Granth Sahib has to be installed and opened ceremonially. Overnight it will have been closed and may have been laid to rest in a room set apart for the purpose. If so it will be carried to the *manji*, placed respectfully on it, *Ardas* will be said (see below), and guidance for the day will be sought through a random reading of one of its verses (*vak*). Then the singing of *kirtan* can begin.

At the end of worship, certain specified hymns are sung, the congregation stands for *Ardas*, and a *vak* is taken. *Karah parshad* will

be shared among the congregation who then disperse to the dining
hall for *langar*. (The liturgy used at the conclusion of Sikh worship
is given at the end of this chapter.)

Christian worship is far more complex, varied, and difficult to
describe. Originally it was based upon the worship of the Temple
and synagogue and used the psalms of Judaism but it soon assumed
content and characteristics of its own. In the Acts of the Apostles it
says tersely that the first followers of Jesus met constantly to 'break
bread' (chapter 2:42 and 46). It is not described in more detail as the
readers would be familiar with the practice. Whatever actual form
this took, there can be little doubt that it evoked memories of the
Last Supper and perhaps other meals which Jesus shared with his
disciples. At one time this may have been a full meal but there is
some evidence that this became an excuse for self-indulgence and
divisive assertions of class superiority (1 Corinthians 11). Quite
soon, within thirty years of the Last Supper, in Corinth at least, it
had become a meal characterised by simplicity and symbolism.

For the vast majority of Christians the Last Supper remains the
focus of worship. The name used may vary. Breaking of bread,
Eucharist, mass, holy communion, Lord's supper, are among the
most popular phrases employed. The Divine Liturgy is the name
used by the Orthodox Church. The presence of Jesus is recognised
in all traditions though the manner in which he is believed to be
present has been the occasion for many disputes and persecution.
Some Christians will call the service a memorial in which Jesus
is called to mind, but this is not usually simply recalling a past
event. The Last Supper is reenacted or rehearsed, the experience of
the original meal is recaptured spiritually. Many more Christians
consider him to be present in the elements of bread and wine in
some special way. Roman Catholic and Orthodox Christians will
affirm the presence of Jesus in the bread and wine which, at the
words of consecration, become his actual body and blood. Other
Christians may prefer to speak of a mystical or spiritual presence.

For those whose focus is the Last Supper, the act of worship
based on it may be simple or complex. It may consist of a group of
Christians reading the words of scripture, either from 1 Corinthians
11, which is the earliest actual written account of the event, or from
one of the gospels, and then passing around a loaf of bread from
which each takes a piece, and a wine goblet, from which each
drinks in turn. On the other hand it may be the highly ritualistic
and elaborate celebration of a Roman Catholic High Mass.

At the Reformation of the seventeenth century, and in more recent times, some Christians have rejected the Last Supper focus, replacing it with an emphasis upon the preaching of the Bible and the singing of hymns based on the Bible. This kind of Christian worship is more akin to that of the Sikhs both in form and spirit. In both the scripture is central. (In passing it might be pointed out that some Christian denominations have rejected the Lord's Supper completely, most notably the Society of Friends or Quakers. They emphasise the inwardness of God's spirit and reject the need for externals. Their meeting for worship is one of silent waiting upon the spirit of God who may speak through the ministry of one of the worshippers or simply in the silence of the gathered meeting.)

TIMES OF WORSHIP

Sunday has become the Christian weekly holiday but this was not always the case. In the Acts of the Apostles we read of the followers of Jesus worshipping in the Jerusalem Temple daily as well as breaking bread in their own homes (2:46). The Jewish Sabbath would, of course, remain special for them. Some Christians, presumably of Jewish background, observed it into the second century and perhaps later. (In the nineteenth century Seventh Day Adventists revived the practice of keeping the Sabbath in the belief that a reason why the expected return of Jesus had not occurred was because of the failure of Christians to keep the Sabbath.)

Sunday eventually became the day identified with Christianity for a number of reasons. It was the first day of the week, the one on which the work of creation had begun. God had said, 'Let there be light' (Genesis 1:3). Jesus was the Light of the World (John 8:12). He rose to life from death on the first day of the week (Mark 16:2). One other reason might be added; the wish to be different from the Jews. To keep the same day might have suggested that the followers of Jesus were no more than a Jewish sect. The endorsement of Sunday by the Emperor Constantine in 321, as a day of rest for all his subjects other than agriculturalists set it on the path of becoming the almost universal holiday which it now is. This does not mean, however, that Christians do not meet for public worship on other days. Many Roman Catholics and Eastern Christians will celebrate the Eucharist daily in the morning and local churches of other denominations hold regular week-day services. Interestingly, the Lord's Supper often took the form of an evening service (Acts 20:7 is an example of such a gathering). These assemblies were apparently declared illegal by the Emperor Trajan in the second century. This may be the origin of the practice of early morning Eucharists. Later still the idea of purifying the body by fasting for about eight hours before receiving the consecrated bread and wine, the body and blood of Jesus, became an added reason for celebrating the Eucharist in the early morning.

Daily worship is a feature of Hindu practice which was taken up by the Gurus. When Guru Nanak settled at Kartarpur in the latter days of his life members of the Sikh community gathered with him each morning to say the Japji and in the evening when work was done they recited two other hymns, Sodar and Arati, together. This has remained the Sikh custom ever since and throughout the world *gurdwaras* open daily from before dawn until after dusk. The only exception to this is in small communities in the Dispersion where no one may be available to attend the Guru Granth Sahib during the working day or because the *sangat* is so scattered that weekday congregational worship is impossible. In such circumstances reliance has to be on private devotions and *diwan* on the weekly holiday, usually Sunday.


## HOLY COMMUNION, *LANGAR* AND *KARAH PARSHAD*

There are distinct similarities between these three aspects of Christian and Sikh worship. It may therefore be appropriate to make some comparison of them if only to eliminate the confusion which may be caused by some Sikhs referring to *karah parshad* as a sacrament.

The word 'sacrament' is the Latin for the Greek *mysterion*, English 'mystery'. In popular usage the word means 'riddle'. This is not quite its religious meaning. In the New Testament the word mystery refers to God's purpose or plan of salvation. It is a revealed secret because God has explained it through the life, death and Resurrection of Jesus. For the Christian believer the riddle no longer exists. St Paul described it as:

> The revelation of that divine secret kept in silence for long ages, but now disclosed. (Romans 16:25)

In Colossians 2:2, God's secret is:

> Christ himself in whom lie hidden all the treasures of wisdom
> and knowledge.

Those who know Christ know the secret. Baptism, the formal
means of entering the Church, became the rite by which one became
a sharer in the mystery of the Gospel. The other sacraments also
have the idea of participation in salvation as at least part of their
purpose. Sacraments came to be called means of grace, acts through
which the participant receives God's grace. If we accept the definition of a sacrament as a means of grace we may choose to include
or exclude the sharing of *karah parshad*! Its inclusion would be on
the grounds that all Sikh ceremonies and activities are means of
grace and Sikhs might extend this teaching to include similar rituals
in other religions. Others, however, would condemn all rituals as
superstitions and assert that any value they possessed were social
in nature. They did not confer spiritual benefits. The most important
Sikh activities from which grace might be said to be received are the
reading of and listening to the Guru Granth Sahib and the practice
of *nam simran*, the Sikh form of meditation which involves the use of
scripture. If Sikhs were ever asked where the 'real presence' of God
is in their worship they would certainly answer, 'In the *gurbani*', the
words of scripture.

There is one feature of Sikh worship which still requires comment,
especially as it has caused Christians of tender conscience some
difficulty when they have attended a Sikh service, that is *karah
parshad* and the practice of touching it with a *kirpan* (short sword),
after the prayer, *Ardas*. This action, known as *deg* and *teg* (Persian
for kettle and sword), signifies the responsibility of the Panth to
provide food and protection for the needy and oppressed. There
is no suggestion that the food has become something other than
a *halwa*, that is a pudding, made of wholemeal flour, sugar and
clarified butter (*ghee*). This is what *karah parshad* is. Its only one
purpose is to enable Sikhs to express unity, equality, and freedom
from caste restrictions against commensality, by eating together. As
the Rahit Maryada puts it:

> In order to remove untouchability and to teach social equality
> Guru Nanak started the custom of distributing *karah parshad*
> among his congregations. (p. 11)

This is also the purpose of *langar*, which is an integral part of worship as well as having a place in Sikh ethics. It is the vegetarian meal which is served in *gurdwaras*. All worshippers and visitors are expected to sit together and eat it. This requirement extends to *Khalsa* members. Though they are taught that they should not eat from the same dish as non-Khalsa Sikhs (Rahit Maryada, p. 22) people never share the same plate (*thali*) at *langar* so the rule is not infringed. The famous story of the emperor Akbar's visit to Guru Amar Das is often told by Sikhs to stress the importance of *langar*.[1]

Before being given an audience he was required to sit in the food line with others who had come to worship and receive *darshan*. The Sikh principle is summed up in the sentence:

'*Pehle pangat, pichle sangat*'. 'First eat together, then worship together'.

This institution of *langar*, like *karah parshad*, has to be understood in the context of the Sikh emphasis upon equality. People of all faiths or none, beggars and worshippers, may enjoy the simple meal. The only restriction is that imposed by the would-be eater. If he or she is unable to share food with people of another religion or another caste, a restriction which some *brahmins*, for example, may still observe, they cannot eat in the *langar*. That, however, is not a limitation placed upon them by Sikhs, who welcome all comers, usually with great kindness and pleasure.

One of the meanings of Holy Communion is that of fellowship. It is a way in which Christians demonstrate their unity with one another as well as with their Lord. In some churches the celebrant may say that the Lord's table is open to anyone who 'loves the Lord Jesus'. Presumably this phrase was intended to encompass members of any denomination as well as those who had not become full members of the church through baptism or the rite of receiving the right hand of fellowship as a church member. Whether it might be extended to include someone of a different religion, a Hindu or Sikh for example, who 'loves the Lord Jesus' as many do, might provoke an interesting discussion at a church meeting!

Generally, however, sharing in the sacrament is restricted to those men and women who are members of the particular denomination or are in good standing with it (i.e. are members of a church which is in communion with it). At the moment of writing members of Protestant denominations are excluded from partaking of the elements consecrated in a Roman Catholic mass, for example, though Roman Catholics would be permitted to receive communion if they attended the Eucharist of another denomination.

Perhaps it is evident from this brief discussion that to use the word sacrament in Sikhism is not helpful. Khalsa initiation, which is dealt with elsewhere (Chapter 9), might be considered to be a *sacramentum* in the sense of an oath of allegiance, which is what the Latin term meant originally, but this is very different from the concept of a sacrament as a means of grace.

## PRIESTHOOD

In most Christian denominations there are ordained men (mostly) or women who conduct worship and administer the sacraments, especially the Eucharist. In some there is a priesthood who are the only people ordained to celebrate the communion service. From the time of the apostles the Church consisted of two kinds of member. The apostles, as we have seen, were Jewish men who had been with Jesus throughout his ministry and were witnesses to his resurrection. They, in turn, appointed men and women from converts to minister to the new Christian congregations which resulted from their evangelistic work. (See Romans 16:1, where Phoebe is named as a minister of the church at Cenchreae, near Corinth). As emphasis upon the sacraments grew so these ministers became set apart more and more, eventually being required to be male and celibate in the western church, and from about the second century the term 'priest' began to be applied to them. With the sixteenth-century Reformation attention often focused more upon what is called the priesthood of all believers than on the ordained clergy but most of the new denominations retained an ordained, paid, and full-time ministry. This might have been the consequence of tradition, the recognition that there were practical advantages, or a continued belief in the need to maintain the apostolic succession.

Some denominations elected ministers from the membership of the individual gathered church. From this a full-time ministry of people set apart, at least to some extent, by ordination, has evolved. The Society of Friends (Quakers) is one of the few denominations which has not done so. All its members exercise an equal ministry. Its officers are chosen to perform purely functional tasks and enjoy no permanency of appointment.

Sikhism has no lay-ordained distinction, it is literally meaning-less. Those who hold offices within the Panth or local *sangats* exercise a purely functional role. There may be people who are paid emoluments for their services but this is because the community feels that it needs them to exercise their office on a full-time basis. This is especially the case outside India where there is a need for the *gurdwara* to undertake the educational functions of the Sikh village or extended family. They are appointed and dismissed at the will of the *sangat* and thereafter revert to the occupation which they previously followed.

In the context of worship there are two functionaries whose duties need explanation. The first is that of *granthi*. As the name implies, this is a person who reads the Guru Granth Sahib on such occasions as worship or weddings. He or she may be a highly educated person or someone who possesses only the basic skills which are required, those of being able to read *gurmukhi* in the intoned way used in public worship and to provide an exegesis of the passages read. The elected *sangat* committee will organise events and decide who should address it on important occasions. There are, however, highly trained *granthis* who combine sound theological knowledge with the requirements mentioned above. In countries of the Diaspora such as Britain, Canada, and the USA, they may teach the young *gurmukhi* and the principles of the Sikh religion. Sometimes they may exercise a pastoral role, but the extended family is the main source of counselling support for Sikhs.

Small *sangats* may not need a *granthi* or have the finances to appoint one. Large and wealthy *gurdwaras* may have as many as five. *Granthis* may have acquired their skills from another *granthi* or have gone for training to a college in the Punjab. Sometimes these are called missionary colleges. These should not be con-fused with Christian colleges which train men and women to evangelise non-Christians. The *granthi's* ministry is only to the Panth.

In western communities *granthis* may have larger responsibilities, those of educating the young in *gurmat*, the teachings of the Gurus. This is likely to include instruction in reading *gurmukhi*, the lan-guage of the Guru Granth Sahib, and how to sing *kirtan*.

Such *granthis* may be highly educated graduates. As Sikh children brought up in the west grow further away from the parental culture of the Punjab the apologetic role of *granthis* will increase in the attempt of Sikhism to wean its young people away from the lure of non-religious values and materialism or Christianity. *Granthis* receive their training in the Punjab, but the time may come when the Diaspora feels the need to set up its own colleges to ensure that the teachers upon which it will come increasingly to rely are familiar with the ideas, issues and cultures of the societies in which they live. *Granthis* may also act as custodians of a *gurdwara*, especially in the west where most Sikhs have the kind of employment which keeps them from attending the *gurdwara* during daytime.

*Ragis*, the second group, are musicians who lead and accompany the singing of *kirtan* in public worship. Their requirements are obvious, musical ability both instrumental and vocal. Most congregations recruit *ragis* from among their own number as the occasion demands but there is a tendency to employ professionals at weddings and festivals. Some famous *ragis* have recorded passages of the Guru Granth Sahib and spend their lives touring internationally. They may be paid a fee or given the money which members of the congregation place in front of them to show appreciation for their skills. Sometimes blind boys are trained to become *ragis* so that they can earn a living in the service of *gurdwara*.

So far Sikhism has succeeded in resisting a tendency for an ordained ministry to evolve. It would certainly seem likely to retain the three principles which underlie this position. They are, first, the belief that no one should be seen to rival or compete with the Guru; secondly, the belief that the Guru is present in the *panth* and therefore the *sangat*, as a corporate body of believers; thirdly, the principle of equality.

To this may be added the awareness that Sikhs still possess of their religion being, at least in part, a protest against the power and authority of the *brahmins*, the priests of the Hindu tradition. For these reasons no development of a separate or ordained ministry is in prospect. If Sikhs describe their *granthi* as a priest it is in a wish to help their non-Sikh listener. Should they be Protestant Christians or Muslims the result may actually be offputting!

A *sant* is a preceptor who has gained a reputation as a teacher and spiritual guide. For this reason they are given the title '*sant*' which may be used as a prefix to their names. The title has no formal validity. Their home may become a *dehra* (literally camp), to which devotees come and where some of them stay permanently. *Sants* may travel locally or internationally, inspiring Sikhs to greater spirituality through their ministry. They have no official place within Sikhism and may be regarded with caution by some Sikhs who fear that devotees may fall into the danger of treating them as gurus are honoured in the Hindu tradition and accord them the kind of respect and allegiance which should be given only to the Panth and the Guru Granth Sahib. The equivalent to saints in the Christian tradition would be the spiritual masters or 'fathers in God' to whom some Christians may attach themselves for the development of their devotional lives. Bede Griffiths is a well-known example of someone who has spanned the Hindu–Christian divide, not always without incurring suspicion, because meditation is still a practice which is considered unacceptable and even dangerous by some Christians. It will be interesting to see whether the Indian Church, as it becomes more free of the influence of western Christianity, the so-called Latin Captivity, produces *sant*-like figures. They would be more acceptable than gurus whose teaching is based on their own doctrines, regarded as divinely revealed. *Sants* should teach *gurmatta*, the message of Sikhism.

## THE CONCLUSION OF *DIWAN*

Whatever the general content of *diwan* the conclusion is always as follows.

(a) Six verses of *The Anand Sahib of Guru Amar Das*.
1.  O joy, my mother, I have found the True Guru. I have found the True Guru and songs of rejoicing fill my heart. Beautiful songs and heavenly singers come to sing praises to God. Those who keep God within ever sing God's praises. Nanak says, my heart is full of joy, for I have found the True Guru.
2.  O my soul, live with God forever. Abide with God and all your sorrows will vanish. You will be acceptable to God who will take charge of all your affairs. The Perfect One is omnipotent; why forget God? Nanak says, live with God forever.
3.  O my True One, is there anything that your house does not contain? Everything is in your house, there for whoever you decide to give it to. The recipient will praise your bounty and honour your name. Strains of heavenly music resound for one

in whose heart your name resides. Says Nanak, is there anything
that your house does not contain?

4. The True Name sustains me forever. the True Name satisfies my
hunger and sustains me. God's Name is awakened in my heart.
It has given me peace and joy and fulfilled all my desires. I will
always be a sacrifice to the Guru who displays such kindness.
Says Nanak, listen O saints, love the Word. The True Name
sustains me forever.

5. Celestial music rings through the house. Music resounds in the
house where God's might has been infused. There God has
conquered the five passions and destroyed fear of death. Those
favoured by destiny are attached to God's Name. Nanak says,
they have found happiness and they hear celestial music in their
hearts.

40. O Listen to my joy, my fortunate friends. All my desires have
been fulfilled. I have attained to God the Supreme Spirit and all
my sorrows have vanished. Sorrow, affliction and suffering have
been dispelled through hearing the true Word. Saints and holy
people are glad on hearing it from the perfect Guru. Pure are
the hearers; stainless the speakers; the True Guru will fill their
hearts. Nanak says, heavenly trumpets sound for those who bow
at the Guru's feet.

(b) Some words from Guru Nanak's *Japji*.
Air, water, and earth, these are the elements from which we are
made. Air, like the Guru's Word, gives breath of life to the baby
born to the great mother earth, sired by the waters. Night and day
are the nurses which watch over us in our infancy. We play in their
lap. The world is our playground. Our right and wrong acts will
receive judgement in your court. Some will be seated near your
throne and some far away. Toil has ended for those who worship
you. O Nanak, their faces are radiant with joy. They free many
others.                                                         —

(c) A section of the Sukhmani Sahib (Hymn of Peace) of Guru
Arjan.
You are the Supreme One; I pray to you. My body and soul are
the gifts for starting life. You are both father and mother, we are
your children. We draw many blessings from your grace. No one
knows your limits; you are the highest of the high. All creation
depends on your will; it has to accept all the comes from you. You

alone know what determines your purpose. I am ever a sacrifice to you.

(d) The Sikh congregational prayer, *Ardas*, is then offered by a member of the congregation.[2] It reads:

Victory to the Eternal One. May almighty God protect us.

First remember almighty God, then call to mind Guru Nanak, Guru Angad, Guru Amar Das and Guru Ram Das, may they help us. Remember Gurus Arjan, Hargobind, Har Rai and Har Krishan whose sight removes all sorrows. May we remember Guru Tegh Bahadur at whose invocation the nine treasures [spiritual blessings] come hastening to our homes. May they help and protect us at all times.[3]

May we always enjoy the protection of the Tenth Guru, Guru Gobind Singh. Disciples of the Gurus, meditate on the Guru Granth Sahib, the visible form of the Guru. Repeat the name of God. Vahiguru.[4]

Think of the glorious deeds of the five beloved ones (*panj piare*),[5] the Guru's four sons,[6] the forty liberated ones,[7] and others who were steadfast and long suffering. Remember them and call on God. Vahiguru.

Call to mind those who kept the Name in their hearts and shared their earnings with others. Vahiguru.

Those who allowed themselves to be cut limb from limb, had their scalps scraped off, were broken on the wheel, were sawn or flayed alive, remember them. Vahiguru.

Think of those who cleansed the *gurdwaras*, permitted themselves to be beaten, imprisoned, shot, maimed or burned alive with neither resistance nor complaint, and call on God. Vahiguru.

As you remember the seats of authority (*takhts*)[8] and other places touched by the Gurus' feet, call on God. Vahiguru.

May the whole Khalsa remember the Wonderful One, and as it does so may it be blessed. May God's protection be upon all members of the Khalsa wherever they may be, and God's glory be proclaimed and way prevail.

May the Khalsa be victorious in battle, uphold its charitable acts and let victory attend it. May the Khalsa choirs, flags and mansions remain forever. May the kingdom of justice come. May Sikhs be united in love and humility, but exalted in the wisdom of remembering God. O Khalsa, say Vahiguru.

(e)                           Vahiguru.
O true king and loving father, we have sung your sweet hymns, heard your word which gives life and talked of your many blessings. May these find a place in our hearts so that our souls may be drawn towards you. O Father, save us from lust, anger, greed, worldly attachment and pride: keep us always attached to your feet. Grant to your Sikhs the gift of discipleship, the gift of your Name, the gift of faith, the gift of reading your word with understanding. O kind and loving father, through your mercy we have passed our days in peace and happiness: grant that we may be obedient to your will. Give us light and understanding so that we may please you. We offer this prayer in your presence, Wonderful One. Forgive us our wrong acts, help us to remain pure. Bring us into the good company of those who love you and remember your Name. Through Nanak may the glory of your Name increase and may the whole world be blessed by your grace.

*Vahiguruji ka Khalsa! Vahiguruji ki fateh. Sat Sri Akal!*[9]

There then follows a random opening of the Guru Granth Sahib. The passage (*vak*) is read aloud to the congregation.

(f) Sharing of *karah parshad*.
The congregation may then disperse for *langar* or notices and *sangat* business may be conducted.

The role of those who conduct Christian worship cannot be divorced completely from the issue of authority. The reader will find this discussed towards the end of Chapter 10.


## FESTIVALS

Festivals provide an important focus of community expression of faith and, perhaps, a public expression of piety and commitment. Holy week, the period leading up to the commemoration of

Jesus' death and the celebration of his Resurrection is observed by a number of processions in a country such as Spain, beginning with Palm Sunday. Elsewhere, where the dominant ethos is Protestant, such demonstrations may be limited to a procession of witness on Good Friday. Sometimes one denomination may observe a festival which other Christians allow to pass unnoticed, Corpus Christi is an example of this. It is important to Roman Catholics but Protestant neighbours may be unaware of it altogether unless it is accompanied by a procession, and even then they may see it only as an opportunity for display. This kind of occasion has been used in the past, less so now, to inform Protestants of the numerical strength of Roman Catholicism in the neighbourhood. The commemoration of the Battle of the Boyne on 12 August each year by Protestants in Northern Ireland is scarcely a date on the Christian calendar but it is used in this provocative way. The practice of carrying the Sikh scripture around the neighbourhood, known as *Nagar Kirtan* or *Jalous*, which can accompany a Sikh festival, can be intimidatory in a similar manner but the purpose of carrying the Guru Granth Sahib around Southall in England or the streets of New Delhi, probably on a lorry and always preceded by five men representing the *Panj Piare*, is to bear witness to and celebrate the Sikh faith.

Festivals are occasions when Christians and Sikhs who may not usually attend church or *gurdwara* are to be found at public worship. The Church of England is an example of a denomination which requires attendance at church on at least two occasions annually (Christmas and Easter), but the reason for this was political, to ensure that the population conformed to the established form of Christianity. However, the religious rule for Christians as well as Sikhs is that they should be regular in worship. The Christian injunction is to be in the Lord's house on the Lord's day. For Sikhs, that is any and every day of the week, as has already been stated.

## THE FORM OF FESTIVAL

Christian festivals focus on Jesus, especially his birth, death and Resurrection. Their equivalent in Sikhism is the *gurpurb*. This is a celebration of the birth or death of one of the Gurus or, occasionally, of some other event in their lives. The August/September anniversary of the installation of the Guru Granth Sahib in Amritsar in 1604 is also a *gurpurb*. Certain *gurpurbs* are observed universally, for example the birth of Guru Nanak, the martyrdom of Guru Arjan and the birth of Guru Gobind Singh. Others may only be local events; the birth of Guru Har Krishan is observed in Delhi in July. In 1956, however, on the three-hundredth anniversary of his birth, the *gurpurb* was time for rejoicing world-wide.

The essential feature of a *gurpurb* is the continuous reading of the Guru Granth Sahib which is timed to commence about forty-eight hours before the *gurpurb* is due to be celebrated. After this reading, known as an *Akhand Path*, has been completed, there will be lectures or homilies on the teachings and achievements of the Guru. If he composed *gurbani* some of his compositions will be sung. Where climate and space permits, as in India, the celebration may take place in the open air with *langar* on the grass at the end. With regard to the precise date, Sikhs are flexible. In one of the historic *gurdwaras*, for example Sis Ganj in Delhi, the martyrdom of Guru Tegh Bahadur, who died there, will be observed on the precise calendar date. Elsewhere it will be held on the following weekend as almost world-wide now this is a time when people can be free from the pressures of paid employment.

Another kind of Sikh festival is the *mela*. Two of these take place everywhere. One is Baisakhi, the other is Divali. The first of these marks the spring new year gathering in 1699 when Guru Gobind Singh instituted the family of the Khalsa and introduced a new method of initiation. The second, Divali, is at autumn harvest time and new year according to other Indian calendars. To wean Sikhs away from Hinduism both these festivals had been made into times of assembly by the Gurus. Divali too came to have a specifically Sikh association as it was at this time in 1612 that Guru Hargobind, himself a prisoner of the Mughal Emperor, Jehangir, for his war-like activities, secured his own release and that of fifty-two Hindu *rajas*. Other *melas* are locally-celebrated events, for example Hola Mohalla at Anandpur Sahib. This assembly of Sikhs was introduced by Guru Gobind Singh as a rally which placed the emphasis upon military manouevres. It took Sikhs away from indulging in the Hindu Holi festival. Nowadays martial arts competitions and exhibitions feature strongly in it. '*Mela*' means 'fair' and Baisakhi, Divali and Hola Mohalla are opportunities for the buying and selling of animals and secular amusement as well as religious observance.

At this point a strong Christian–Sikh similarity appears. Both religions have used festivals to turn adherents from their parental traditions to their own and have reinterpreted the meaning and significance of existing festivals in so doing. (This, of course is not a feature peculiar only to the religions being discussed here.) Christianity took over the winter solstice celebrations common in the northern hemisphere and 'baptised' them. No one knows at what time of year Jesus was actually born. The first record of his birth being celebrated only occurs in a calendar which cites its observance in Rome in 336. In the Roman world the season was linked with Saturn and in 274 December 25th was inaugurated as the birthday of the Unconquerable Sun, the rival of Jesus, the Persian god Mithras. His devotees doubtless also chose the date in their desire to focus on a similar attempt to the Christian to take over the symbolism of light defeating darkness. Easter, of course, replaced the great Jewish festival of deliverance, Passover (*Pesach*) with the Christian one. On this occasion, however, the historical event did occur at the time when it was remembered and celebrated. Jesus died at Passover time. For Christians, however, he became their deliverer, not from the Egyptians but from sin. The Passover lamb became his symbol. St Paul described Jesus as 'Christ, our Passover, sacrificed for us' (1 Corinthians 5:7). Some words of Bhai Gurdas might apply with equal relevance to Christianity as well as to Sikhism. Doubtless expressing the view of his Guru, he wrote: 'Hindu days cannot be compared with *gurpurbs*' (Var 7, pauri 10). And the tradition grew up that: 'non-Sikh festivals should not be celebrated. Even if we observe the same day we do it in our own way'.[10] As 'derived faiths' the two religions share a common need to affirm their distinct identity. Festivals (as well as the Christian Sunday which has no equivalent in Sikhism), have provided opportunities to do this.


THE CALENDAR

The Christian year, like worship, focuses on Jesus. It begins in Advent with four weeks of preparation for the festival of Jesus' birth, Christmas. The principal festivals which follow are centred upon Jesus and follow sequentially the main events of his life, ending with his Ascension into heaven. Then come a group of festivals which emphasis the consequences of his ministry, for example, the gift of the Holy Spirit to his followers at Pentecost, and Corpus Christi which celebrates the gift of the Eucharist. This pattern is intentionally devised. It is supplemented by a lectionary of recommended biblical readings. The purpose of what is known as the liturgical year is to cover the great events in Jesus' life and also to ensure that anyone who participates in all the important occasions enshrined in it will be conversant with the major teachings of the Church.

*Gurpurbs* serve the same function but the Sikh calendar is simply a commemoration of historical events which are observed on the dates of their anniversaries. There has been no attempt to create a pattern or sequence, a liturgical year.

Christianity and Sikhism, however, are at one in that their calendars are subordinated to the now internationally established Gregorian calendar which has January 1st as New Year's Day. For some time, however, it was the 25th March, the Feast of the Annunciation, when Mary was told that she would be the mother of Jesus, which marked its beginning. Many Christians, especially those who belong to churches which put little store upon the annual liturgical cycle, and some Sikhs, no longer know that Advent and Baisakhi have new year significance for their respective traditions. Although the (miscalculated) date of Jesus' birth was eventually used to divide history into two eras, BC (before Christ) and AD (Anno Domini, the year of our Lord), Sikhs exchanged the Indian Bikrami/Samvat era dating for that of BC/AD. For the most part they have not shown any concern to begin a Sikh era with the birth of Guru Nanak in 1469 CE, though occasionally Bikrami/Samvat dates as well as Gregorian are provided side-by-side, especially in books covering the period of the Gurus.[11]

## Major Christian Festivals and Seasons

| Nov./Dec. | Advent |
|---|---|
| Dec. | Christmas (25). 6 Jan. in those eastern Churches which retain the Julian calendar |
| Jan. | Epiphany (6) |
| Feb. | Candlemas (2) |
| Feb./March | Lent |
| March/April | Holy Week, Easter |
| May/June | Ascension Day (Thursday after 4th Sunday |

after Easter
Pentecost (Whit Sunday) 7 Sundays after Easter
Trinity Sunday, Sunday after Pentecost
Corpus Christi (Thursday after Trinity Sunday,
Sacred Heart of Jesus (Friday of 3rd week after
Pentecost).

There are a number of feasts dedicated to the Virgin Mary, Jesus'
mother. They are: Mary's Nativity, 8 September; Immaculate Conception, 8 December; the Annunciation of the Lord, 25 March; her
Assumption, 15 August; the Solemnity of Mary, the mother of God,
1 January.

**Major Sikh *Gurpurbs* and *Melas* according to the Gregorian
Calendar**

Sikh observances are based on the lunar calendar with the exception
of Baisakhi.

| | |
|---|---|
| January | Maghi *mela*, Muktsar, near Ferozepore. Commemorates Guru Gobind Singh's battle there. |
| | Amritsar commemoration of Baba Deep Singh, scribe of Sikh scriptures who died attempting to recover the Darbar Sahib (later called Golden Temple), from Mughal occupation. |
| | Chheharta Sahib *mela* (near Amritsar), where Guru Arjan sank six wells. |
| February/March | Hola Mohalla *mela*, Anandpur Sahib. |
| March | *Mela* at Dera Baba Nanak opposite Kartarpur where Guru Nanak spent the last years of his life. |
| April 13 | Baisakhi *mela* (every 36 years on 14th). |
| May/June | Martyrdom of Guru Arjan. |
| June | Death of Maharaja Ranjit Singh, celebrated in towns associated with his reign. |
| July | Birthday of Guru Har Krishan, Delhi. |
| August | *Mela* Baba Bakale, at Bakala near Amritsar |

|                     | where Guru Tegh Bahadur was proclaimed Guru. |
|---------------------|-----------------------------------------------|
| Aug./Sept.          | Installation of the Adi Granth in 1604, Amritsar. (*Gurpurb*). |
| September           | Goindwal *mela* to commemorate death (Immersion into Eternal Light) of Guru Amar Das. |
| October/November    | Divali *mela*. |
| November            | Guru Nanak's birthday. |
|                     | Achal Sahib, Batala, *mela*, at Gurdaspur where Guru Nanak disputed with a group of yogis. |
| December            | Martyrdom of Guru Tegh Bahadur, Delhi. |
|                     | Martyrdom of Zorawar Singh and Fateh Singh, young sons of Guru Gobind Singh, Fatehgarh Sahib, near Sirhind. |
|                     | Martyrdom of Ajit Singh and Jujhar Singh, sons of Guru Gobind Singh, Chamkaur Sahib. |
|                     | Birthday of Guru Gobind Singh. Sometimes falls in January. (In 1993 no celebration; in 1992 two, in January and December). |

# 8
# Personal Devotion

The most intimate aspect of a religion, little known even to specialist students, is private devotion. Christians and Sikhs have usually only a slight awareness of what actually happens in the homes of their co-religionists, let alone behind the closed doors of people of another faith. Ignorance, however, is no justification for supposing that personal prayer does not happen. It does. Here it might be added that many Indians, some Sikhs among them, would not be inclined to talk about such things or describe their personal religious experience. They are matters between God and themselves, not to be shared with other mortals. It is like a guru's *mantra*, something entrusted to them which would lose value and potency by being divulged to anyone else. Here is a very different view from that of many Christians for whom it is an important witness to offer personal testimony of God's love, mercy and forgiveness. Reticence should never be taken to indicate a lack of anything to say or share.

A noteworthy contrast between Christian personal devotion and Sikh is the degree of variety within Christian practice. This may have something to do with the immense number of denominations and with cultural diversity but just as significant may be the fact that Jesus did not lay down a pattern of prayer for his disciples. He taught them what to pray about and the spiritual conditions for prayer rather than how and when they should pray. As Jews they already possessed this discipline. Like Daniel they would face towards Jerusalem and offer prayer three times a day (Daniel 6:10).

When Christianity left its Jewish milieu the form of private devotion must have been affected but if it is correctly deduced that a Latin *Pater Noster* was found in Pompeii it might be concluded that the Lord's Prayer was already playing such an important part in Christian spirituality that it had been rendered into the daily spoken language of Italian people. It can be said with certainty, on the other hand, that Sikhism has always focused upon the *gurbani*, the hymns of the Gurus, for private devotion as well as public worship. Consequently, many Sikh homes will have 'Babaji's room', where a copy of the Guru Granth Sahib is kept and to which the whole family may go early in the morning and/or in the evening. They may gather at other times too, or individually quietly go there for prayer, sitting in front of the book or reading from it. Other Sikhs may use a *nitnem or gutka*, a collection of the hymns prescribed for daily use. Some will listen to cassettes of *kirtan*, hymns recorded by famous Sikh musicians (*ragis*) who also comment upon the verses. *Amritvela* is a time particularly recommended for devotion, that is the period of the night just before sunrise. Guru Nanak said:

> A godly person who contemplates the Name through the Word, in the early morning, shedding love of the world, wins, while the world loses. (AG 1330)

The Sikh Code of Discipline, the Rahit Maryada, states that a

> Sikh is expected to rise early in the morning [at about 3 a.m.], and, after taking a bath, meditate on the Name of God.

The breadth of Christian devotion extends from reading the Bible, often aided by printed notes which include a prayer, to meditation, sharing in services broadcast on the radio, reading liturgies as in church, reflecting upon a poem or a devotional classic such as the writings of Julian of Norwich, and using a rosary. Usually the content will include the Lord's Prayer. As for timing the most popular times are probably at the beginning of the day before embarking upon the daily routine, or at night before going to bed, but there is nothing to prevent Christian or Sikh turning their thoughts to God at any time and place, as they travel, as they prepare a meal, or as they work in the fields or an office. It is more a matter of mind than body. Kneeling, standing, sitting in a particular position, none of these is really important, in fact Guru Nanak criticised the *yogis* who taught that austere practices, breath control and physical postures were essential for success in meditiation. He said:

> Listen, O yogi! The quintessence of the Divine Word is this. Yoga cannot be practised without contemplating the Name of God.

They who are imbued with the Name remain absorbed in God night and day and thereby attain peace and bliss. The Name is obtained through the True Guru, O yogi, and one comes to know the way of yoga thereby. Reflect on this therefore, that without the Name no one is liberated. (AG 946)

Jesus warned his followers not to take to the rooftops where their piety might be seen and admired by observers. Such devotion was no more than hypocrisy, the concern being more for the audience and their adulation than for communion with God.

When you pray do not be like the hypocrites; they love to say their prayers standing up in synagogues and at street corners for everyone to see them. Truly I tell you: they have their reward already. But when you pray go into a room by yourself, shut the door and pray to your Father who is in secret; and your Father who sees what is done in secret will reward you. (Matthew 6:6)

Here Jesus had in mind some Jews, but by no means all, whose piety was insincere. The Indian parallel was the *pandits*, the priests, who studied and expounded the scriptures but were unaffected by what they read. Guru Nanak's words imply a blanket condemnation, as Jesus' did, but today many Sikhs would acknowledge, as Christians do, the need for selectivity in applying them.

Hear me, O pandit, ritualist. The one rite which brings peace and bliss is meditation upon spiritual reality. You stand reciting the Shastras and Vedas but act and behave in a worldly manner. You are dirty within with moral defilement which cannot be cleansed through hypocrisy, brother. You are caught like a spider and tossed upside down in the web you have spun. (AG 635)

The only restriction that the Christian or Sikh would put upon where or when to pray is the obvious one that the mind cannot be doing two things at once. Prayer and meditation demand the whole of one's concentration. That is why many spiritual teachers advocate the early morning before the mind is cluttered with the cares which the day must bring and so that personality may be adjusted to cope with them as a result of time having been spent with God.

To aid concentration some Christians use a circle of beads called a Rosary and some Sikhs use a *mala* which is a circle made of wool with 108 knots tied in it.

Defining personal devotion is never easy. The underlying belief for Christian and Sikh, as in public worship, is that God is a being with whom communication is possible and who desires the kind of relationship which includes speaking, listening, and sharing concerns. When Guru Nanak uttered the words: 'You are my mother and father. We are your children. In your grace lie many comforts' (AG 268) he was expressing belief in a God who cares and protects and seeks the company of created beings. This, in one aspect, is what Sikhs say the purpose of revelation is. Private devotion is the conscious realisation of that intention. Christians would go along with this. The word 'Father' when used in the Lord's prayer sounds rather formal today, somewhat Victorian, but the Aramaic word used by Jesus would be 'Abba', 'daddy', which conjures up thoughts of protection and love.

The purpose of personal devotion is to become one with God. This having been said, Christian and Sikh would explain the same sentence in different ways. For most Christians God is wholly other, the Creator; humanity is his creation. At best the vision of the Garden of Eden before the Fall might be contemplated, where 'The Lord God walked in the Garden in the cool of the day' (Genesis 3:8) and Adam and Eve were able to speak with him.

Elsewhere it is said that Moses spoke with God 'as a man speaks to his friend' (Exodus 33:11). These pictures describe the ideal which Christians might hope to reach, but it is one which preserves the distinction between the divine and the human. Quakers who have gone beyond this and spoken of 'that of God in everyone' and mystics who claim to have experienced unity with God, have often been vilified or even persecuted by other Christians for stressing immanence as against transcendence. As we have seen the trancendence of God has a place in Sikh thought (Chapter 3) but the belief that 'God's light infuses all' (AG 279) is also important, so unity with God may be described as the goal of devotion. This goal was beautifully expressed by Guru Tegh Bahadur in many verses, one of which reads:

Just as fragrance is in the flower and reflection in the mirror, in the same way, God is within you. Search for God in your heart. (AG 684)

*Nam* itself has been discussed already. The method of becoming one with God is known as *Nam Simran*, God remembrance. This is not like remembering a holiday which one once enjoyed, it is nearer to the way that Christians remember the Lord's death in the communion service. It is a calling to mind in which God becomes consciously present. There are many different concepts of God, especially within the Indian religious tradition, and a number of them use *simran* as a technique for realising God.[1] Hence the Sikh insistence on the need to meditate upon the Gurus' hymns. The most important of these for the purpose of *Nam Simran* at least is his *Japji*. The words give meaning to the concept 'God' as well as having the power to help the user to achieve mystical unity, to become aware of the God who is within. Guru Nanak taught that:

> Without the Name there is no liberation (*mukti*). The liberating Name is obtained by the Guru's grace. Without the Name birth into this world is fruitless. Without the Name of God one eats poison, speaks poison, dies without merit, and is condemned to wander. (AG 1127)

The contrast with this state is clearly stated in the Sukhmani Sahib by Guru Arjan. It is another important devotional *bani* which might be translated as the Hymn of Peace:

> One who nurtures *Nam* within will find God, ever present there. Gone forever the pain of rebirth, the soul is instantly freed. Noble are the actions, gracious the speech of the one whose spirit is merged in the blessed Name. All suffering, fear and doubts are ended. Such a person is renowned for faith and virtuous deeds, raised to honour and fame. Priceless is the pearl, God's glorious Name. (AG 296)

Running through its two thousand lines is the refrain:

> The Name of God is sweet ambrosia (*amrit*), sourse of all inner peace and joy. The Name of God brings blissful peace to the hearts of the truly devout.

*Nam Simran* is one of the ways supplied by God's grace to be the means of becoming God-filled and removing the taint of one's unregenerate nature. This, becoming *gurmukh* as opposed to *manmukh*, is the highest goal of spiritual aspiration. It is not prayer but carefully disciplined meditation, focused firmly upon the Word so that Guru Nanak's promise can be fulfilled:

> One who meditates on the True Name by means of the Guru's Word is accepted in the court of the True One. (AG 355)

Christians also use their aids to prayer for the same kind of reason, to provide a discipline so that the mind may be concentrated and the danger of creating God in one's own image may be avoided. Bible notes or a lectionary are especially valuable for overcoming the natural tendency always to read the passages one agrees with whether they be of a strong judgemental God or a rather indulgent father!

A feature of eastern or Orthodox Christianity is the Jesus Prayer. This usually takes the form of 'Lord Jesus, son of God, have mercy upon me'. Discussions upon this prayer by, for example, Per-Olaf Sjörgren or Kallistos Ware,[2] stress its use as a method of inner spiritual development. Sjörgren describes three stages in the relationship to Jesus. The first is when people feel drawn to him. The second is when they begin to count themselves as a followers of Jesus. The third is union with Christ.[3] Then, such words as: 'If anyone acknowledges that Jesus is God's son, God dwells in him and he in God' (I John 4:15), and, 'God is love; he who dwells in love is dwelling in God, and God in him' (I John 4:16) become realised in personal experience. Our first reason for mentioning the Jesus Prayer lies in this emphasis upon God as immanent. The consequence of prayer is that the believer 'may share in the very being of God' (2 Peter 1:4). The purpose, as Ware puts it, is 'to become what you are' (p. 4). The biblical words just quoted are reminiscent of those passages from the Guru Granth Sahib relating to *Nam Simran*.

The second reason, and one which may be even more important, is the stress which writers on the Jesus Prayer place upon method and the Name. The method is also akin to that used by Sikhs. Ware says: 'To pray is to be silent. You yourself must be silent; let the prayer speak – more precisely, let God speak. True prayer is to stop talking and listen to the wordless voice of God within our heart; it is to cease doing things on our own, and enter into the action of God' (p. 3). Of course, repeating the Jesus Prayer perhaps hundreds of times in one period of meditation, is not vain repetition, any more than reciting the Japji is; underlying the word 'Jesus', for example, is scriptural knowledge of Jesus, though Ware counsels against meditating upon particular incidents in the life of Jesus, laying aside thoughts and above all, trying to shape in the mind any visual image of Jesus (p. 14). In fact it is encouraged to pray in darkness rather than in the presence of an icon. In such meditation there should be no image interposed between the mind and God.

In discussing the importance of Name, Ware quotes an early Christian writing, *The Shepherd of Hermas*. In the Similitudes, ix, 14, Hermas affirms that: 'The Name of the Son of God is great and boundless and upholds the entire universe'. A modern writer, Father Bulgakov, gives a different emphasis: 'Shining through the heart, the light of the Name of Jesus illuminates the entire universe' (Ware, p. 25). These again are passages with affinities with teachings of the Gurus on *nam* as the instrument of creation which can be perceived in creation by one who has become enlightened. A final similarity might be noted. For the Sikh the practice of *Nam Simran* may be reduced to meditating upon the single word 'Vahiguru'; the Jesus Prayer may only entail use of the word 'Jesus'.

Of course meditation upon the Jesus Prayer and *Nam Simran* are not one and the same thing. The most notable difference is probably that for the Christian the indwelling of God is realised through the Holy Spirit entering the believer; for the Sikh *nam* is naturally immanent, but its presence is unknown until God's grace becomes effective.

Prayer might be said to be the natural inclination of the religious person but if some kind of justification is needed both Christian and Sikh can cite the practice of their founders. Jesus and Guru Nanak both went away into a quiet place for some time before beginning their ministries. What the precise meaning of 'being taken to God's court' was in the experience of Guru Nanak (AG 150) only God and he knew, the Sikh must say, but many would explain it as a time of intense private prayer.

Supplication as an element in prayer sometimes needs justification. If God knows a person's needs even before the petitioner (Matthew 6:8 and AG 5) there would appear to be no reason for asking! But, again, there is the example of Jesus and the Gurus. In the Garden of Gethsemane Jesus supplicated God so strongly that the disciples saw that the beads of sweat on his brow were like drops of blood as he prayed:

'Father, if it be your will, take this cup from me. Yet not my will but yours be done'. (Luke 22:39–44)

The prayer which Christians believe that Jesus taught his disciples has been referred to several times. Supplication has its place in that prayer which reads:

Our Father in heaven, may your name be hallowed; your kingdom come, your will be done, on earth as in heaven. Give us today our daily bread. Forgive us the wrong we have done, as we have forgiven those who have wronged us. And do not put us to the test, but save us from the evil one. (Matthew 6:9–14; Luke 11:2–4 gives a slightly different reading)

There are a number of features of the prayer which belong particularly to the Judaic tradition but there are others which have strong parallels in the teachings of the Gurus. There is the description of God as father, though Sikhs include mother too. The importance of *nam* has been mentioned frequently in this book. Sikhs affirm the rule of God's will (*hukam*), and in their prayer that the kingdom of justice may be established, they express their belief in the manifest sovereignty of God as Christians do. In requesting food sufficient for the day the Christian is acknowledging God's providence rather than indulgence. Sikhs believe that God is the supreme giver, but that they should be moderate in their petitions, seeking enough, not selfishly expecting abundance. God is also the Deliverer, and as for forgiveness, Guru Nanak said:

For one who imbibes its spirit forgiveness is as virtuous as fasting, good conduct, and contentment. One who can forgive is tormented neither by any ailment or by death. (AG 223)

Guru Arjan successfully prayed that the Mughal chieftain of the Amritsar region, Sulhi Khan, would be deflected from his intention to attack the city.[4] Later he wrote:

God has protected me from Sulhi who could do no harm and died the death of an unholy person. (AG 825)

Not that either groups of disciples were ever taught that their prayers would be answered in accordance with their wishes. Jesus

was not spared the Cross and Guru Arjan eventually died the death
of a martyr. Guru Nanak warned his followers with some humour:

> If the seeker cries out and begs at the Lord's door, he will be
> heard. Whether he is blessed or given a kick it is all for his good!
> (AG 349)

There is a place for prayer as well as meditation in Sikh devotional
life as there is in congregational worship, through *Ardas*, but it is
secondary in importance to *Nam Simran*. Bhai Khan Singh justified
it and described the manner in which it should be performed:

> The Guru has decreed that petitionary prayer should be offered
> for the fulfilment of worthy ambitions; for the forgiveness of
> transgressions (both of omission and commission); for deliver-
> ance from acts of pride and arrogance; and for dedication of
> oneself to the will of God . . . the sacred scripture clearly states
> that prayers of petition are to be offered only to God, and that one
> should stand with palms joined while reciting a prayer . . . He
> who violates the fundamental principle by offering prayers of
> petition to gods, goddesses, temples, or any other feature of
> God's creation, justifying his error by appealing to some spurious
> authority, is ignorant of the precepts of Sikhism . . . There is no
> particular direction which one should face while offering prayer,
> and one may do so in a sitting or lying position if suffering from
> any disability . . . One should not pray with head uncovered.
> Shoes should be removed, except when actually travelling or if
> offering prayer while on horseback.[5]

Sikhs will cover their heads if using a *gutka* but otherwise Bhai
Kahn Singh's instructions about how Sikhs should pray may not be
widely observed, though the head is normally covered whether or
not a Sikh is praying.

Boon prayers have never been condemned outright. Christians
and Sikhs might argue that the founders were too wise, compassionate and aware of human frailty for them to do that and they
could be said to have offered them themselves. Teaching the concept
of a caring God carries with it the idea that the devotee may ask
for help, as a child would a mother or father. It is possible to find
examples in Christian liturgies of prayers for rain, for peace, for

material wealth, and relief from famine for example, and these are things Sikhs also request, though they are written in hearts, not in books and so cannot be quoted. In the New Testament and the Guru Granth Sahib there are instead, admonitions that prayer should be focused more on seeking the will of God than trying to get one's own way:

> The whole world begs at your door but receives only what you are pleased to give. (Guru Arjan, AG 1321)
> Prayers are offered for material gain but these come to one as is the writ of one's karma. (AG 937)

Guru Nanak gave the assurance:

> God's benevolence is great and beyond description; the great giver who gives all and covets nothing. (AG 5)

Jesus confirmed that the rain falls on the just and the unjust alike (Matthew 5:45). God should not be prayed to for favours. But the Lord's Prayer does contain the words:

> Give us this day our daily bread. (Matthew 6:11)

On the other hand, the Sermon on the Mount also contains advice not to be anxious about food, drink and clothing. These are things which occupy the minds of the heathen, Jesus said, God knows human needs for them and will provide; so, he continued:

> Set your mind on God's kingdom and his justice above everything else, and all the rest will come to you as well. (Matthew 6:25–33)

When the Sikh reads Guru Nanak's promise that: 'The gracious God ferries people through life by his grace' (AG 465) they receive similar assurance.

The devotees, whatever the particular religion, seldom find it easy to accept God's will, except when it fits in with their own. 'Set your mind on God's kingdom' is what is required of the Christian who prays: 'Your will be done'. The equivalent for the Sikh is obeying the *Hukam*, the will of God: 'Only those who obey God's will become nobles at the divine court' (Guru Nanak, AG 142). Guidance to know the will of God and strength to perform it successfully are among the purposes of prayer and *Nam Simran*. Thus Guru Arjan said: 'Those who meditate on God do good to others' (AG 263), while St Paul spoke about the harvest of the Spirit, the disposition of those who belong to Jesus Christ:

> The harvest of the Spirit is love, joy, peace, patience, kindness, goodness, fidelity, gentleness, and self-control. Those who belong to Jesus Christ have crucified the old nature with its passions and desires. If the Spirit is the source of our life, let the Spirit also direct its course. (Galatians 5:22–24)

St Paul has previously catalogued 'the behaviour that belongs to the unspiritual nature' (Galatians 5:19–21). The impressive list reads:

> fornication, indecency, and debauchery; idolatry and sorcery; quarrels, a contentious temper, envy, fits of rage, selfish ambitions, dissensions and party intrigues; and jealousies, drinking bouts, orgies, and the like.

There is nowhere in the Guru Granth Sahib where virtues and vices are stated so precisely but Sikhs number the vices as five, which Guru Amar Das describes as five thieves because they deprive the people they rob of *amrit*, the life-giving nectar, that is the *shabad* or *nam*.

> God has blessed the devotees with the treasure of worship, brimful of the True Name. This treasure is inexhaustible, no one can discover its worth. Blessed with it one's countenance becomes beautiful and one attains the True One. O my mind, through the Guru's Word one ascends to God. Without the Word the world is led astray and punished in God's Court. Within this body five thieves are hidden, lust, wrath, greed, attachment, and ego. They steal away the nectar (from within us); but they are unaware being lost in ego, and no one hears their lamentations. The world is blind and so are its ways. Without the Guru there is pitch darkness. Indulging in self-reliance (*haumai*), mortals waste their lives. Nothing goes with them (at death). The God-oriented (*gurmukh*) think only of the Name and cherish it. (AG 600)

St Paul wrote about being 'united to Christ' in his second letter to the Church in Corinth (5:17): 'For anyone united to Christ, there is a new creation: the old order has gone; and a new order has already begun'.

The differences between Christian and Sikh teaching about union in Christ and *Nam* are considerable. 'Christ' implies exclusivity whereas *Nam* is inclusive; 'Christ' refers to faith in a person and in the effectiveness of the saving act of death and resurrection which is wholly absent from the concept of *Nam*. But there may be similarities too. Christ is the *logos*, the eternal Word, and *Nam* is also the eternal expression of God:

> The self-existent God became manifest in *Nam*. Second came the creation of the universe. (AG 463)

As the passages from Guru Amar Das and St Paul indicate, being in Christ, or possessing the Holy Spirit, and being filled with *Nam* are essential if vice is to be replaced with virtue.

The Christian emphasis upon the transcendence of God and the importance attached to the Eucharist may have resulted in some Christian neglect of sanctifying, transforming effect of the Holy Spirit on the life of the believer, through prayer, at least in the western church. The Sikh requirement to practice *Nam Simran* daily might certainly remind Christians of God's inner presence and encourage them to realise it in prayer.

Prayer, however, is not a way of escaping from social responsibilities. Jesus spoke of taking up one's cross every day (Luke 9:23), and St Paul described 'fruits of the Spirit', which included goodness, kindness, fidelity, gentleness and self-control (Galatians 5:22), which are social virtues. These can be seen as the fruits or consequences of spirituality. Guru Nanak taught that 'one becomes like the one who serves' (AG 224), so that when 'meditating on the Lord removes the scum from your mind' (Guru Arjan, AG 284) one should then turn to worshipping God through the service of one's fellow human beings. *Seva* for the Sikh and love of neighbour for the Christian are fruits of piety. 'To pray is to work', taught the monk, St Benedict. Both Christians and Sikhs would frown upon forms of religion which encourage permissiveness, or a spirituality which is aimed at self-gratification of any kind. Moral conduct is regarded as an essential part of the process of an individual's spiritual development.

# 9

# Ceremonies

Originally, Christianity and Sikhism had only one ceremony, that of initiation. It remains undisputably the most important as far as Sikhs are concerned. However, as the two religions became distanced from their parent traditions the need to develop their own ceremonies became increasingly important. Probably this was more true of Sikhism than of Christianity. The Panth could easily be perceived as one of many Hindu guru-cults; in fact this is how some observers still regard it today. Thus, even though acceptance of the teachings of the Gurus and faith in the lordship of Jesus, with all that that implied, were the only essentials of being a Sikh or a Christian, sooner or later the movements acquired their distinctive rites and ceremonies. Had this not happened Sikhs would never have broken away from Hindu influence because the Panth remained rooted in India. It would probably been reabsorbed into the parent tradition. Hinduism with its belief that the passage through life from conception to death is surrounded by many threats places great emphasis upon the proper performance of ceremonies to ensure safety. Sikhs reject these as superstitions, but some of them still take place in some families in the twentieth century and the Gurus must have been aware of a need to wean their followers from them by providing alternative ceremonies, not simply by condemning existing practices. Guru Amar Das and his nephew, Bhai Gurdas (1551–1637), were particularly concerned to replace Hindu rites with those which were distinctively Sikh. Because Christianity soon became severed from Judaism its need to develop more than a form of initiation may have been less urgent and there is evidence of an inclination to accept the customs of Gentile converts while giving them a Christian meaning.

For both Sikh and Christian, initiation is supposed to be a time for affirming commitment. There are, however, people connected with both communities who regard Christian baptism or Sikh *amrit pahul* as no more than formalities. It is therefore possible to meet men and

151

women who were christened, to use the popular term, and have never been to church since, and to see a ten-year-old Sikh given *amrit* while his mother stands by with a towel to wipe his face and hair so that none of the sticky nectar gets onto his best clothes! Formalism in religion, something which Jesus and the Gurus criticised most strongly, is something which has happened as the religions based on their teachings developed. From time to time Christian and Sikh voices have been raised decrying the process of institutionalisation as a threat to them both.

## CHRISTIAN BAPTISM

The first Christians were the Jewish disciples who are mentioned in the New Testament. There is no record of them undergoing any kind of initiation into discipleship. The use of a baptismal rite is first mentioned in some detail in the story of the conversion of the Ethiopian courtier. When non-Jews were admitted into the Church the need to consider the form of initiation became more acute. Male converts to Judaism were required to undergo circumcision, men and women would have to take a *mikvah*, a ritual purificatory bath. Should this requirement be laid upon non-Jewish followers of Jesus who had been brought up to deride the Jewish practice of circumcision? Upon the answer to this question could depend the future of Christianity. It might develop as a liberal Jewish group distinct from other Jews only in affirming that the Messiah had come and was the Son of God or as a movement in which no one had a birthright claim to membership but into which everyone had to be initiated. A rite was devised which required everyone, whatever their background, to confess their faith in Jesus as Lord and to be immersed in water as a sign that their sins have been remitted. Male circumcision was not made a requirement of membership (Acts 15).

The focus became new life in Christ, not whether one's past had been within the covenant of Judaism or outside it. The use of water at significant times in life was a Jewish custom which Jesus observed by being baptised, but it was and is almost universal. It was certainly a common feature of many cults in Jesus' day so Christians were taking a familiar practice and investing it with new meaning.

Jesus himself accepted baptism from John the Baptist. This is a fact of such importance that it is mentioned in all the New

Testament gospels. The Gospel of John (4:2) records that Jesus' disciples baptised people in his name, and the closing words of Matthew contain the command of Jesus to make

> disciples of all nations, baptising them in the name of the Father and of the Son and of the Holy Spirit. (28:19)

Clearly the church regarded baptism as more than the non-controversial rite to which Jew and Gentile could both accede without either losing face. It was believed to have the authority of Jesus himself.

It is impossible to state categorically whether the early Christian communities did or did not baptise infants. Most believers would be mature adults but if a husband and wife were converted the question of their children's religious state arose. Were they within the household of faith or outside it? The Acts of the Apostles often says that a person was baptised with all his or her household (e.g. Acts 16:34). Who they were, spouse, slaves, children, no one knows for certain but obviously parents would be most concerned that their children might receive the assurance of salvation which baptism made. (There is evidence in 1 Corinthians 15:29 that converts were baptised on behalf of their loved ones who had died before they could hear the Gospel, so it is likely that there would be a desire that their own living children could receive the benefits they wanted for the dead.) However, it was when Christianity became a legal religion, in 313 CE, that the tendency to nominal membership rather than personal commitment grew and with it the natural acceptance that the right to baptism should be extended to include children.

Today there are denominations which baptise only believers, people who personally and publicly affirm or 'confess', to use the favoured expression, that Jesus is their Lord. They often hold a service of blessing for babies, recognising that the children of Christian parents do have some place within the church. Those denominations which baptise infants have a second rite, that of confirmation or church membership at which the believer makes personal vows of faith and allegiance to 'confirm' those made by the parents.

The Salvation Army and Society of Friends are probably the two best known groups which are non-sacramental. They believe, in common with all denominations, that it is the Holy Spirit who baptises but they therefore conclude that outward rituals are unnecessary. At best they could only confirm the action of the Spirit, at worst they might deceive the initiate into believing that they had received the Spirit as a result of the ceremony, so encouraging ritualism.

All denominations which practise the rite of baptism believe it to be a sacrament, a means of grace. In the New Testament the phrase 'baptism for the remission of sins' is to be found (e.g. Mark 1:4; Acts 2:38), and very early teaching linked it with Adam's sin and Jesus' redemptive work. St Paul, in his Letter to the Romans, teaches that Adam's sin has brought sin, condemnation and death upon the human race, his descendants. Jesus' death has reversed the process and offers eternal life to all who believe in him. Then he writes:

> Have you forgotten that when we were baptised into union with Jesus Christ we were baptised into his death? By that baptism into his death we were buried with him, in order that, as Christ was raised from the dead by the glorious power of the Father, so also we might set out on a new life. (Romans 6:3,4)

Immersion in water symbolised burial. One emerged from it into a new life.

Baptism, then, is more than the means whereby one affirms belief in Jesus as saviour and Lord and becomes a member of the Church, but it does also embrace these meanings. (The very proper stress on the remission of past sins led to converts in the fourth century deferring baptism until as near death as possible in the belief that all previous sins were washed away and the prospect of committing further ones seemed to be extremely limited! An interesting contrast with the earlier eagerness to enable deceased relatives to share in the benefits of baptism as mentioned in 1 Corinthians 15:29!)

## SIKH INITIATION

The tradition of gurus initiating disciples (*chelas*) dates from Vedic times. Guru Nanak would therefore have a custom and practice ready to hand. The method was that of *charn pahul*. *Amrit* produced from water poured over the foot of the Guru, was collected in a bowl and then drunk by the initiate. As it is not the practice of Hindu children under the age of about nine years to be initiated, the issue of the reception of babies into the Panth would not have exercised the minds of Sikhs as much as it eventually did Christians. Sikh initiation should always be of reasonably mature people. The Rahit Maryada says, 'the recipients should not be too young' (p. 19).

*Charn pahul* was used by successive Gurus until 1699 when the tenth, Guru Gobind Singh, devised a new initiation ceremony, *amrit sanskar* or *khande di pahul*, initiation by the sword. This involved the use of water but now it was mixed together with sugar crystals in an iron bowl and stirred with a double-edged sword by five people, the *panj piare*, as they recited some compositions of the Gurus.[1] There are at least two reasons why the Guru introduced this form of *amrit* ceremony in 1699. One was to place the emphasis upon a readiness to fight in the cause of righteousness. The sword symbolised this. The other was to focus the ceremony upon the Panth represented by the *panj piare*, not the Guru. He was already talking about the Guru Panth, that is, the community as the embodiment of guruship. The new ceremony provided a practical demonstration of it. From now on Sikhs were initiated into a family instead of becoming individually *chelas* of the Guru.

## THE SIKH NAMING CEREMONY

For members of the three twice-born castes of Hinduism there were many rites of passage or *sanskaras*, sixteen in all, beginning with one undertaken by a couple who wish to have a child and ending with ceremonies on behalf of ancestors. One of the *sanskaras* is *jatakarma*, an act of purification performed on the day the child is born.

There is no Sikh birth ceremony, though naturally Sikh families visit and give presents and some may follow traditional Hindu practices. Naming, however, should take place in the presence of the Guru Granth Sahib as soon as mother and baby are well enough to go to the *gurdwara*, though the ceremony can take place at home. *Amrit* will be prepared and administered and then the scripture will be opened at random. The first word on the left-hand page will be read aloud to the parents who will then decide on a name beginning with its initial letter. The *granthi* will announce their choice publicly adding '*Kaur*' for a girl and '*Singh*' in the case of a boy and the congregation will express corporate approval.

Here, of course there is a difference with Christian custom. Baptism is not a naming ceremony. The minister should say 'X I baptise you in the name of the Father and of the Son and of the Holy Spirit', not 'I baptise you X'.


## MARRIAGE

The Roman Catholic and Orthodox churches consider marriage to be a sacrament. All denominations hold it in high regard; many liturgies include a reference to Jesus attending a wedding at Cana (John 2) as an indication that he is present at the wedding of a Christian couple just as he was on that occasion. Nevertheless there has been and is a counter tradition in Christianity which recommends celibacy and suggests that marriage is a concession to the weakness of those who cannot exercise sexual self-control. This tradition originated with the teaching of St Paul, himself unmarried, who wrote:

> To the unmarried and to widows I say this: it is a good thing if they stay as I am myself; but if they cannot control themselves, they should marry. (1 Corinthians 7:8–9)

Christians might also point to the fact that Jesus did not marry. In recent statements about the purpose of marriage, churches have been more positive than St Paul was.

They tend to give three reasons:

1. To have children,
2. To provide a right relationship for sexual intercourse,
3. To give one another help, comfort, and protection.

The Methodist Church in England expresses the purpose of marriage thus in its wedding service. Its tone and content would be endorsed by all Christians today:

> According to the teaching of Christ, marriage is the lifelong union in body, mind and spirit, of one man and one woman. It is his will that in marriage the love of man and woman should be fulfilled in the wholeness of their life together, in mutual companionship, helpfulness and care. By the help of God this love grows and deepens with the years. Such marriage is the foundation of the true family, and when blessed with the gift of children, is God's

chosen way for the continuance of mankind and the bringing up of children in security and trust.

Sikhism rejects asceticism. It denies it is either a prerequisite of or an aid to spiritual growth and fulfilment. Guru Nanak said:

> Attempts to subdue the desires through self-torture only wear out the body. The mind is not subdued by fasting and penances. (AG 905)

On the contrary, the Gurus positively affirmed the householder family life as the one which God commended. The world was God's creation to be used wisely but not rejected. Holiness did not come from asceticism, that could lead to *haumai*, pride and a belief in the efficacy of one's own effort to attain liberation. Guru Nanak taught:

> Contemplation of the True Name brings that illumination which enables one to live detached in the midst of evil. Such is the distinctive greatness of the True Guru through whose grace and guidance salvation can be attained even though one may be surrounded by one's wife and children. (AG 661)

These words in themselves may sound rather negative, suggesting that marriage is likely to be a hindrance to spiritual development. To this Sikhs might respond by saying that the Guru was being realistic, that marriage can have that consequence. They might add that Jesus once gave such a warning (Luke 14:26). However, they would also remind the critic that all the Gurus, with the exception of Guru Har Krishan, who died at the age of eight, were married, and that Guru Ram Das composed a hymn, *Lavan*, for use at a wedding. This is used universally in Sikh weddings today. The hymn, which occurs on page 774 of the Guru Granth Sahib, commends the marriage union which is being embarked upon but also stresses the spiritual unity with God which marriage symbolises. In the first of its four verses it describes the Householder life, focused on God's Word, as divinely ordained. The second affirms that the union has been brought about by God. The third speaks of the couple's membership of the *sangat* in which God's praises are sung. The last congratulates them upon gaining their hearts' desire, union with God.

Christian and Sikh marriages, strictly speaking, are performed by the couple in the presence of God (represented in Sikhism by the Guru Granth Sahib). Those who conduct the service merely witness an agreement freely entered into by those being married.

Sometimes marriages end in divorce. Christians and Sikhs reluctantly recognise this. Sikhism has no reservations about a second marriage, where one of the partners has been divorced, taking place in the presence of the Guru Granth Sahib. In some Christian denominations a divorcee cannot be given Christian marriage, in others it is allowed. Sikhs have always recognised the right of a widow to remarry, unlike many Hindus. Though St Paul did not favour widows remarrying, this has always been permissible too in Christianity.

## FUNERAL RITES

Death, when it comes, should not be an occasion for hopeless grief as both Christians and Sikhs believe that it marks the transition from a life in which the knowledge and experience of God may sometimes be obscured by worldly cares and distractions to one in which the joy of being in the presence of God eternally can be realised.

The evidence for a life beyond the present one lies for the Christian primarily in the Resurrection of Jesus. For the Sikh it lies in the assurances of the Gurus, in the belief that they themselves had been living in the divine presence when they were commanded to resume a human form to preach God's message to humanity, and in personal experience. Some people become *jivan mukt*, that is, they attain liberation while still in their human bodies. This would be considered the logical conclusion of the Gurus' emphasis upon God as immanent. Here both Christian and Sikh would speak of a relationship with God which they could not envisage as ending at physical death. God's love is eternal.

Funeral services should proclaim the hope and promise of eternal life. Sorrow is natural but the mourners should be reminded of the fuller life which the departed now enjoys. Christians from Afro-Caribbean backgrounds sometimes combine grief and joy by walking to the cemetery to the sounds of a single drum beaten in slow time. On the way back they sing and dance to the strains of 'When the saints go marching in . . . I'll be there in their number!' This composition has become a jazz classic, but it was a Christian hymn long before it acquired its world-wide popularity. Christian liturgies vary between denominations but generally include biblical passages such as the twenty-third psalm, and the words of Jesus:

'I am the resurrection and the life. Whoever has faith in me shall live even though he dies'. (John 11:25)

St Paul's famous affirmation of resurrection may also be read (1 Corinthians 15).

Sikhs tend to prepare the body themselves and dress it in the five Ks. In rural Punjab *Vahiguru* and hymns will be sung as the procession walks to the cremation ground. In the west these are chanted in the *gurdwaras* by the congregation. The *Rahit Maryada* lays down the order of service which will therefore be the same throughout the Sikh world. Its injunctions read as follows:

The dead body is washed and clothed (complete with the five symbols) before it is taken out on a bier to the cremation ground. The procession starts after a prayer and sings suitable hymns from the Guru Granth Sahib on the way. At the cremation ground the body is placed on the pyre, the *Ardas* is recited, and the nearest relatives light the pyre. When the pyre is fully ablaze, someone reads *Sohila* and offers prayers for the benefit of the dead. Then the people come away, and leave the relatives of the deceased at their door, where they are thanked before departing. (pp. 7–18)

## DISPOSAL OF THE DEAD

The cultural environments into which they were born influenced Christianity and Sikhism to the extent that the Jewish practice of burial became the Christian method of disposing of the dead even though the prevalent Roman custom at the beginning of the Common Era was cremation. Later this tradition was justified by reference to the Christian belief in the resurrection of the body. Roman Catholic and Orthodox Christians still tend to follow the practice of inhumation but during the last hundred years cremation has become acceptable and even popular among many Protestants.

Guru Nanak was asked whether the Hindu custom of cremation

or the Islamic method, inhumation, was the correct one. He refused to enter into the controversy but did humorously point out that the best clay for making pots seemed to be found in cemeteries so there was a chance that the decomposed body ended up by being burned! (AG 466). There was a continuing argument among his followers as the story is told that when the Guru was dying those who came from a Hindu background asked for permission to cremate him; the Muslim devotees wished to bury him. Guru Nanak told them to cover his body in a cloth and place flowers by it, Hindu one side Muslim the other. Those whose flowers remained fresh may dispose of the corpse as they wished. In the morning they found both groups of flowers still fresh but the body had gone![2] The Guru was indifferent to how the body should be dealt with. The only thing that mattered was the state of the soul. If it had not achieved liberation its prospects were bleak indeed. In fact, Sikhs today accept the customs of the land in which they live. For choice they cremate but in Arab countries where this is not possible they are content to bury their dead.

Linked to the attitude to the survival of the body in eternity may be a view about transplant surgery. Sikhs support the use of organs from dead people to improve the quality of life of the living. There still seems to be some ambivalence among Christians with regard to this aspect of medical ethics. On the other hand Sikhs dislike the almost customary western practice of *post mortem* examinations for two reasons. First, following Indian custom, the funeral should take place before sunset on the day of death if at all possible. Otherwise it should be performed during the following morning, though postponements are permitted to allow relatives living some distance away to attend. A *post mortem* causes delay and adds to the distress of bereavement by preventing the grieving from performing their traditional religious and cultural duties. Secondly, the corpse should be treated respectfully. In Sikh eyes *post mortems* seem to be routine, casual and lacking any reverence.

Finally, the Rahit Maryada forbids 'the erection of monuments over the remains of the dead' (p. 17). This is because of the Hindu and Indian Muslim custom of making the burial place of a saintly person a focus of devotion, just as the relics of saints are for some Christians. Only God can respond to the needs of those who require help, though the *sangat* can give spiritual as well as physical comfort and moral support. *Samadhis*, resting places for the remains of devout men and women, encourage practices which Sikhs regard as superstitious. For some Christians, shrines and places where God has become manifest such as the holy sites associated with Jesus in Israel, or Lourdes, where the Virgin Mary appeared to St Bernadette, are points on earth where his grace is available to those who present themselves in faith and with sincerity.

# 10

# Authority

Jesus and Gurus were the respective authorities for their disciples during their earthly ministries. Each rejected implicitly or explicitly the authority of the scriptures, the Torah and the Vedas. So we find Jesus saying, in the Sermon on the Mount:

> You have heard that our forefathers were told, 'Do not commit murder; anyone who commits murder must be brought to justice.' But I tell you this: Anyone who nurses anger against his brother must be brought to justice. (Matthew 5:21)

This formula is repeated several times, covering such issues as adultery, divorce, oath taking and personal vengeance. Christians often consider these teachings to be far more than the normal Jewish sage's comments upon the Torah. The contrast between 'you have heard', referring to the Torah, and the statement 'but I tell you', is one which places the Torah's authority in a subordinate position to his own. In John's Gospel there are a series of sayings of Jesus which begin with the words, 'I am'. They have the same implication.

When a group of ascetics asked Guru Nanak the name of his sect, the path which he follows and the seat of his authority, he replied:

> 'I have come from God and shall go wherever God's will directs me'. (AG 938)

His commission was from God, the Guru of gurus.

In Sikhism authority passed to the other Gurus and eventually to the Guru Granth Sahib and the Guru Panth. Where it now resides is a matter which will concern us after we have examined the complexities of Christianity.

## AUTHORITY IN CHRISTIANITY

In Matthew's Gospel there is an account of Peter intuitively recognising the true nature of Jesus. He says:

'You are the Messiah, the Son of the living God'.

Jesus replies:

> 'You are favoured indeed! You did not learn this from any human being; it was revealed to you by my heavenly Father. And I say to you: you are Peter, the Rock: and on this rock I will build my church, and the powers of death shall never conquer it. I will give you the keys of the kingdom of Heaven; what you forbid on earth shall be forgiven in heaven, and what you allow on earth shall be allowed in heaven'. (Matthew 16:17–20)

Roman Catholic Christians see in this promise of transference of authority from Jesus to Peter. This is finally effected at the end of John's Gospel where Jesus, risen from death, commands Peter three times to tend his sheep (John 21:15,17). This is interpreted by Roman Catholics as a commissioning charge to St Peter to assume responsibility for the community of Jesus' followers.

There is a tradition that St Peter ended his days in Rome where he was executed in the persecution which took place in that city in 64CE. This is highly likely. Roman Catholics also believe that he was the leader of the Church there, its bishop, and consequently the first pope. (The word literally means 'father' and was used of any bishop but eventually its usage was restricted to references to the bishop of Rome.)

In 313 Constantine declared Christianiity to be a legal religion in the Roman Empire and began to take an interest in its affairs. A process of centralisation could now begin. In the western empire the focus became Rome. A succession of able bishops meant that it came to enjoy in practice the authority that it claimed in theory. By the end of the fourth century its status was ensured. In the east, however, the patriarchs of Constantinople acknowledged its primacy only in terms of dignity, not authority.

When, in 1054, the doctrinal division between east and west became final, the underlying issue had to do with authority.

The supremacy of the popes of Rome in western Europe survived all challenges until the sixteenth century. Whereas in the past popes had actually appointed or deposed kings and had been able to count on the help of princes to counter threats, now secular rulers took advantage of the arguments of the monk and doctor of the faith, Martin Luther, to strengthen their own national positions by combining a measure of religious authority to that which they enjoyed as monarchs and free themselves of the claim that popes had to be their sovereigns. This may well explain why Luther in 1517 did not suffer the fate of the Bohemian critic John Huss who was burnt to death in 1415. Thus, in England, for example, Henry VIII established the Church of England by act of parliament and became its 'supreme governor'. In its articles it declared that

the Bishop of Rome hath no jurisdiction in this Realm of England. (Article 37)

Protestants who rejected the authority of the pope had to find an alternative and in the process reinterpret the meaning of Matthew 16:17–21. This they did by saying that Jesus was referring to Peter's faith, not to him as a person. This faith is enshrined in the Bible. This, therefore, should be the authority. The way was clear for some very idiosyncratic doctrines to be postulated and many of those who had rejected papal authority affirmed that the church should be the interpreter of scripture and should take account of the views of the great teachers and leaders of the church in the early centuries, the church Fathers.

At the end of the twentieth century there is no agreement where authority lies in Christianity. For Roman Catholics the pope remains supreme, though there are members of that denomination who would wish to give greater place to senior bishops and, perhaps the laity, non-ordained Christians. The collegiality of bishops and laity is very important in the Orthodox church. As its patriarchs (senior bishops) wrote to the pope in 1848:

Among us neither patriarchs nor Councils could ever produce new teaching, for the guardian of religion is the very body of the church, that is, the people themselves.

Other denominations will stress the authority of scripture and tradition. Yet others will quote other words of Jesus and base their views on them. On one occasion he said; 'Where two or

three are gathered together in my name there I am with them'
(Matthew 18:20). Such Christians believe that the only authority
is this gathered church, that is, the congregation. Among such are
Baptists and Quakers. They may organise themselves into a Baptist
Union or Quaker Yearly Meeting but ultimately authority lies in
the individual, local church or meeting. To pursue the matter a
little further, a Baptist congregation would decide a doctrinal or
ethical issue on the basis of holy scripture, the Quakers would
emphasise the inspiration of the Holy Spirit speaking in the hearts
of individuals and the Meeting (a word which they use in preference
to 'congregation').

All Christian groups would argue that they conform to the practice of the early Christians of Jerusalem who said, through their
leader, James the brother of Jesus:

> 'It seemed good to the Holy Spirit and to us'. (Acts of the
> Apostles 15:28)

The question at issue is whether 'us' refers to James and the
apostles, or the whole community of believers.

## AUTHORITY IN SIKHISM

The Panth is smaller in numbers than the church and remains more
unified so the discussion of authority may seem to be simpler.

The Gurus had always stressed the priority of the *bani* and the
importance of the Panth. The story of Guru Nanak and Mardana
at Saidpur has already been told. With regard to the importance of
the Sikh community there are many passages in the Guru Granth
Sahib which affirm the importance of 'the company of the saints',
'the devotees' or 'the holy congregation' which are the phrases used
in English translations of the Guru Granth Sahib for members of the
*sangat* or Panth. A typical example reads:

> I am attuned to the lotus feet of God, who has mercifully blessed
> me. O God, I crave for the dust of your devotees' feet, and I con-
> template you as I remain in your presence always. (AG 1183)

The Gurus saw themselves and the *sangat* or Panth as being one
with all who have ever praised God. Guru Ram Das said:

When I attain to the society of holy people I am rid of a sense of being caught in the net of worldly things. (AG 1335)

In 1604, when the Adi Granth had been compiled, Guru Arjan installed it in the newly completed Harmandir Sahib (known now as the Golden Temple). He prostrated himself before it, showing, by this act of obeisance that he acknowledged the supremacy of the Word. Ninety years later, at the Baisakhi assembly of 1699, Guru Gobind Singh initiated the first five members of the Khalsa and then instructed them to administer *amrit* to him. In this way he was demonstrating the authority of the Khalsa Panth.

In Gur Sobha (The Radiance of the Guru), a poem composed between 1711 and 1745 by a writer called Sainapati, there is an important passage which deals with this issue of authority. After describing the death of Guru Gobind Singh and the concern of his followers about the future, he continues:

On an earlier occasion the Guru had been approached by his Sikhs and had been asked what form the [eternal] Guru would assume [after he had departed this earthly life]. He had replied that it would be the Khalsa. 'The Khalsa is the focus of my hopes and desires', he had declared. 'Upon the Khalsa which I have created I will bestow the succession. The Khalsa is my physical form and I am one with the Khalsa. To all eternity I shall be manifest in the Khalsa. They whose hearts are purged of falsehood will be known as the true Khalsa; and the Khalsa, freed from error and illusion, will be my true Guru'.

'And my true Guru, boundless and infinite, is the eternal Word, the Word of wisdom which the devout contemplate in their hearts, the Word which brings ineffable peace to all who utter it, the Word which is wisdom immeasurably unfolded, the Word which none may ever describe. This is the light which is given to you, the refuge of all who inhabit the world, and the abode of all who renounce it.' (Quoted in McLeod, 1984, p. 38)

These words are the basis of the Sikh concept of the belief that authority in Sikhism lies in the Khalsa Panth gathered around the Guru Granth Sahib.

This completed a trend which had begun with Guru Nanak who always spoke of the *sangat* in deeply respectful terms:

Friends have come to my home. The True One has brought about my association with them. When God, I met them. I have obtained bliss through meeting the holy company. I have obtained the very thing for which my mind longed. My soul is enraptured day and night through this meeting. (AG 764)

He affirmed elsewhere that:

The company of those who cherish God within themselves, turns mortals into enlightened beings. (AG 228)

Guru Arjan attributed his enlightenment to the *sangat*. He said:

By the saints' grace I have obtained supreme bliss and peace. (AG 614)

His respect for the *sangat* was not merely theoretical. When he was looking for a partner for his son Hargobind, he considered a proposal that he should marry Sada Kaur, the daughter of Chandu, the Emperor Akbar's finance minister. Members of the *sangat* opposed the liaison and Guru Arjan withdrew his offer.[1]

Writing at approximately this time, Bhai Gurdas said:

One is a Sikh, two is a *sangat*; where five are, God is there. (Var 13:19)

In his first epic poem (*var*) about Guru Nanak, he wrote:

The Guru (Nanak) said; 'I have nothing to show; I have no refuge other than the Guru (God), the congregation of believers (*sangat*), and the sacred utterance (*bani*)'. (1:42)

Sikhs use the phrase 'Guru Panth' to describe this concept.

Guru Gobind Singh submitted himself to the *panj piare* for initiation when he created the Khalsa in 1699 and submitted himself to its discipline on a number of occasions. He spoke of the Khalsa Panth as successor to his authority. However, in practice no insistence has been made that rather than the Panth as a whole it is the group which enjoys supreme authority. Even if a *gurdwara* committee is *amritdhari* the decisions they take will be taken to the whole *sangat* for approval.

Before Guru Gobind Singh died he appointed Banda Singh to be military leader of the Sikhs, but as servant of the Khalsa whose sovereignty he was commanded to accept. Banda Singh, however, aspired to the guruship and consequently forfeited their support. After Banda Singh there followed a number of military and political leaders known as *misldars*. One of these was Maharaja Ranjit Singh who eventually established a Punjab which was free of Mughal rule. It survived until the Punjab was annexed by Britain in 1849. These men had no standing in religious terms. In fact they were themselves subject to the discipline of the Panth.

The story is told of the Maharaja being brought to book by Phula Singh (1761–1823), *jathedar* of the Akal Takht. Ranjit Singh had been associating with dancing girls. On another occasion he had married a Muslim without requiring her to convert and was either given twenty-one lashes or this was commuted. (Sources seem to disagree on whether the corporal punishment was actually carried out.) He was also criticised for making a gift to the Akal Takht of a ceremonial canopy which he had already put to his own use. He gave the taxes (*jagir*) of two districts to the Harmandir Sahib, in reparation, a gift which was eventually stopped by the British in 1892.

Minor matters affecting a local community could be decided by the *sangat* and still are, but greater decisions, be they doctrinal, ethical or disciplinary, were decided by *gurmatta*. This was done by a properly constituted assembly of the whole Khalsa, known as a *Sarbat Khalsa*. Such assemblies could be summoned at any time and were reminiscent of those which the Gurus held at Baisakhi, Diwali and Hola Mohalla. Maharaja Ranjit Singh abolished assemblies of the *Sarbat Khalsa* in 1805. Their purpose had often been to appoint a military leader of the Panth and doubtless the Maharaja considered this to be no longer necessary, but the abolition also removed the potential threat of these assemblies issuing *gurmatta* which might conflict with his political authority or provide a focus for opposition.

The practice of convening a *Sarbat Khalsa* has recently been revived, especially in an attempt to unite Sikhs in their agitation against the Indian government's policies in the Punjab during the years following Operation Bluestar in 1984 when the army was deployed to storm the Golden Temple.

Specifically religious matters have become the preoccupation of the Shiromani Gurdwara Parbandhak Committee (SGPC) and a group of five men known as *jathedars*. The Committee was set up in

1920 in anticipation of the Gurdwaras Act of 1925 and was intended to be responsible for the administration of historical *gurdwaras* in the Punjab, that is, places associated with the Gurus. (For this purpose 'Punjab' means the modern states of Hariyanna, Himachal Pradesh, and the city of Chandigarh, as well as the Punjab itself.) Its members are elected by Sikhs at elections administered by the central Indian government. It has gradually turned its attention to all matters to do with the Panth and regards itself as the voice of Sikhism. It claims to be the body which the Indian government should deal with in the crisis which led to and has continued after Operation Bluestar.

The SGPC appoints the *jathedars* of the Akal Takht, Amritsar, and of the *gurdwaras* Keshgarh Sahib at Anandpur, and Damdama Sahib at Talwandi Sabo, Batinda, three of the five seats of authority. These *Takhts* were established at shrines associated with particular events in the lives of the Gurus. The Akal Takht was the first of these, enjoying its authority by at least the mid-eighteenth century when it was the venue for gatherings of the *Sarbat Khalsa*. Keshgarh Sahib, Patna Sahib and Hazur Sahib in Nander became *Takhts* in the eighteenth century and Damdama Sahib was designated in 1963.

*Jathedars* are religious figures with political and administrative roles and influence. Originally they were intended to decide on matters of orthodoxy and orthopraxy in *gurdwaras* of the regions in which they served. They may possess considerable theological knowledge but the criteria for appointing them varies and can have to do with party political allegiance and the vague term 'standing within the Panth'. The authority enjoyed by the *jathedars* depends largely on personal influence and respect which are important criteria for selecting them. The names of people being considered for appointment are known publicly and discussed so that the SGPC is aware of popular feeling when it makes appointments. Women could be appointed to the post of *jathedar* but this has not yet happened.

As Sikhs enter the twenty-first century it has to be acknowledged that they have no individual or body which is able to speak on their behalf or act as a spiritual authority world-wide. The SGPC was only intended to have authority in the Punjab but during the Emergency in India of 1975–77 it spoke as the voice of Sikhism, denouncing the enforced use of vasectomy as part of the government of India's policy of birth control. It has also pronounced upon such groups as the Nirankaris, declaring them not to be Sikh. Maybe it will come to possess an authority which stretches to the USA, New

Zealand, Britain and other communities of the Sikh Diaspora, but if it does, presumably it will have to adapt its electoral system and membership to provide the populations of these countries with representation. So far no serious discussions have taken place about a body which might speak and act universally on behalf of Sikhs.

Should such an organisation exist? It will be for Sikhs to decide how this question should be answered, not because outsiders would like a national or international body with which councils of Christian churches can confer, but because Sikhs themselves feel the need for such a body. They are unlikely to be pressurised by developments in other religions to conform and break with their own principles. It must also be remembered that the movement which led to the formation of the World Council of Churches in 1948 only began in 1910 with the World Missionary Conference at Edinburgh and that it was prompted by its own inner concerns. Roman Catholic Christians only attended its gatherings as observers, even at Canberra in 1991. The scandal of division has inspired the ecumenical movement but has not, so far, provoked many denominations into giving up their particular authority for a greater unity. Sikhism possesses greater unity and cohesion even if these are not always to be regarded as unalloyed virtues.

So far it has not needed to create instruments of authority. If it does these will not be to the detriment of the concept of the Panth in the way that some Protestants might say, that within Christianity they have been damaging to the concept of the role of the ministry in the church. Such Christians would argue that the administrative hierarchy has often emerged which has resulted in the imposition of something very like the episcopal system that their forebears rejected. They would say that it has divided the church into professionals, the ministry who take decisions, and laity who are expected to endorse and implement them. In Sikhism responsibility remains clearly vested in the local *sangat* whose elected officers depend on it for the authority which they possess. In the Punjab the SGPC, in Delhi the Delhi GPC may intervene in the affairs of a local *sangat*, but in practice this could be difficult. Elsewhere the *sangat* is supreme. There is no authority beyond it. In the Diaspora secular courts have occasionally been used to settle disputes related to the interpretation of a *gurdwara*'s constitution, in effect this means that they have been invited to take sides in a factional disagreement. If, of course, the *sangat* becomes docile the committee can become an oligarchy and tensions develop based upon personal rivalry, or caste or family power struggles (the two may be indistinguishable to an outsider). The result may be a split which leads to a new *sangat* being formed, a consequence with which Christian churches have long been familiar.

## DEFINING ORTHODOXY

The parameters of orthodoxy are matters of perennial concern within religions though they may go unnoticed by the outside world. Contemporary societies are generally more liberal and tolerant than those of the past when heretics, those who held views unacceptable to established canons of orthodoxy, were imprisoned or even put to death. Some people might argue that this results from the weakening of religious power rather than enlightenment, of course. However, the fundamental issue of defining such words as 'Jew', 'Muslim', 'Sikh' or 'Christian' remains.

Ecumenical Roman Catholic Christians will no longer require recognition of the Pope as God's earthly vice-regent to be a condition of interdenominational co-operation, as witness their recent decision to join the British Council of Churches which in its broader form has become the Council of Churches for Britain and Ireland. However, the relationship of the Roman Catholic Church to the World Council of Churches is significant. Officially it still holds the view that the Protestant and Orthodox churches are in a state of schism and must accept the authority of the Pope before full reconciliation and Christian unity can be achieved. In defining the church the Roman Catholic Council known as Vatican II (1962–65), described it as 'the Catholic church under the government of Peter's successors and the bishops in communion with him' (1:8).

The basis of membership of the World Council of Churches is acceptance of the following statement:

> The World Council of Churches is a fellowship of churches which confess the Lord Jesus Christ as God and Saviour according to the Scriptures and therefore seek to fulfil together their common calling to the glory of the one God, Father, Son, and Holy Spirit.

It is clearly Trinitarian and is sometimes used to define whether a particular group is Christian or not. Unitarians, who reject the

Trinity and the deity of Jesus, would be refused admission to the World Council of Churches were they to seek it. So would Mormons and members of the Unification Church, for a variety of reasons, one being that they have other scriptures than the Bible, another that the uniqueness of Jesus and the finality of his mission seems to be questioned in or rejected by their teachings. Jehovah's Witnesses too are not included in the category of 'Christian' as Jesus is believed to be the first and highest created being, a man, not the divine, eternal Son of God.

The definition of 'Sikh' was formalised in the Sikh Gurdwaras Act of 1925.

> Sikh means a person who professes the Sikh religion or, in the case of a deceased person, who professed the Sikh religion or was known to be a Sikh during his lifetime. If any question arises as to whether any living person is a Sikh, he shall be deemed respectively to be or not be a Sikh according as he makes or refuses to make in such a manner as the State Government may prescribe the following declaration:
> 'I solemnly affirm that I am a Sikh, that I believe in the Guru Granth Sahib, that I believe in the Ten Gurus, and that I have no other religion.'

The Gurdwaras Act gave custody of the historic *gurdwaras* of the Punjab to the Panth through the elected Shromani Gurdwara Parbandhak Committee. Some kind of definition was necessary to decide who had the right to vote or stand in elections to the SGPC. The concern about 'a deceased person' had to do with property rights. It was caused by the ownership of many *gurdwaras* being in the hands of Hindu families as ancestoral possessions. A conversion of convenience could result in such families retaining ownership and thus being able to perpetuate the kind of practices found in Hindu temples. The Act tried to provide safeguards to meet this possibility.

The 1971 Delhi Gurdwaras Act, giving control of its *gurdwaras* to an elected Delhi SGPC, added greater precision to the 1925 definition. It reads:

> Sikh means a person who professes the Sikh religion, believes and follows the teachings of Sri Guru Granth Sahib and the Ten Gurus only, and keeps unshorn hair. For the purposes of this Act,

if anyone poses the question whether a living person is a Sikh or not, he shall be deemed respectively to be a Sikh according as he makes or refuses to make in the manner prescribed by rules the following declaration:

'I solemnly affirm that I am a *keshdhari* Sikh, that I believe in and follow the teachings of Sri Guru Granth Sahib and the Ten Gurus only, and that I have no other religion.'

Three aspects of these statements might be noted. First, the movement towards sharper definition. Once a Sikh was simply a devotee of the Gurus. By 1925 it was felt that there was a need to stress three features in the act of affirmation, namely belief in the Ten Gurus, the Guru Granth Sahib, and the exclusive statement of having no other religion. Behind this requirement lay the awareness that some Sikhs described themselves as *Nanak panthis*, that is, devotees of Guru Nanak who rejected the developments associated with Guru Gobind Singh embodied in the *Khalsa* tradition. Secondly, there was also a tendency among some Sikhs to value some of the hymns of the Guru Granth Sahib more than others. For example, *chamars*, members of the leather-worker *jati*, honoured Ravidas, a cobbler who has forty-one hymns in the Guru Granth Sahib. *Sangats* comprised solely of *chamars* might use only his compositions. They also came to regard Ravidas as a guru, a status denied him by Sikhs. The reference to Ten Gurus could be applied against this tendency as well as that of Nirankaris and Namdharis to call their leaders gurus. Thirdly, while Sikhs at the popular level of their religion may declare themselves to be Sikh and Hindu or even Sikh and Christian, the condition of the Panth at the turn of the century required the inclusion of the phrase 'no other religion' when the opportunity came to use it. *Arya Samaj* and Christian conversions were sufficient in number to cause alarm. The most positive response to this perceived danger was the Singh Sabha movement. Associations, *sabhas*, were organised locally and centrally throughout the Punjab. The recently arrived printing presses were put to good use in producing cheaply available literature. One of the most important books was *Hum Hindu Nehi* (We Are Not Hindus).[2] Khalsa colleges were also established so that Sikhs had alternatives, especially at higher education level, to the provisions made available to them by Christians or Hindus. In such a climate religions often also turn inwards upon themselves. 'No other religion' is the product of such a response. The Rahit Maryada, however, adds the provision that,

'Sikhs must in no way give offence to other faiths' (p. 12). During this period pressure was successfully brought upon the British government to permit only *keshdhari* Sikhs to serve in the Indian army. These were men who kept the beard and uncut hair, and wore the turban, the person most people have in mind when the word 'Sikh' is mentioned. In fact, not all Sikh men fall into this category either outside India, in the Diaspora, or even in the Punjab itself. A large percentage are *sahajdhari*, the word literally means 'slow adopters', men or women who have not been initiated and do not keep the uncut hair. Insistence upon the outward form, however, is a way of visually distinguishing Sikhs from other groups. Other Indians have beards, do not cut the hair, and some wear turbans, but none keep all three as Sikhs do. This distinctive appearance is obligatory upon all initiated males and many Sikhs would like it to be the form adopted by them all. Hence the Delhi Gurdwaras Act's inclusion of the word *keshdhari* in the required declaration. Under the Act only such Sikhs may vote in elections. In *gurdwaras* in Britain at least, there is a tendency to insist upon men and women being *keshdhari* Sikhs if they wish to be candidates for *gurdwara* committees. Some *sangats* demand that they must be *amritdhari* (initiated members of the Khalsa). Occasionally there is a requirement that the electors should also be *amritdhari*. No one is barred from worship in a *gurdwara* because they do not keep the outward form or have not been initiated. The only requirements are they should cover the head, remove their shoes and respect the Guru Granth Sahib, but they may well be subjected to lectures in which the importance of being a Sikh in appearance as well as spirituality is stressed.

A proposal for an Act to place all the *gurdwaras* of India under the control of one body is being considered at the time of writing. It will be interesting to see how it defines a Sikh. Mention has already been made of Ravidasis, people who belong to the same social group as the mystic Ravidas (c. 1414–c. 1526). They tried to improve their untouchable status[3] by becoming Sikhs because Sikhs were considered to be egalitarian and included compositions of Ravidas in their scriptures. The attempt was not successful, as was the effort which some made to improve their lot through conversion to Christianity. They were permitted to participate in the religious life of the Panth but usually not to serve on committees and Sikhs of other social groups would not intermarry with them. They have responded by establishing their own religious institutions though they keep the Sikh outward form and use the Guru Granth Sahib as the focus of their worship. Often they now prefer to call their place of worship a *sabha* (association) rather than *gurdwara*. An edition of the works of Ravidas is being prepared which may replace the Guru Granth Sahib in worship.

Equally unfortunate is the *chuhra* (sweeper/cleaner caste) experience. This untouchable group found its attempt to gain full acceptance within the Panth equally difficult. It has therefore turned from Sikhism and Christianity to Balmiki (Valmiki), the legendary author of the great Hindu epic the Ramayana, recognised him as their founder guru and installed the Ramayana as their worship focus, sometimes together with the Guru Granth Sahib. However, Balmikis tend no longer to keep the uncut hair and turban and seem closer now to Hinduism than Sikhism. They would insist, like the Ravidasis, on their distinctiveness but also on their wish to remain in good standing with Sikhs as well as other religious groups.

The nineteenth century saw the emergence of two important Sikh reform movements led by Dayal Das (died 1855) and Baba Balak Singh (died 1861). Both of these remained within the Panth but produced a succession of their own gurus. These groups became respectively Nirankaris and Namdharis. It is against such groups that the emphasis upon 'Ten Gurus' in the Gurdwaras Acts of 1925 and 1971 was intended, and also the Radhasoamis. They also originated in the nineteenth century but outside the Punjab, in Agra in 1861, and outside the Panth. They have never regarded the Guru Granth Sahib as their scripture as have the four groups previously mentioned. However, some of their gurus have come from Sikh backgrounds and Sikhs in the Punjab and elsewhere sometimes attend their gatherings at Beas following the common Indian practice of seeking spiritual guidance wherever it might be found. The constitution of the Singh Sabha *gurdwara* in Southall, UK, which says that members should 'reject belief in any other gurus' (than the ten Sikh), is specifically intended to discourage Sikhs from religious association with these groups whose danger lies in their apparent proximity to the beliefs and practices of the Panth as well as their physical presence in a very multi-religious conurbation. Unlike the Punjabi village it has no one group which can assert domination, especially as the context is one of a Britain in which the norms have changed only slightly from what they were fifty years ago. Whichever community gains local ascendancy it remains a fairly powerless minority subgroup in broader social terms.

In our conclusion to this discussion of a search for uniformity within the Panth we must point to the Rahit Maryada's pervading emphasis upon the desirability that all Sikhs should become *amritdhari*. Although, as has been seen, the Gurdwaras Acts do not define 'Sikh' so rigidly, it is clearly perceived as the norm towards which all should strive. Pressure to accept this definition of orthodoxy is growing both in India and in parts of the Diaspora.


## CLERGY AND MINISTRY

The first difficulty here lies in terminology, especially the use of the word 'clergy'. Some Protestant Christian denominations might not wish to use the word. It seems to suggest a distinction between the ordained and lay church members which they seek to avoid rather than emphasise. Some Anglicans as well as Roman Catholics might confine 'clergy' to those who are ordained within their (apostolic) tradition. Sikhs find either word puzzling as the Panth allows for no distinctions whatsoever of this kind.

Sikh ministry is uncomplicated and straightforward. It derives from Guru Nanak's teaching on the oneness of God and the indivisible unity of humanity. In Sikhism there is no priest–laity distinction. The very notion of a priesthood is alien to Sikhs who belong to a movement which long ago rejected the authority and ritual specialisation of the *brahmins*. Every aspect of ministry is open to all Sikhs, both men and women, though, of course only Khalsa Sikh may conduct the initiation ceremony.

The student of Sikhism may soon come across the terms '*granthi*', '*giani*' and also '*sant*'. Sometimes the first two may be used synonymously and translated into English as 'priest' by Sikhs who wish to be helpful. However, a *granthi*, as has already been mentioned, is strictly speaking only the custodian of the Guru Granth Sahib and, by extension, of a *gurdwara*.

Traditionally, a *giani* is a person of spiritual knowledge who has achieved unity with God, someone who is *brahmgiani*. It is also an academic qualification in Punjabi language and literature, possibly including the Sikh scriptures. A *granthi* may sometimes be respectfully addressed as *gianiji* without any implication of knowledge being intended. '*Bhaisahib*', brother, is a more usual respectful title. *Sants* influence *sangats* but do not operate within them, so they will be discussed below.

Christian ministry is of three kinds.

1. There is a priesthood of men and now, to an increasing degree, women, who are set apart to administer the sacraments, especially the Eucharist, and preserve doctrinal fidelity. These are seen to be the successors of the apostles and are specially ordained as, it is claimed, the apostles were ordained by Jesus. Such a priesthood is a self-perpetuating order, though of course it has never become a distinct group like the *cohens* of Judaism or the *brahmins* of Hinduism. The eventual insistence in the Roman Catholic branch of the church that priests should be celibate would have prevented this from happening anyway. Even more important, however, has been the recognition that any man might be called to the vocation of priest. None of the Apostles was a priest in the Jewish tradition; in fact they came from many walks of life, as did Jewish teachers traditionally. (Rabbis were usually expected to earn their own livelihood.) The priestly ministry operates from the top downwards, from Jesus, through the apostles to the laity. Its members are usually called 'clergy'.

2. There are churches which have an ordained ministry but recognise that these are men and women set apart to perform certain functions on behalf of the congregation. At one time they were elected and would revert to their original position of church member at the end of their period of service. With the passage of time, however, this ministry has evolved in such a way that men and women once ordained retain the title 'Reverend' for the rest of their lives, whether they are exercising the functions for which they entered the full-time ministry or not. Although this kind of ministry has moved in the direction of the one previously described, it is really one which works from the bottom upwards, though the use of the term 'bottom' to describe the congregation might be abhorrent! The emphasis is on the congregation, 'the priesthood of all believers'. 'Minister' rather than 'clergyman/woman' or clergy-person is the preferred term because the primary function is that of ministering on behalf of, rather than to, the church.

3. There are some denominations for whom the priesthood of all believers and the promise, 'Where two or three are gathered in my name I am in the midst of them' (Matthew 18:20) are taken

so seriously and literally that there are no ministers. Men or women, known for their piety and competence, conduct services at the request of the congregation. From these beginnings the kind of ministry described in point 2 above evolved, but such a development is not inevitable.

Ministry in the Panth is closest to this third kind. It could move in the direction of the second but certainly not towards the first. The insistence of Guru Gobind Singh that authority should be vested in the Guru Granth Sahib and the *Khalsa Panth* forbid a return to what Sikhs would condemn as *brahminism*.

For this reason there is ambivalence in the attitude of Sikhs towards *sants*.

A *sant* is a preceptor who has gained a reputation as a teacher and spiritual guide. For this reason they are given the title *sant*. In the *gurbani* a *sant* is an enlightened individual. *Sant* (holy person) may be used as a prefix to a Sikh's name, for example Sant Puran Singh. The title has no formal validity. Their spirituality and knowledge of Sikh teachings (*gurmat*) is so considerably developed that they acquire a respect and with it a following of devotees similar to that enjoyed by Hindu gurus. *Sants* are influential guides who assist those who come to them in organising their spiritual and everyday lives. They may have a *dehra*, an encampment or group of houses which some Sikhs visit occasionally, but others stay more permanently. Followers may be encouraged to adopt strict regimes which will usually have taking *amrit* at the centre but may also stress vegetarianism and periods of celibacy. *Sants* may travel internationally with their closest companions by invitation or as missionaries to *sangats* abroad.

The line between a *sant* and a Namdhari or Nirankari guru can become very indistinct in practice. The true *sant*, however, should always point Sikhs away from himself and towards the *gurmat*.

Such spiritual guides have, of course, existed within Christianity for a long time. Their position has often been regularised in the form of chaplains, especially to royal households and other families as well as statespeople. From time to time they too have been criticised for wielding excessive power and influencing the course of government. Perhaps the most recently notorious example is Rasputin, the monk who was associated with the Romanov family during the reign of the last Tsar.

Very different is Bede Griffiths, who established an *ashram* in

South India to which many Hindus and Christians have trav-
elled over the years, attracted by his spirituality and his openness
to the ways of eastern spirituality. His theology is firmly and
unequivocally Christian but meditation, the use of *mantras*, and
the inclusion of other practices outside the experience of Christians
in the west have sometimes made his ministry suspect. Others
have seen it as a sign of the ability of Christianity to make use
of the experiences which it encounters as it becomes aware of
the spirituality of other traditions. Perhaps this development has
parallels with the *sant* in Sikhism both in the matter of its dangers
and its value.

Religion can appear to be more a matter of administration, organisation and a power game than the story of an effort to make real the
message preached by a Christ or the Sikh Gurus. The bureaucracy
discussed in this chapter and found wherever there are Christians
or Sikhs should be viewed in the context of such claims as that of
the popes to be servants of the servants of God and Guru Gobind
Singh's, 'Know me only as God's slave'.

# 11

# Ethics

Value systems are based on beliefs but the moral issues which religions address in their scriptures often reflect the relationship of eternal principles to particular historical and social circumstances. Christians and Sikhs, as we have seen, believe in a God who is the creator and sustainer of the universe and who is the parent of humanity. It is the responsibility and duty of those who share these concepts to work as God's co-partners in the world, using its resources but not exploiting them as if no other world existed, and caring for all people as one's own kin. Christians encapsulate this teaching in the injunction to 'love your neighbour as yourself' (Leviticus 19:18) supplemented by the parable of the Good Samaritan (Luke 10:25–37) which Jesus told to reinforce the Jewish view that one's neighbour is anyone in need, not the person one would like to help. Sikhs make the same point by telling the story of Bhai Kanaya, a follower of the tenth Guru who, during a battle between Sikh forces and a Mughal army, was commended by the Guru for treating the wounded irrespective of whether they were Sikhs or their foes.[1] This principle of service to humanity, called *seva*, has been mentioned already. It is the greatest Sikh virtue. It characterises communities wherever they are found.

Christianity and Sikhism, as has been noted before, but there is a need to repeat the point here, grew up in positions of weakness. The use of force to persuade the emperors Tiberius and Babur of the errors of their ways was not an option. The abolition of the slavery upon which the Roman Empire was based was not something which Christians could bring about any more than the Gurus could legislate against the practice of wives immolating themselves on their husbands' funeral pyres (*sati*). However, Christian slave owners were told how they should treat their slaves (viz. Philemon 1:16):

> no longer as a slave but more than a slave, as a dear brother, very dear to you, and still dearer to me, both as a man and a Christian.

The letter was written by Paul to a Christian slave owner. The author of Colossians wrote:

> Masters, be just and fair to your slaves, knowing that you too have a master in heaven. (4:1)

The Gurus forbade members of the Panth to commit *sati* or permit female infanticide. Guru Amar Das expressed his views on the former thus:

> Wives burn themselves in the fire with their husbands. If they deeply love their spouse they will anyway suffer the bodily and mental pangs of separation for ever. If they do not, why should they immolate themselves? Whether the husband be alive or dead such a woman remains far from him. (AG 747)

He is also responsible for the one possible reference to infanticide in the Guru Granth Sahib, it reads:

> Cursed is he who kills a *brahmin*, a cow, or a daughter, or who accepts offerings from an evil man. His sins will stick like leprosy to such a proud person. (AG 1413)

An accumulation of evidence suggest that it might have been an aspect of this Guru's policy not to go out of his way to oppose Hindu traditions in his wish to win converts to what was now emerging as a distinct Panth. This may lie behind his comments on the treatment of *brahmins* and sacred (*kapila*) cows, but this can only be a matter of speculation, of course. However, to class a girl with them would be rare indeed. To kill a daughter at birth was an accepted custom among many Indian castes. It is a practice that may still exist though cases would be hard to prove and often the use of amniocentesis and the aborting of a foetus which is shown to be female has taken its place. The crime of engineering the death of a bride whose family fail to deliver an adequate dowry or to add to it after marriage if the husband's family make continued demands, is also something which is not unknown in contemporary Sikhism in India and in the Diaspora. Murder for any reason and the dowry system are completely contrary to the Sikh tradition. They are explicitly forbidden in the early Rahat Namas upon which the Rahit Maryada is based.

The earliest, attributed to Chaupa Singh, a disciple of the tenth Guru, and dating from the mid-eighteenth century, denounces female infanticide several times. One prohibition which sums up the others reads:

> A *gursikh* must never kill a female baby. He must have no dealings with anyone who has committed this unpardonable offence. (Section 14:ii)

The Rahit Maryada expressly condemns the dowry system and infanticide (p. 22).

We do not find Jesus or Guru Nanak providing their followers or emperors with a detailed blueprint for the perfect society, though Christians and Sikhs believe that if their respective teachings were accepted sincerely by humankind a new world order would be the inevitable consequence. What the New Testament and the Guru Granth Sahib do reveal is a serious concern for the way that ordinary men and women, the early members of the church and the Panth, should live their lives. If Jesus and St Paul seem to be more concerned about individual personal ethics than the Gurus, whose overall emphasis may be upon the family and the village community, it must be realised that Indian society was based on these to the extent that individual autonomy was very limited, as it sometimes still is. Someone who accepted the spiritual message of Guru Nanak and began to practice *nam simran* might not attract much notice or hostility; orthodoxy has never been a strong characteristic of Indian religion, but any attempt to go against the *mores* of the family and the social structure of the village would cause instant and severe opposition. The eager convert who decided to arrange an inter-caste marriage to affirm the principle of equality would quickly provoke anger, as he might today, be he Sikh or Christian in India where neither those religions (nor any others) have yet enjoyed much success in breaking down the caste barriers which each repudiates!

Even before Jesus began to preach, his forerunner John the Baptist was admonishing soldiers to be content with their pay and to treat civilians justly. Tax collectors were told only to take the money due to them (Luke 3:12–14). This may be a faithful record of what he actually said but the fact that it was included in the gospel also presumably indicates that there were soldiers and tax collectors among the Christians for whom the gospels were written and that they had to be advised as to the conduct expected of them. The Sermon on the Mount (Matthew, chapters 5 to 7) makes it clear that the high ethical code of Judaism is incumbent upon Christians and that it is the spirit of Torah, not merely the letter, that should be the basis of their behaviour.

Family issues, of course, concerned the church just as individual conduct was important to the Gurus. Conversion could be disruptive to the family and still is. 'Should a woman married to a partner who does not become a Christian still honour and obey him?, Paul was asked. The answer is 'Yes' (1 Corinthians 7:12–13). However, being yoked with unbelievers, a phrase which may have had marriage in mind, was discouraged (2 Corinthians 6:14). Mixed marriages, even between Christians of different denominations, have usually been condemned or regarded as inadvisable. Such marriages are more common now as the interaction of faiths throughout the world increases, and the evidence is that such marriages can be successful and spiritually enriching, but they may require more effort and grace than even that needed by people of similar persuasions!

Care for the individual in the Guru Granth Sahib and the Rahit Namas often takes the form of comment upon the existing social structure. For example, besides condemning the common custom of female infanticide and *sati*, the tendency to despise people of low caste (AG 1128), women (AG 473), and especially widows was also repudiated. In fact, the remarriage of widows has always been approved by the Panth.[2]

It is perhaps on the issue of woman that Christian and Sikh ethics seem most at variance. In the Jewish and Roman context of Christianity women did not enjoy equal rights with men. In synagogues women had no need to attend worship. In the Jerusalem Temple there was a courtyard for women beyond which they could not go. Sages did not teach women; Jesus was an exception to this rule. He had women disciples. When St Paul was writing to the young church at Corinth, however, he instructed women to keep silent in the church: 'as in all congregations of God's people. It is a shocking thing for a woman to talk at the meeting' (1 Corinthians 14:34–36). This contrasts strongly with the attitude of Jesus who applauded Mary for choosing 'what is best'. She 'sat at the Lord's feet and listened to his words' (Luke 11:38–42), presumably joining in the discussion.

In Hindu society women were a potent source of ritual pollution,

a matter of considerable importance within that tradition. Also it
was believed that a woman would tempt the would-be pietist from
the path of spiritual liberation to destruction. Guru Nanak rejected
the notion of ritual pollution. Spirituality was only affected by one's
inner condition:

> If the mind is unclean it cannot be purified by worshipping
> stones, visiting holy places, living in forests, and wandering
> about as ascetics do. Honour is acquired only by one who
> cherishes the Lord's Name. (AG 586)

Here he seems to have been at one with Jesus who said:

> Alas for you, scribes and Pharisees, hypocrites! You clean the
> outside of the cup or dish but leave the inside full of greed and
> self-indulgence. (Matthew 23:25)

Guru Nanak accepted women as disciples and denounced the lack
of respect given to them. One of his most famous affirmations was:

> Why should we revile the one who gives birth to great men?
> (AG 473)

The Gurus were married men who rejected asceticism. Furthermore, the wives of the Gurus and other women played an important
part in the propagation of Sikhism in the sixteenth century and
later. The disciples of Jesus included women but they were not
among the inner group of twelve who became the apostles. As
the church evolved and western Christendom came under the
leadership of a male, celibate priesthood, the part which women
had played at the beginning of the Christian story was forgotten,
with the exception of Mary, the mother of Jesus who became a
role model of submission and piety. Only now is an effort being
made by some scholars to reconstruct the history of the early
church and demonstrate that the place of women as leaders was
far more significant than has been suggested. Meanwhile, a number
of Protestant denominations ordain women as ministers. If pressed
on the New Testament passages which seem to subordinate women
to men and the words of St Paul quoted above, supporters of female
ordination argue that he was writing at a particular time for specific
circumstances. He was not making a pronouncement which applies

to the very different society of the late twentieth century. Opponents of the ordination of women would not accept their interpretation of scripture, of course.

What we find here is an issue which began as a matter of ethics taking on theological significance. Interestingly, the place of women in the Sikh tradition has gone the other way. As we have seen, Guru Nanak affirmed the status of women. It is surely not accidental that Guru Gobind Singh at the first Baisakhi initiation ceremony asked his wife, Mata Sahib Kaur, to assist in the preparation of *amrit*, something which would have rendered it unacceptable to pollution-conscious Hindus. Yet, today, the Shromani Gurdwara Parbandhak Committee has few women members and there are no Sikh *jathedars*. Most *gurdwara* management committees are controlled by men and, in short, the equality which the Gurus gave women is now more notional than real. The Gurus settled the theology, the matter has now become one of ethics and perhaps the kind of self-assertiveness by women which Punjabi culture regards as unbecoming!

There are also ethical issues involved in the Christian sacrament of the Eucharist and the non-sacramental Sikh meal of *langar*. One dimension of the Eucharist in the early church was that it signified unity and equality. These are important teachings in John, chapters 13 to 17. St Paul reminded a divided church:

> When we break the bread is it not a sharing in the body of Christ? Because there is one loaf, we, though many, are one body; for it is one loaf of which we all partake. (1 Corinthians 10:17)

In fact the form which the Eucharist came to assume, the sharing of one cup and a piece of bread torn from one loaf, seems to have been the result of a divisiveness among Christians who used the meal as an opportunity for ostentation. St Paul condemned those who used it as an occasion for debauchery:

> When you meet as a congregation it is not the Lord's supper that you eat; when it comes to eating, each of you takes his own supper, one goes hungry and another has too much to drink. (1 Corinthians 11:20–21)

The Eucharist came to symbolise the unity of the church and the equality of all believers. Converts from Hinduism to Christianity have sometimes experienced difficulty in sharing the Eucharist

with members of different castes. They have had to lay aside their
traditional ideas which rejected commensality and regarded those
beneath them as a source of impurity. Occasionally one still hears
of *brahmin* Christians refusing to share the common cup or insisting
on drinking from it before people of lower castes. The notion of
the communion service as an act of Christian unity has also been
obscured by an emphasis upon the nature of the priesthood and
the consecrated bread and wine so that it has become a testimony
to disunity.

*Langar* is a meal open to anyone who can accept the Sikh belief
in social equality. It is served by men and women of any caste. The
meal is simple as a matter of principle and only vegetarian food is
provided so that no one is caused offence. When the emperor Akbar
sought an audience with Guru Amar Das he was required first to
take *langar* with everyone else. Sometimes there have been local
attempts to deprive low-caste people of the right to provide langar
or *karah parshad*. Such tendencies are well known to be completely
contrary to Sikh teaching and have been quickly overruled.

At this point it is necessary to recognise that precept and practice
do not always go hand-in-hand. St Paul said:

> There is no such thing as Jew and Greek, slave and freeman, male
> and female; for you are all one person in Christ Jesus. (Galatians
> 3:20, cf. 1 Corinthians 12:12–13)

But there is no denying that the reality has been far different in
churches in South Africa, the United States, India, Britain and
elsewhere. The Christian record on racial equality has not been
a good one any more than Sikhs have succeeded in eliminating
caste discrimination as well as sexism from the Panth despite Guru
Nanak's words:

> We [all humanity] are God's own people, neither high nor low
> born, nor in between. (AG 504)

> God does not mind our caste or birth. So let us learn the way of
> truthful living, for one's deeds proclaim one's caste and respect.
> (AG 1330)

When Guru Gobind Singh formed the *Khalsa* he reinforced precept
with practice by initiating as its first five members a *jat* farmer,
a washerman, a baker, and a potter, as well as a *kshatriya*, the

only member of a twice-born caste. The Guru's wife also received initiation.

Caste and the treatment of women, racism and the status of women in ministry are the Achilles' heels of the two religions being reviewed in this book. Social justice lies at the heart of both religions. When they gained some numerical strength, in the case of Sikhism, and political influence, as Christians did from the time of the emperor Constantine and especially in medieval Europe, the issue of war and peace arose. Peace was dear to the hearts of Jesus and Guru Nanak but war was endemic in the times in which they lived. Over the centuries, as the religion came to have political influence, a Christian doctrine of the just war was promulgated. The conditions for going to war should be:

1. It must be on the authority of the sovereign;
2. The cause must be just, the enemy must deserve to be attacked;
3. The intentions must be rightful, that is to seek to establish peace and justice;
4. The good resulting from war must outweigh the evil involved in waging it;
5. War must be the last resort;
6. Minimum force must be used with care being taken not to harm innocent non-combatants.

The Sikh doctrine is almost the same. It was laid down by Guru Gobind Singh who complained to the Mughal emperor, Aurangzeb, that his policy of oppression and forcible conversion, contrary to the teachings of Islam, left him no choice but to make war against his sovereign. He wrote:

When all efforts to restore peace prove useless and no words avail, the flash of steel is lawful, it is right to draw the sword. (Zafarnama or Letter of Admonition)

The five conditions for a *dharam yudh* (just war) are:

1. It should be the last resort;
2. It should be waged without enmity or a desire for revenge;
3. Territory should not be annexed, property captured in the

course of war should be restored; there should be no looting or taking of booty;

4. The army must be made up of soldiers committed to the cause, mercenaries should not be employed and military discipline must match the righteousness of the cause; Sikhs should be 'saint-soldiers'. Codes of Conduct of the period commanded them; 'not to drink, smoke or molest the womenfolk of your adversaries';

5. The minimum amount of force needed to achieve the objective should be used, but a just war should be undertaken regardless of the odds or the likely outcome.


## PACIFISM

The breakdown of formal unity in western Christendom during the sixteenth century led to the emergence of many European Christian groups interpreting scripture and the Gospel according to the insight which they believed they were given by God. One of these was the Mennonites whose founder was Menno Simons (1496–1561). His followers refused to hold public office and undertake military service. In Britain, in 1660, a religious movement which had begun during the Civil War, the Society of Friends (Quakers), presented a Peace Testimony to King Charles II which began: 'We utterly denounce all outward wars and strife'.

Whether Jesus was a pacifist is a matter of dispute and it cannot be claimed that the New Testament is unequivocal in its attitude but Christians often describe their religion as the Gospel of Peace and it is significant that it was the task of theologians to justify war, not peace. There is probably enough evidence available to argue that there were Christian soldiers before the time of the emperor Constantine, so any case for pacifism must be based upon moral and philosophical grounds, the principle of Christian love, the ethics of the Sermon on the Mount, and not the use of particular proof texts.

No such pacifist movement exists within Sikhism, although peace groups are active in the troubled state of Punjab. It is one of the articles of Khalsa teaching that Sikhs should be prepared to take up arms in defence of righteousness against oppression. The eminent historian, Khushwant Singh, entitled the fifth chapter of his *History of the Sikhs* (1963), 'From Pacifist Sikh to Militant Khalsa', but did not produce any strong evidence to demonstrate an attitude on the part of Guru Nanak for or against war. Views that a major purpose of his mission was to reconcile Hindus and Muslims, as Mahatma Gandhi did later, find little support among scholars today, though they agree that he would have favoured attempts to bring communities together rather than endorse communalism. Such information as exists indicates that his concern in this respect was more with spiritual dialogue, not communal harmony. Sikh writers stress his support for justice, noting that he chided the emperor Babur for his treatment of non-combatants during the seige of Saidpur and when it had been captured. They would say that this concern was identical with that which led to Guru Gobind's use of outward force almost two hundred years later.

Hand-in-hand with the theory of the just war is a recognition by Christian and Sikh of the importance of the United Nations' Declaration of Human Rights and, as a consequence, support for all agencies which promote social justice and seek to alleviate suffering.


THE BODY

The teachings of the Gurus and the Rahit Maryada specifically forbid the use of alcohol, tobacco and drugs, the reason being that the body should not be abused. Some individual Christians share the same views for the same kinds of reason, but prohibition has only occasionally been as strong as it is in the Panth, where, however, it must be admitted that many who are not *amritdhari* do drink alcohol, despite the Panth's disapproval. Were Amritsar ever to be declared a holy city, as Varanasi and Kurukshetra are, alcohol and tobacco as well as other non-medicinal drugs would be banned from its precincts.

Developments in science and technology which have taken place during the twentieth century and have resulted in transplant surgery, genetic engineering, medical ethical issues and others which result from social changes often related to them, such as the easy availability of contraceptives and abortion, have challenged Christians and Sikhs. Christian reactions have varied. The Roman Catholic Church, for example, condemns abortion and rejects the use of artificial methods of birth control. Other Christians argue that these and many other ethical matters are for the individual conscience to decide. Unless the SGPC makes a pronouncement there is no Sikh body which can express *the* Sikh position on any of these subjects (see Chapter 10).

However, there are guidelines within Sikh teaching in general which may be applied. For example, genetic engineering might not be acceptable because it would be tampering with the natural form (a reason why Sikhs should not cut the hair) and also attempting to flout the *karmic* process, thus going against the divine will. Similarly abortion should be condemned unless the health of the mother is threatened and certainly the growing practice in India of aborting a foetus when it has been discovered through amniocentesis to be female is rejected. A child is a gift from God whatever its gender. Artificial insemination or the use of surrogacy would also be unacceptable because it must be a matter of absolute certainty that the child is the offspring of the married couple. With this guarantee, *in vitro* fertilisation could be practised. One looks forward to Sikhs sharing their insights on the new ethical issues which are arising with people of other faiths and contributing to the moral debate but it must be remembered that these questions have arisen in the western world and are often the consequence of affluence. Not many Sikh doctors in India face the challenge of switching off the current to life-support machines. These are situations which they are now meeting in the wealthy west where they encounter divided opinion among Christians.

# 12
# Attitudes to Other Religions

In Chapter 2 we noted that both Christianity and Sikhism took up stances towards their parent faiths and that in the case of Christianity this had a theological basis but that it is not systematically worked out in the New Testament. The Sikh Gurus never considered it necessary to reflect theologically on Hinduism or Islam as such; they dealt more pragmatically with particular aspects of the religions as they encountered them, for example the concepts of *avatar* or ritual pollution. Now both religions find themselves sharing a global village. How Christians and Sikhs may regard other religions *per se* is not a matter which can be ignored. For some this may be because they belong to one or other of them and are interested in dialogue with the other. This concern will be discussed later in the chapter. Many readers, however, may belong to neither tradition and perhaps have no religious beliefs at all. For them the need to know will be related to such things as how two neighbours in the global village in which they too live interact, or their curiosity may be purely intellectual.

Christians do not hold one coherent belief about other faiths though it may be true to say that most Christians who consider the question start with a residual belief that it is the only true religion. It was this conviction which sent them far and wide from Europe to India, Africa, China, Japan and South America, mostly in the nineteenth century, though there had been earlier phases, most notably that which evangelised Europe itself. Mission gave rise to such a hymn as:

> From Greenland's icy mountains
> From India's coral strand,
> Where Afric's sunny fountains
> Roll down their golden sand,
> From many an ancient river,
> From many a palmy plain,

They call us to deliver
Their land from error's chain.

What though the spicy breezes
Blow soft oe'r Ceylon's isle,
Though every prospect pleases
And only man is vile,
In vain with loving kindness
The gifts of God are strown,
The heathen, in his blindness,
Bows down to wood and stone.

Most of the missionary hymns of the nineteenth century are of this kind. They colour the perception which Christians have of other cultures, faiths, and non-Caucasian races to this day.

There are several attitudes which Christians hold towards other religions. One gives them no salvic status at all. Salvation is through Jesus alone. Other religions may be human searches for God at best. However, the longings they seek to satisfy cannot be met through the systems they have created, only through Jesus, the one who was provided by God to deal with such yearnings.

This view, sometimes described as exclusivist for obvious reasons, is justified and substantiated by an appeal to a number of verses in the New Testament and a belief that all humanity is condemned as the result of Adam's sin. It can only be spiritually saved by faith in the work of Jesus, the second Adam; an argument made by Paul in his Letter to the Romans.

At the other extreme there are those who consider Christianity to be one of many religions, seeing it as one of the paths leading to God and provided by God. Such Christians would argue that they do not devalue the ministry or death of Jesus he was a perfect example of human commitment and divine love. However, they would also share the kind of attitude which Arnold Toynbee expressed in the following sentences:

> I think it is possible for us, while holding that our own convictions are true and right, to recognise that, in some measure, all the higher religions are revelations of what is true and right. They also come from God, and each presents some facet of God's truth.[1]

This position is often described as pluralist. Some critics would condemn it as relativist, claiming that it is really based on the belief that religions are relatively true but none is completely true. This is certainly not what is being suggested in the passage just quoted. Other critics might wish to ask what criteria there are for asserting that 'the higher religions' whichever they are, are revelations from God but that lower ones, by implication, are not? Modern anthropologists and writers on pre-literate, traditional religions (note the rejection nowadays of the term 'primitive'), have drawn attention to the degree of spirituality which they possess and their sophisticated concepts of God.[2] Those who would delete the phrase 'higher religions' from the above sentences might be called universalist.

Some Christians hold an intermediate position which sees the presence of the Holy Spirit in other religions but nevertheless safeguards belief in the 'finality of Christ', to use a popular phrase. This means that no matter how authentic a religion like Sikhism, for example, may be, Jesus is God's Word in terms of revelation. There is a point, then, they might argue, at which Sikhs will accept the authority of Jesus, realising that it is in him that the aspirations and ideals of the Gurus receive their fullest expression. Some Christians expect this to be through eventual conversion. Some might argue that it happens when Sikhs accept the Christ-like qualities of the Gurus and come to emphasise these in their lines. They might claim that Jesus Christ is to be found in Sikhism, albeit in an unacknowledged form in such aspects as the Gurus' insistence on social justice and equality, their monotheism and rejection of idol worship. Perhaps their reverence for the Name and practice of *Nam Simran* also indicate the presence of Christ. A famous Christian, J. N. Farquhar, who worked for the YMCA in India at the beginning of the twentieth century, summed up this view in some words about Hinduism:

> Christ provides the fulfilment of the highest aspirations of Hinduism . . . In him is focused every ray of light that shines in Hinduism. He is the Crown of the Faith of India.[3]

According to this view, in the end Christ will be recognised as the source of the light which is to be found in other religions. It is described as inclusivist as it finds a way of including other religions in the divine plan of salvation.

Whether Christians could admit that through the teachings of the Gurus the Holy Spirit was giving Christians a nudge in the direction of the equality of women with men is less certain! The spirit of reciprocity, the recognition that God might be speaking to Christians through the other religions of the world, is one which most Christian theologians have scarcely begun to consider.

Unless they do, and thereby open up Christianity to critical scrutiny by members of other faiths, their position is likely to be dismissed as paternalistic at best and, by Sikhs and other inhabitants of the subcontinent, as an indication that the influence of the *raj* upon the British psyche at least, lives on.

The extent to which religions can amend their beliefs in the light of fresh knowledge and the criticisms of other traditions is as important as it is contentious. For the religions being examined in this book the traditional lines of discussion lie between Christian and Jew and Sikh and Hindu (and to a lesser extent Muslim) rather than between Christian and Sikh, whose contact with each other is relatively recent. However, the same question is posed to each of them. It is, to what extent is it possible, through listening to the religions against which you reacted, to reconsider your own teachings? Can Sikhs reassess their views on Hindu polytheism and idol worship or the meaning and efficacy of pilgrimage, for example? Is it possible for Christians to recognise that the portrayal of Pharisees in the gospels may be biased and prejudiced, that the reference to 'an eye for an eye' (Matthew 5:38) is certainly not an accurate portrayal of the spirit of the Oral Torah, which requires monetary compensation for such injuries? There are signs that such reappraisal is possible. During the last quarter of the twentieth century there has been a growing appreciation of the contribution of Jewish scholars to New Testament studies. An evangelical Christian who served for many years as a missionary in India, Roger Hooker, has recently published a brief reconsideration of traditional Christian teaching about idolatry, entitled *What is Idolatry?* (British Council of Churches, 1986). It would be interesting to learn how Sikhs might respond to it.

Sikhism, in both theory and practice, has a long history of accepting the authenticity of other religions. This attitude derives, at least in part, from the eclectic nature of Indian religion in general. Although the *brahmins* emphasised a caste system which resulted in social and ritualistic separation it was nevertheless one which allowed a valid place and status to other castes. Their teachings, derived from the Vedas, accepted the existence of six orthodox philosophical interpretations, one of them atheistic. A denial of the possibility that there were many paths to spiritual liberation was never part of Guru Nanak's heritage in the way that it was one aspect of Jesus' and, in his day, the dominant one.

Acceptance of other forms of religion dates back to Guru Nanak himself. His musician companion, Mardana, was a Muslim from his own village, Mardana. According to the *janam sakhis* they accepted food from anyone who would give it to them, preached to Hindu and Muslim alike, and accepted Sufi hospitality. Guru Amar Das employed a Muslim preacher, Alayar Khan.[4] Obviously he accepted the teachings of the Guru but there is no evidence that he had to become a Sikh.

According to some traditions the Sufi Mian Mir laid the foundation stone of what is now called the Golden Temple at Amritsar.[5] Whilst it is more likely that he took part in the ceremony but that the actual act was performed by Guru Arjan, his presence indicated a liberalism of attitude by the Sikhs as well as his own outlook. Guru Hargobind provided money to build a mosque. Other examples could be given but these must suffice to demonstrate a pluralist attitude by the Gurus towards other religions, tempered, of course, by the rejection of practices or beliefs which they considered to be immoral, like *sati* or female infanticide, the worship of idols and formal ritualism.

It seems that Guru Nanak wished Muslims to become better Muslims, and Hindus better Hindus. So he taught:

> There are five prayers, five times, and five names given to them. Let truthfulness be the first, honest living the second, charity in God's Name be the third, purity of mind and good intention the fourth. The fifth the praise and adoration of God. Let good deeds be your article of faith. Thus will you be called a true Muslim. (AG 141)

And:

> There are six systems, six teachers and six doctrines. But the teacher of teachers is one, though the Lord has many vestures. The system where God's praise is uttered, that is the one to respect. (AG 358)

It cannot be said that he despaired of liberation being achieved through these two religions though the overall evidence of the Guru

Granth Sahib and his own conviction that he had been sent to the
current age of decadence which Indians call the *Kalyug* because God
was being forgotten, may be put forward as arguments in support
of that view. The truth was difficult to perceive, at least, obscured
by so much formalism.

Against it is the evidence of the *bhagat bani* and certain other
passages from the Gurus and Bhai Gurdas.

The presence of the *bani* of non-Sikhs in the Guru Granth Sahib is
seen by Sikhs today as an explicit acceptance of religious pluralism.
It has already been mentioned in Chapter 6 but attention must be
drawn to it again. The *bhagat bani* comprises hymns by such men
as Kabir who explicitly rejected any sectarian affiliation. However,
there were others such as Sheikh Farid, the *sufi*, who must be
placed within the Muslim tradition, and Ramanand, the *brahmin*
Hindu, who is represented by one composition (AG 1195). Even if,
individually, they are to be regarded as liberal and anti-sectarian,
devotees of the one true God, men whose teachings reinforced those
of Guru Nanak, cumulatively they form an impressive list of medieval Hindu and Muslim holy men. For Sikhs they are a testimony
to the openness of the Gurus to spiritual insights, whatever their
origin.

The theological foundation of this view is contained in such a
verse as:

> There is light among all; and that light is God's own self which
> pervades and enlightens everyone, but which becomes manifest
> only through the teaching and leading of the Guru. (AG 663)

The 'Guru' in this verse is, of course, God. The passage emphasises
dependence upon God as being absolutely essential if one is to speak
or respond to the Word. Read together with the previous quotation
from page 358 of the Adi Granth, it stresses the pluralistic nature of
Guru Nanak's teaching even if the case that he was the collector of
the *bhagat bani* is considered to be not proven.

Elsewhere Guru Nanak affirmed:

> He who holds fast to the Lord's Name and causes others to
> repeat it; Nanak says such a *Vaishnava* obtains supreme libera-
> tion . . . .
> He is a scholar (*pandit*) who instructs his mind, searches for
> the Lord's Name in his heart, and drinks the *amrit* of the Lord's

Name. The world lives by the instruction of that *pandit*. The *pandit*
who implants God's instruction in his heart does not go and
return (transmigrate); he understands the essence of the Vedas,
Puranas and Smirtis, recognises the apparent in the subtle and
instructs all four castes. Nanak says, I always salute such a *pandit*.
(AG 274)

He might be a rare Hindu for most would teach only the three
twice-born *varnas*, but Guru Nanak does not say 'If I were to find
one I would respect him'. The verse should be interpreted as read.

In a part of the evening hymn, Sodar Rahiras, there is a section
by Guru Gobind Singh known as Benati Chaupai. Two lines from
it are relevant to the present discussion. They read:

God created Shiva and Brahma, the Vedic king.

And:

As Brahma clothed in might you sit, as Shiva the yogi's lord.

Bhai Gurdas, contemporary and relative of the fourth and fifth
Gurus, criticised the sectarian divisiveness of Hinduism and Islam
and invited Hindus and Muslims to recognise the unifying and
eirenic teaching of the Gurus:

Thus there exist the four Hindu castes, and with them the four
sects of Muslims; all of them involved in vanity and avarice,
in pride, in discord, in violence. Hindus turn to the Ganga and
Banaras, Muslims to Makkah and the Ka'ba; Muslims cling to the
rite of circumcision, Hindus to the *tilak* and *janeu*. Though Ram
and Rahim are one and the same, Hindu and Muslim follow
paths that are separate. Forgetting the words of their own sacred
scripture, both have succumbed to the world's satanic greed.
(McLeod, pp. 63–64)

The claim of the Sikh Gurus was that God spoke through them.
In putting forward that view they did not feel the need to deny
the authenticity of other paths but they did denounce dependence
on rituals and formalism which, they said, led nowhere. All true
religion was inspired by the Sat Guru, God. It was with this concept

in mind that Kal, one of the poets at Guru Arjan's court was able
to say:

> In the third age you were Krishna who killed Mur the demon
> and delivered Kans . . . .
> In the fourth age you are the Gurus Nanak, Angad, and Amar
> Das. (AG 390)

This eulogy should not be read as a statement of fact but it does
demonstrate the Sikh belief in revelation as continuous. This is not
the belief that revelation proceeded from a simple level to a more
sophisticated one as humankind grew up and was better able to
understand the mysteries of God, a view which owed much to
theories of human evolutionary progress. Sikhs would deny the
truth of this idea. The emphasis is not on a fuller or further
divine revelation. The message and gracious activity which leads
to liberation does not change. There may be enlighteners after the
Gurus but they will not contradict what has been revealed through
the Gurus. They will come, as the Gurus did, to minister to an age
which had lost its way in spiritual darkness.

To sum up:

> There is light among all, and that light is God's own self which
> pervades and enlightens everyone. (AG 663)

Understanding of the light may improve but not the quality or
intensity of the illumination which God provides. Among Christians
only the Quakers and some mystics might feel able to support this
belief.

At this point we might look at two often quoted New Testament
verses which are used to assert that salvation is possible only
through Jesus and see what Sikhs might make of them. The first
is some words of Jesus in John's Gospel (14:6):

> I am the way, the truth and the life; no one comes to the Father
> but by me.

If a Christian were to argue that these words were to be understood in an exclusive sense, that only Christians can be saved,
Sikhs would disagree. It would go against their own experience of
spiritual liberation as well as the theology which has been outlined

in this chapter. If, on the other hand, these are the words of the *Logos*, God as the eternal Word, and declare the necessity for God to effect salvation, then they would agree. Human effort cannot win salvation, only God's grace. That grace comes through the Word of God. The other verse is part of a speech delivered by St Peter:

> There is no salvation through anyone else; in all the world no other name has been granted to mankind by which we can be saved. (Acts 4:12)

This would be seen as affirming the uniqueness of *Nam*, which Sikhs would be equally emphatic in defending. (See the section on *Nam Simran* in Chapter 8.) It accords with such passages as:

> That person reaches the highest stage (liberation) whom God yokes benevolently to the Name. (AG 298)

And:

> Without the Name true life is not possible. (AG 40, Guru Ram Das)

## Possible Attitudes to Religions Other than One's Own

There are perhaps nine possible attitudes which the believer in one religion can have to others. It might be useful to outline them here and consider how Christians and Sikhs might respond to them. In doing so it is necessary to recognise that individual Sikhs as well as Christians might hold eccentric views which straddle categories or are held to be unorthodox by most adherents.

1. *My religion is true: the rest are false.*
   There are many Christians who hold this view. No Sikh should.
2. *All earlier religions are ways provided by God to prepare the way for my religion.*
   Many Christians hold this view of Judaism and might extend it to Hinduism and Sikhism or tribal religions. Some passages in the Guru Granth Sahib might be capable of this interpretation but it is not one widely accepted by Sikhs, whose concept of time is not linear and who do not believe in what would

seem to them to be the kind of theory which suggests that God is progressively revealed.

3.   *My religion is seeking the Truth; this cannot be said of others.*
Revelation, a strong feature of both our religions, is excluded from the first part of this statement. Neither faith could accept that religion is a human invention. Salvation ultimately depends upon grace, not personal effort.

4.   *My religion is from God; the rest are human searches.*
Any believer must accept the first clause. Many Christians might accept the second. No Sikh should whose beliefs are based on the *gurbani*.

5.   *All religions are searches for the Truth.*
Again the insistence on revelation which the two religions share would make this idea unacceptable to them both.

6.   *All paths lead to God.*
Many Christians would reject this notion completely. It would appear to make the ministry of Jesus, and especially his death, irrelevant. Sikhs might have reservations about the word 'all' and the suggestion that the movement was *towards* God rather than initiated by God. Members of both faiths might well want to enter the *caveat* that any religion which they might accept as leading to God would have to preach a high code of personal morality as well as be monotheistic. Hinduism might exercise the minds of them both.

7.   *Revelation is ongoing, beginning with Time and part of the creative process, ending only when and if Time ends.*
This is a position which Sikhs could accept. The message of the Gurus is never believed to be God's last Word though it is the Word of God. The eternal Word can have neither beginning nor end. Belief in the finality of Christ would seem to make it difficult for some Christians to accept.

8.   *In different environments God becomes manifest in different ways.*
This too is an idea which Sikhs could accept, though they would want to say that Sikhism has a universal and timeless message which is independent of its Indian environment. Christians might look favourably upon this as an explanation for the existence of other religions but would want, like Sikhs, to maintain the universality and finality of the Gospel.

9.   *God may be found in the religions but is more than the sum of the parts to which they all add up.*
The *logos* doctrine of Christianity might allow some place for

this view but it would probably find more acceptance among Sikhs.

## INTERFAITH WORSHIP

A Sikh would have little difficulty in attending a Christian act of worship. Men would, of course, wish to retain the turban and this would attract attention to say the least but need not create a barrier. It might test hospitality and tolerance though it was, of course, the custom of Jesus to cover his head in the synagogue, probably by pulling the edge of his prayer shawl over it. Sikh women who wore a head scarf would only be emulating their sisters in the early church and the practice of many still.

A Sikh might be prepared to bow towards the altar as some Christians do, but not towards pictures of Jesus or Mary. The Eucharist might seem to resemble *langar* or the sharing of *karah parshad* so that the Sikh would expect to receive the elements of bread and wine at a Lord's Supper open to 'all who love the Lord Jesus'. The obstacle here would be practical, not theological. A Sikh should not drink wine! Often the Trinitarian formula and hymns addressed to Jesus would be quite acceptable, as would be the Lord's Prayer, for God is 'our Father'. A Sikh should interpret this phrase as meaning 'our parent' and would apply it to all humankind whether they acknowledge his parenthood or not.

If the Christian were to discuss the service with the Sikh visitor afterwards the rationalisations and interpretations of the experience might surprise the Christian but unless the hymns, sermon or readings had been of the kind found in the missionary sections of hymn books, the Sikh would not have been intimidated.

Once a western Christian had overcome the cultural obstacles of covering the head, taking off the shoes, being prepared to sit on the floor, and understanding Punjabi, there would be the question of whether to bow towards the Guru Granth Sahib or not. The Sikh should be bowing to God as Word, not worshipping the book, so the issue of idol worship does not arise. If there are pictures of the human Gurus in the *gurdwara* the visitor will not be expected to bow to them. Sikhs themselves will not. They are simply pictures of men, not of the formless Supreme Being. Those Christians who insist that worship must be offered 'through Jesus Christ' will not be able to agree that what is taking place is worship, of course. This may be the most important stumbling block for some Christians. *Karah parshad* and *langar* cannot be considered sacramental, so no alarm need be caused by the invitation to partake of either of them.

At the end of the day it is up to individuals to decide what they can do with a good conscience and without upsetting the feelings of the host community but it has to be acknowledged at this point that Sikhs are more used to visitors than Christians and many churches have yet to consider what provision they should make for observers, participant or non-participant. For a Christian to attend *diwan* at a *gurdwara* or a Sikh to go to a church service would be welcomed but it might be prudent to contact someone in the respective community so that the visit might be as successful and fulfilling as possible. The purpose of the visit should be clearly explained and understood. The person to contact is usually the Christian clergy person and the secretary of the *gurdwara* whose English may well be better than that of the *granthi*, and who is likely to be more familiar with the local culture than someone who may only have arrived recently from India and whose life is spent entirely within the Sikh community.

For over a century Sikhs have been aware of the church in their midst and have learned to accommodate it. The *gurdwara*, which may now stand in the same street as a church, is a new experience for many Christians outside India. It provides a challenge. Some Christians see this in terms of evangelism. For others it raises questions about the purpose of a God who allows such alternative belief systems to exist, and whether the Holy Spirit can be present outside the walls of the church in other religions. How the two religions may and will interact only the future can reveal. Perhaps this book has demonstrated something of the challenge and fascination which can result from the meeting of two faiths. It is a conversation or encounter which is just beginning. It cannot be forced. The point which the authors have reached has only been arrived at after twenty years of collaboration and friendship. Some years ago the British Council of Churches (now the Council of Churches for Britian and Ireland) said that there were four conditions for dialogue. We would endorse them in our experience. They are:

1.  *Dialogue begins when people meet each other.* (But not always. Readiness to listen is more important than eagerness to speak and sometimes believers are more ready to witness than to learn.) We might remember what some Christian dissenters in Britain used to say with regard to the Lord's Supper: 'Come,

not to express an opinion, but to seek a presence'. People coming to the church, *gurdwara*, *mandir* or mosque in this spirit might leave saying with Jacob: 'Truly, the Lord is in this place and I did not know it' . . . This is none other than the house of God. It is the gateway to heaven (Genesis 28:16). Actually, this is not a bad interpretation of the word '*gurdwara*'!

2.  *Dialogue depends on mutual understanding and mutual trust.* (And this takes time and demands patience. It cannot be rushed or forced.)
3.  *Dialogue makes it possible to share in service to the community.* (But such opportunities should not be created artificially.)
4.  *Dialogue becomes the medium for mutual witness.* (But this comes fourth in order, time and purpose. Those who set out to achieve it are likely never to reach this stage. Those who do not have such a preset purpose may well discover that it implicitly permeates the relationship.)

There will, of course, be users of this book whose interest is purely intellectual. It is the conviction of the authors that real knowledge about religions involves meeting people who try to follow them. Only then can their beliefs, practices and values really be understood. That necessitates observing the first two principles listed above if not also principles three and four. Above all it requires a readiness to listen and not impose one's own presuppositions upon what one sees, hears, and reads. This may be especially true of the westerner who encounters an eastern expression of religion. The tendency towards orientalism which was referred to elsewhere should always be kept in mind.

The late Max Warren, secretary of the Church Missionary Society, said that it:

requires us to take off our shoes and recognise that we are standing on the other person's holy ground. If we refuse to do this we might find ourselves trampling on their dreams.[6]

Finally, religions are gradually changing their perspectives. The challenge facing them is not only that posed by the very persistence and dynamism of other faiths which ought to have disappeared when confronted by so-called higher religions. It is also the demand placed upon religions when they are seen in a global context. Poverty, racism, war and peace, as well as pressing ecological issues, are requiring religions to offer a spirituality of commensurate proportions. There is a need for religions to rediscover the original visions which inspired them and interpret them in ways which speak to the condition of those who will be the men and women of the next century. When Jesus and the apostles, and the Sikh Gurus, proclaimed their messages there was really no alternative to religion in providing hope or a world view; now there seem to be many, and those offered by religions, which may seem to rival one another, are often considered to be of questionable worth from the standpoint of the outsider. There are Sikhs and Christians who believe that hope lies in restating the fundamentals of their religions with greater fervour, commitment, and sincerity. The fault lies in their lack of a conviction which will, through God's grace, overcome the ignorance or sinfulness of the unbeliever. There are other people of faith who are beginning to assert that renewal of a different kind must take place, one whose vision will result in a spirituality and theology which is global rather than sectarian. Some writers who are glancing in this direction are listed in the final section of the Bibliography. It is too soon to say that any of them has yet had a strong influence on church or Panth.

# Notes

## Chapter 1

1. St Augustine, Bishop of Hippo (354–430), On Baptism, IV, 17; also attributed to St Cyprian.

## Chapter 2

1. The word *sant* in this context refers to a group of north Indian teachers belonging to the fourteenth and fifteenth centuries CE. They shared a belief in the oneness of God, who is formless (*nirguna*), and does not become incarnate. They also rejected caste. It is also used by Sikhs to describe some respected teachers in their tradition. On the *sant* tradition, see McLeod (1968), pp. 1–6, and Khushwant Singh (1977), vol. 1, chapter 2.
2. Jesus came from the Galilean village of Nazareth, hence the tendency of Jews to call his followers 'Nazarenes'. 'Christian' was a nickname given at Antioch (Acts 11:26) to those who said that Jesus was the Christ. ('Christ' is Greek for the Hebrew word 'Messiah', the anointed one.)
3. The single word 'caste' is frequently used outside India to refer to a highly complex system of considerable social as well as religious importance. Generally it covers two words, *varna*, literally 'colour', the fourfold division of society into *brahmins, kshatriyas, vaishyas,* and *shudras*, with the scheduled classes beyond it (hence the pejorative terms outcaste or untouchable), and *jati*. It is actually this word which is of most practical significance for the majority of Indians (including Sikhs and Christians as well as Hindus). *Jati* means 'birth'. It is used as a name for the group into which one is born, status being inherited from the father. It is normally endogamous. Its place within the social hierarchy of a village is determined mainly by the ritual purity or pollution derived from the group's traditional occupation. Thus a tanner or a washerman, who are most impure because they handle animal skins and clothes which may be stained with blood or at least sweat, come low in the scale. *Brahmins*, born pure, come first in the hierarchy.

    Within a *jati* (Punjabi *zat*), there are a number of exogamous kinship groups known as *gotras, gots* in Punjabi. These are recognisable by their 'surname' such as Kalsi, Sambhi, or Arora. Sometimes the *varna* status of a group may be disputed. Not so the *jati* and *gotra*. From early years children are brought up to know their place and everyone else's. Guru Nanak was a *khatri*.

Sometimes books say that he was a *kshatriya*, others describe him as a *vaishya*. The traditional family occupation was business. His *jati* was *khatri*, his *gotra* was *Bedi*. All the Gurus were *khatris* but only from the fourth Guru did they belong to the same *gotra*, *Sodhi*.

Even though one may change one's occupation, as many Indians now do, the ritual status of purity or pollution remains unaltered. It is the consequence of birth. See further Kalsi (1992), 1.1, 2.2, and 2.3.

*Jat* is the name given to a particular *jati* found in Punjab. *Jats* are landowning farmers, and constitute the largest group in the Sikh community.

4.  The generally accepted CE, Common Era, is preferred to the Christian AD, *Anno Domini*, 'the year of our Lord' by writers and teachers of Religious Studies. Similarly BCE, Before the Common Era, is used rather than BC, 'Before Christ', which Jews consider insensitive.

5.  The two main Jewish religious groups mentioned in the New Testament are Pharisees and Sadducees. The Sadducees were a Jewish group closely associated with the Temple and a strict literal interpretation of the Torah (the five books of Moses). They rejected, therefore, belief in the resurrection of the dead as it could not be clearly established from the Torah, the scripture of Judaism. With the destruction of the Temple in 70 CE they passed into history. The Pharisees were the other most important group mentioned in the New Testament. They were men of high ethical principle, willing to consider new ideas such as the Resurrection in their interpretation of the Torah. This did not mean that they were slack in observing it as the clashes which they and Jesus had show. The hostility described in the New Testament may suggest that he hoped they would accept his views on the Torah which was not far from theirs, and that during the period in which the writings which came to be the New Testament were being produced, the debate with the Pharisees was continuing. In fact the Pharisees came to be identified with Judaism after 70 CE so the disputes which Jesus had with them reflect the tension between his followers and Judaism at this time. See further E. P. Sanders, *Judaism, Practice and Belief* (London and Philadelphia, 1992), sections 15, 18, 19.

6.  The Vedas, literally 'knowledge', are the primary authoritative scripture of Hindus for whom they are the eternal sacred texts.

7.  *Logos* is one of the most important words of *John's Gospel*. Much of its value comes from the fact that it had a history of usage in Greek philosophy, and in the writings of Philo Judaeus, who lived at the time of Jesus. In *John* it should be seen as a claim that Jesus, the Christ, is the creative Word of the Jewish scriptures and the principle of natural and moral law of the Stoics. *Logos* was, of course, extensively used in the Greek version of the Old Testament, the Septuagint. See further C. H. Dodd, *Interpretation of the Fourth*

*Gospel* (Cambridge, 1953), and C. K. Barrett, *The Gospel According to St John* (London: SPCK, 1956).
8.   The *Kal Yug* is the fourth, last, longest, and most degenerate in the cycle of cosmic eras. It is characterised by neglect of *dharma*, right living and social stability.
9.   A version of the story in to be found in Macauliffe (1978 reprint) vol. I, p. 112.
10.  The quotations are taken from McLeod (1984), pp. 135, 136.

## Chapter 3

1.   On Kabir and Ramanand see Vaudeville (1974), ch. 4, section 4. An introduction to Hindu philosophy can be found in Brockington (1981), which also places Sikhism within its Indian historical and religious context.
2.   The Trinity and the development of Christian doctrine are discussed in Kelly (1960; rev. 1978) *passim* and Lindbeck (1984), ch. 4.
3.   D. Brown, *All our Splendours* (Fount, 1982), examines the importance of 'Word' in a number of religions, though, in common with many other writers, he omits Sikhism from his survey.
4.   G. W. Briggs, *Gorakhnath and the Kanphata Yogis* (Calcutta, 1938, rep. Motilal, Delhi, 1973), is still the most convenient introduction.
5.   See again Dasgupta but also the medieval philosopher Shankara's *Crest Jewel of Discrimination* (Mentor Books, 1947, rep. 1970).
6.   See J. Morley and H. Ward, *Celebrating Women* (Movement for the Ordination of Women and Women in Theology, 1986); also R. R. Ruether, *Sexism and God-Talk* (SCM, 1983).
7.   In the township (of the body) lives the king, ever fresh, He is neither man, nor woman, nor bird; he is the very embodiment of wisdom. (Gopal Singh)

     In the village of the body, abides my master, with child-like ever-fresh body, and he stages wondrous plays. The wise and beauteous True Lord is neither a woman, nor a man, nor a bird. (Manmohan Singh)

     The Lord is master of the self's city, the divine child, full of unique miracles. He is neither woman nor man nor bird – holy embodiment of wisdom. (Gurbachan Singh Talib)

## Chapter 4

1.   Parrinder in Harbans Singh (1975), p. 88.
2.   Parrinder *op. cit.*, p. 88. He also quotes Dasgupta (1932), vol. II, p. 533.
3.   Kartar Singh, *Life of Guru Nanak Dev* (Lahore bookshop, Ludhiana, 1958), pp. 306–7.

**Chapter 5**

1.  'Neither *teshuvah* (repentance), nor *Yom Kippur* can wipe away the hurt between one person and another until that hurt has been healed. It is therefore a vital custom within the community for Jews to ask forgiveness of each other, on the eve of *Yom Kippur*, for any wrong they may have committed or any pain they may have caused'. A. Wood and H. Gryn in *Festivals in World Religions*, ed. A. Brown (Longman, 1986), p. 197.
2.  Dunn (1991), p. 177.
3.  A convenient outline and analysis of theories of the Atonement is contained in Baillie (1963), chapters 7 and 8.
4.  McLeod (1968), pp. 38–9.
5.  Grewal and Bal (1967), p. 126. Macauliffe (1978), vol. V, p. 96. See also McLeod (1976), chapter 1 and J. S. Grewal, *From Guru Nanak to Maharaja Ranjit Singh* (Amritsar, 1972), chapter 9.
6.  Macauliffe (1978), vol. V, pp. 243–4.

**Chapter 6**

1.  *The Laws of Manu* are probably most easily accessible in the translation by G. Buhler as vol. XXV of *Sacred Books of the East* (Oxford 1886, reprinted by Motilal Banaridass, Delhi, 1967). Extracts are contained in de Bary (1958).
2.  Maccoby (1989), pp. 2–4, 72–80.
3.  R. Allchin, *Katavali* (London: Allen & Unwin, 1964), p. 49; W. O. Cole, *Sikhism and its Indian Context* (London: Darton, Longman and Todd, 1984), p. 65. The Kabir–Ramanand relationship is discussed in Vaudeville (1973), pp. 110–17.
4.  McLeod (1980), p. 126.
5.  Trepp (1973 edn), pp. 39, 47, 62, 93, 94.
6.  S. S. Kohli, *A Critical Study of the Adi Granth* (New Delhi, 1961), p. 11. McLeod (1976), pp. 60–1.
7.  Teja Singh, *The Holy Guru Granth Sahib*, Introduction, p. xv.
8.  The Rahit Maryada, The Sikh Code of Discipline, was published by the Shromani Gurdwara Parbandhak Committee, Amritsar, in 1945. It was based on the Khalsa code of Guru Gobind Singh dating back to the eighteenth century. It provides the standard against which Sikh individuals and communities should measure themselves and covers personal ethics, the conduct of worship, and ceremonies. It has had great influence in creating or maintaining unity of belief and practice within the Panth. It presupposes and endorses the Khalsa ideal as being the Sikh norm.
9.  McLeod (1968), chapter 2 provides a detailed introduction to the *janam sakhis*. The most convenient one to read is B40, translated with invaluable notes by the same scholar (W. H. McLeod, *The B40 Janam Sakhi*, Guru Nanak Dev University, Amritsar, 1980).

10. R. C. Zaehner, *The Bhagavad Gita* (Oxford, 1969).
11. McLeod, *op. cit.* p. 11.
12. *The Sikh Review*, January 1976, contains a full discussion of the issue.
13. Harbans Singh (1975), chapter 37.
14. This is the view particularly of Ram K. Vepa in *Guru Nanak*, Publications Division, Government of India (1969), chapter 8, where there is an explicit reference to Gandhi. Reconciliation is a theme which runs through that volume of essays and also *Guru Nanak, His Life, Times and Teachings* (Delhi: National Publishing House, 1969). It is not exclusive to Hindu writers. In *The Sikhs Today* (Orient Longman, 1959, rev. 1967), Khushwant Singh wrote; 'Now that religious factionalism has lost its purpose in secular India, the Sikhs have a unique opportunity of fulfilling the mission of the founder of their faith and bringing the two parent communities together' (p. 28). The idea also occurs in the preface to his *History of the Sikhs*, vol. 1, p. vii.
15. *Confessions of St Augustine* (New York: Grosset and Dunlap, n.d.), Book VIII, XII, 29, pp. 173–4. The authors are indebted to the Reverend Donald Johnson for drawing their attention to this passage.
16. Papias (c. 140) wrote that 'Matthew, however, composed the *logia* in the Hebrew dialect, but each one interpreted it as he was able' (quoted Eusebius, *Ecclesiastical History*, iii, 39). This is thought to refer to a collection of sayings (*logia*) which may be included in *Matthew* and to Aramaic which was certainly the spoken language of Jews in the time of Jesus. A. H. M'Neile, *Gospel According to St Matthew*, pp. xxviii and xxx–xxxii, discusses the possibility of an Aramaic original but dismisses it, in common with most scholars.
17. Details are given by Henry Chadwick, *The Early Church* (Penguin, 1967), p. 62. An identical acrostic may be seen in the Cirencester (Corinium) Roman Museum in Britain though this is of a much later date.
18. Gopal Singh, *A History of the Sikh People* (New Delhi: World Sikh University Press, 1979), p. 240; Teja Singh and Ganda Singh, *A Short History of the Sikhs* (Patiāla: Punjabi University, 3rd rep., 1989), p. 46.
19. The International Sacred Literature Trust, Manchester, England, has recently launched a project to publish a modern English translation of the Guru Granth Sahib. It is hoped that this will be completed in time for the tercentenary celebrations of the foundation of the Khalsa in 1999.

## Chapter 7

1. Macauliffe, vol. II, p. 97.
2. The content of Ardas, the Sikh congregational prayer, varies considerably. The form given here is that found in Cole and Sambhi (1978),

Appendix 2. Teja Singh (1938) provides another but similar version. See also McLeod (1984).

3. The above passage comes from the Dasam Granth, p. 119.
4. Vahiguru means literally, 'Praise to the Guru'. It is also used as a popular way of addressing or speaking about God.
5. The *panj piare* were the first five Sikhs to be initiated into the Khalsa.
6. Guru Gobind Singh's four sons, who were all killed in the struggle against the Mughals.
7. These were deserters who were forgiven by Guru Gobind Singh and later fell in battle.
8. The five seats of religious authority (see Chapter 10).
9. These words are often uttered before or after a Sikh speaks in the *gurdwara* and on other occasions. They mean 'Hail to the Guru's Khalsa! Hail to the victory of the Guru! God is True!'
10. Jarnail Singh's translation of *Hum Hindu Nahim* (Sikhs . . . We Are Not Hindus). Kahn Singh, in a section on rites of naming, initiation, marriage, and death, affirms; 'We state four rites that we perform according to *gurmat* (Guru's way)' (p. 141). Later, on the same page, are the words; 'whatever the Sikhs do they do it according to the Guru's *hukam*'. This principle governs all rites and ceremonies. The purpose of this book was to demonstrate that the Khalsa (and therefore Sikhism) was quite distinct from Hinduism. It is largely a collection of proof texts taken from the Guru Granth Sahib and the Dasam Granth. Though it was written to meet the needs of the Panth at the turn of the last century many Sikhs would see it as equally pertinent to conditions almost a hundred years later. Hence Dr Jarnail Singh's decision to undertake the task of providing his translation.
11. The Samvat calendar attributed to King Vikramitra starts in 58 BCE. Guru Nanak was born in Samrat or Bikrami/Vikrami, 1526 or 1469 CE.

## Chapter 8

1. For a wider discussion of *Nam Simran* see Vaudeville (1974), p. 140; on Sikh devotional aspects J. S. Guleria, *Rediscovering Religion* (New Delhi, 1983), chapters 8 to 11. The passages of scripture used in daily devotions are contained in *Nitnem: Daily Prayer of the Sikhs* (Delhi: Guru Nanak Foundation, 1983). The translation was made by Professor Gurbachan Singh Talib.
2. Per-Olaf Sjögren, *The Jesus Prayer* (SPCK, 1975), and Kallistos Ware, *The Power of the Name* (Oxford: Fairacres Publications, 1976).
3. Sjörgen (1975), pp. 38–9.
4. Macauliffe (1978), vol. III, 16.
5. Kahn Singh, *Gurmat Martand*, quoted McLeod (1984), p. 114.

**Chapter 9**

1.  These are *Japji* of Guru Nanak, *Jap*, ten *swayyas*, and *Chaupai* by Guru Gobind Singh, and six stanzas of the *Anand* by Guru Amar Das. Translations can be found in McLeod (1984).
2.  Macauliffe (1978), vol. I, pp. 191–2.

**Chapter 10**

1.  Macauliffe, vol. III, pp. 74–5.
2.  See above Chapter 7, note 10.
3.  Mark Juergensmeyer, *Religion as Social Vision* (University of California, 1982), examines attempts by members of the scheduled classes to improve their social status by changes in religious affiliation. The Ravidasis are discussed on pages 83–92 especially. See also chapter 17 on similar attempts through conversion to Christianity.

**Chapter 11**

1.  A rather restrained account compared to those given in addresses in *gurdwaras* is found in Macauliffe (1978), vol. III, pp. 173–4.
2.  In the nineteenth century M. G. Ranade campaigned for the right of Hindu widows to remarry and for this to be accepted in practice. (See de Bary 1958, pp. 681, 687). See also the work of Vidyasagar, David Kopf, *The Brahmo Samaj* (Princeton, 1979), pp. 56–7. In 1856 the Widow Remarriage Act became law.

**Chapter 12**

1.  A. Toynbee, *Christianity among the Religions of the World* (Oxford, 1958), pp. 99–100.
2.  The chapter on Religions in Primal Societies, Hinnells (1984), is a useful starting point for those wishing to consider recent thinking about these expressions of religion. They might then wish to proceed to books listed in the bibliography, especially those written by Mbiti and Idowu (p. 452).
3.  Quoted by Race (1983), p. 47.
4.  Macauliffe (1978) vol. II, p. 77.
5.  Madanjit Kaur (1983), pp. 11–12, after discussing the evidence concludes that the foundation of the Golden Temple was laid by Guru Arjan himself. Khushwant Singh (1977), vol. I, p. 28, note 8, accepts the popular tradition that the foundation was laid by the Sufi, Mian Mir.
6.  Max Warren, general introduction to the Christian Presence series, S.C.M., London, beginning 1959.

# Select Bibliography

The purpose of this bibliography is to enable the reader to follow up some of the issues which are discussed in the text. The books referred to usually contain bibliographies through which the students who wish to pursue their studies to a greater depth can do so. In drawing up this list we have been constrained by the fact that books from India may not be easy to obtain and that there seems to be an alarming tendency world-wide for books to go out of print within a short time of publication.

In 1964 a conference of Christians and Sikhs took place in India. From it came a number of articles published under the title Sikhism and Christianity, in the Bulletin of the Christian Institute for the Study of Religion and Society, Bangalore, vol. XI, no. 1, March 1964. It was edited by H. J. Singh, R. W. Taylor and M. M. Thomas. This seems to have been the only conference of its kind which resulted in a publication. No decision has yet been made as to whether an ongoing consultation instigated by the United Reformed Church in England and convened by the Reverend John Parry of the Northern College, Manchester, will publish any studies beyond the reports contained in the annual Sikh Bulletin, which is printed at the West Sussex Institute of Higher Education, Chichester.

Baring Union Christian College, Batala, Punjab, has a Christian Institute of Sikh Studies which publishes a Bulletin. This is essential reading for anyone interested in Christian–Sikh relations.

## Introductions

Few scholars have written about Christianity with the outsider in mind. Most seem to assume basic knowledge and usually belief. We would refer readers to: J. R. Hinnells (ed.), *A Handbook of Living Religions*, Viking, 1984; and Huston Smith, *The World's Religions*, San Francisco, Harper, revised edn, 1991. These have sections on Christianity and on Sikhism, though Smith's includes it in the article on Hinduism. R. C. Zaehner (ed.), *The Concise Encyclopedia of Living Faiths*, Hutchinson, 2nd edition revised, 1988, includes an excellent introduction to Sikhism by Eleonor Nesbitt but as usual there is little on Christian practices in the introduction to that religion. See also W. O. Cole, *Christianity*, Stanley Thornes & Hulton, 1989.

## More Detailed Introductions to Christianity

Barrett, D. B. (ed.), *World Christian Encyclopedia: A Comparative Study of Churches and Religions in the Modern World, A.D. 1900–2000*. Nairobi: Oxford University Press, 1982.

Moore, P., *Christianity, Ward Lock Educational*. London, 1982
Smart, N., *The Phenomenon of Christianity*. London: Collins, 1979. This is not an easy read.

Additional information can be obtained from:

Cross, F. L., and Livingstone, E. A. (eds), *Oxford Dictionary of the Christian Church*. London and New York: Oxford University Press, 2nd edn, 1974.
Douglas, J. D. (ed.), *Dictionary of the Christian Church*. Zondervan, Michigan, and Paternoster Press, Exeter, 1974.

### Introductions to Sikhism

Basham, A. L. (ed.), *A Cultural History of India*. Oxford, 1975, places the Sikh religion in its historical context. The chapter on the Sikh religion is by W. H. McLeod.
Cole, W. O., and Sambhi, P. S., *The Sikhs: Their Religious Beliefs and Practices*. London and Boston ( Mass.): Routledge, 1978, 3rd rep. 1989. As the title suggest this covers all aspects of the Sikh religion and is not confined to theology.
Cole, W. O., and Sambhi, P. S., *A Popular Dictionary of Sikhism*. Curzon, UK, and Riverdale, USA, 1990.
Hinnells, J. R. (ed.), *The Penguin Dictionary of Religions*. London, 1984, contains brief entries on Christian and Sikh subjects.
Macauliffe, M. A., *The Sikh Religion*, 6 vols. Oxford, 1909, rep. Delhi, 1963 and 1978. A faithful and comprehensive presentation of the Sikh tradition from 1469 to 1708 with translations on many passages from the Sikh scriptures.
McLeod, W. H., *Guru Nanak and the Sikh Religion*. Oxford University Press, Oxford, 1968. It is included at this point because the second part of the book provides the best available introduction to Sikh theology.
Sambhi, P. S., *Sikhism*. Stanley Thornes & Hulton, 1989.

### Scriptures

Many translations of the Bible have been made during the twentieth century, presumably because the English language has changed so much in the period and there have been considerable developments in biblical scholarship. The King James' version has been found to have academic shortcomings and to be inaccessible to many people, especially the young. We have used the Revised English Bible with Apocrypha, Oxford and Cambridge University Presses, 1989.

English translations of the Guru Granth Sahib tend to use the language of the King James' version or attempt to keep to the original poetic form and can present English-speaking readers with difficulties. Macauliffe (*op. cit.*) can be recommended but only sections are included and page numbers to the Guru Granth Sahib are not given. (Perhaps they will be provided in future reprints.)

McLeod, W. H., *Textual Sources for the Study of Sikhism*, Manchester University Press (Manchester UK and Dover NH), 1984, includes translations of most major scriptural passages and many other important works, such as the Rahit Maryada and Ardas. This is an indispensable anthology for students of Sikhism to possess.

## Complete Translations of the Guru Granth Sahib

Gopal Singh, *Sri Guru Granth Sahib*, Gur Das Kapur and World Book Centre, Delhi, 1962 (4 vols).

Gurbachan Singh Talib, *Sri Guru Granth Sahib*. Patiala: Punjabi University, 1984–89 (4 vols).

Manmohan Singh, *Sri Guru Granth Sahib*, Shromani Gurdwara Parbandhak Committee, Amritsar, 1964–69 (8 vols). This provides the original, English translation, and modern Punjabi, in parallel columns. It can often be obtained from *gurdwaras*.

Mansukhani, G. S., *Hymns from Bhai Gurdas Compositions*, Sikh Missionary Society, Southall, 1988, provides an introduction to the verses of this important Sikh, additional to those contained in McLeod (*op. cit.*).

Teja Singh, *The Holy Guru Granth Sahib*, Patiala: Punjabi University, 1985. This is a posthumous publication of passages which the scholar had translated before death interrupted his work.

## Anthologies which Include Christian and Sikh Scriptural Passages

Smart, N., and Hecht, R. D. (eds), *Sacred Texts of the World a Universal Anthology*. Macmillan, 1982.

Wilson, A. (ed.), *World Scripture, A Comparative Anthology of Sacred Texts*. New York: Paragon, 1991.

There is no English commentary on the Guru Granth Sahib. On the Bible generally there are many. We would refer to:

Grant, F. C. and Rowley, H. H. (eds), *Dictionary of the Bible*, 2nd edn, 1963.

Richardson, A. (ed.), *A Theological Word Book of the Bible*. London: S.C.M., 1950.

Jewish and Christian scholars, sometimes together, have increasingly turned their attention to the Jewish context of early Christianity. We include a few books which have resulted from this reassessment. So far Sikh writers tend to turn only to the Guru Granth Sahib in their studies of Sikh origins:

Dunn, J. D. G., *The Parting of the Ways*. London: S.C.M., 1991.
Rabbi Hilton, M., with Father Marshall, G., *The Gospels & Rabbinic Judaism*, London: S.C.M., 1988. the result of a Jewish–Christian study course.
Maccoby, H., *Judaism in the First Century*. London: Sheldon, 1989.
Sanders, E. P., *Judaism, Practices and Belief*, 63 BCE–66 CE, Philadelphia and London, 1992.
Trepp, L., *History of the Jewish Experience*. New York: Behrman, 1973 revision. A very useful and readable introduction to Jewish belief and practice for anyone wishing to read the other books listed in this section.
Vermes, G., *Jesus the Jew*. London: S.C.M., 1983, 2nd edn. One of the earliest of recent studies.

**General List**

Avtar Singh, *Sikh Ethics*. Patiala: Punjabi University, 1970.
Baillie, D. M., *God was in Christ*. London: Faber, 1947.
Bal, S. S., and Grewal, J. S., *Guru Gobind Singh*. Chandigarh, 1967.
Barrett, C. K., *The Gospel According to St. John*. London: S.P.C.K., 1975.
Barrier, N. G., and Dusenbury, V. A., *The Sikh Diaspora*. Manohar (1991) surveys and examines the presence of Sikhs world-wide.
Bosch, D. J., *Witness to the World: The Christian Mission in Theological Perspective*. Marshall, Morgan and Scott, London, John Knox, Atlanta, 1980.
*Cambridge History of the Bible*, various authors and editors, 3 vols, Cambridge University Press, 1963–70.
Darshan Singh, *Western Perspective on the Sikh Religion*. New Delhi: Sehgal, 1991.
Dasgupta, S., *A History of Indian Philosophy*. Cambridge, 1922–55.
de Bary, W. T. (ed.), *Sources of Indian Tradition*. Columbia, New York, and Oxford University Press, Oxford, 1958.
Dharam Singh, *Sikh Theology of Liberation*. Delhi: Harman Publishing House, 1991.
Dodd, C. H., *The Founder of Christianity*. Collins, London, and Macmillan, New York, 1970.
Dupre, L. and Wiseman, J. (eds), *Light from Light: an Anthology of Christian Mysticism*. New York: Paulist Press, 1988.
Elwes, T. (ed.), *Women's Voices: Essays in Contemporary Feminist Theology*. London: Marshall Pickering, 1992.
Ganda Singh (ed.), *The Singh Sabha and Other Socio-Religious Movements in the Punjab*. Patiala: Punjabi University, 2nd edn 1984. The Nirankari and Namdhari contributions to the Panth are covered as well as the work of Christian and Hindu movements in the Punjab. Some of the themes are continued in O'Connell (see below).

# Index

General references – e.g. afterlife, sin – are to both religions. Certain terms – e.g. atonement, baptism or *giani* – are, of course, specific to one religion.